MUSLIMS ON THE MAP

Serena Hussain completed her PhD at the University of Bristol and is currently working on a project exploring migration and ethnic geographies at the University of Leeds. Though her principal expertise is in Muslims in Britain, she has also worked on community tolerance, young people and unemployment, asylum seekers and 'hidden' ethnic communities.

MUSLIMS ON THE MAP

A National Survey of
Social Trends in Britain

SERENA HUSSAIN

Tauris Academic Studies
LONDON • NEW YORK

Published in 2008 by Tauris Academic Studies,
an imprint of I.B.Tauris & Co Ltd
6 Salem Road, London W2 4BU
175 Fifth Avenue, New York NY 10010
www.ibtauris.com

In the United States of America and Canada distributed by
Palgrave Macmillan, a division of St. Martin's Press
175 Fifth Avenue, New York NY 10010

International Library of Human Geography 13
ISBN : 978 1 84511 471 8

A full CIP record for this book is available from the British Library
A full CIP record for this book is available from the Library of Congress

Library of Congress Catalog Card Number : available

Printed and bound in India by Thomson Press India Limited
camera-ready copy edited and supplied by the author

This book is dedicated to my late father Manzoor Hussain and all the victims of the 2005 earthquakes in Azad Kashmir. The author's profits from any sales of this book will go towards sponsoring the education of an orphan or orphans in the region.

Preface

This project was initiated by the Muslim Council of Britain, the main Muslim umbrella organisation and pressure group in the United Kingdom. The Council was at the forefront of campaigning for a religion question in the 2001 Census of Population and for data on Muslims more generally. They sought to address the lacuna of information available on Muslims as a community, rather than Muslims as ethnic subgroups.

The availability of data on Muslims became particularly pressing for this and similar non-governmental organisations, as there was increasing evidence that Muslims were severely disadvantaged across a number of measures.

Since beginning the analysis, the author has received regular inquiries from Muslim organisations, central and local government, the media and academics for statistics and up to date analysis on Muslims. It was the research findings from this project that prompted discussion on Muslim lone parent households, a finding which took both Muslims and academics by surprise (paper presented at the British Muslims Research Network Meeting at Selly Oak, University of Birmingham, September 2004).

Many current texts on Muslims in Britain place greater emphasis on religious practice, political activity, identity and historical accounts, or are ethnographic studies of specific locations such as Bradford (Lewis 1994) or Manchester (Werbner 2002). This study however is primarily a national socio-economic profiling exercise, something which has been lacking until recently for Muslims as a faith community.

There are a number of texts emerging which discuss Muslims' reactions to key global and local events such as 11 September 2001 and 7 July 2005. Although discourse on disadvantage and the Muslim community's socio-economic position has increasingly come under discussion, particularly during the aftermath of 7 July bombings in London in 2005, there has been less focus on this so far in the work produced and more emphasis on reactions to media coverage and the government policy on anti-terror and religious discrimination. This study is therefore particularly relevant and timely in providing an insight into Muslims as a community in Britain, allowing a greater understanding for those wishing to contribute to the debate.

Acknowledgements

I was extremely fortunate in having Professor Tariq Modood and Professor David Gordon as supervisors for my PhD. I am grateful for their direction and advice and for the genuine interest they showed in the subject for this book. I would also like to thank Professor Ceri Peach and Dr Eldin Fahmy for their guidance and the Muslim Council of Britain for their involvement, particularly in the initial stages.

My sincere gratitude and thanks to those whose friendship supported, encouraged and at times carried me during the course of this work: Shazia Chughtai, Nazia Naheed, Lisa Flannigan and Dr Hisham Hellyer.

For the many hours spent reading through chapters I would like to thank Bharat Vijay Bilimoria who believed in this work just as much as I did, if not more so at times, and my sister Safina for her time and support. Finally I'd like to thank Tariq Aziz for all his encouragement over the years.

SH
Teesside, UK
15 August 2007

Contents

Introduction

In recent times Muslims living in the United Kingdom have become more visible as a political group of actors. The prevailing idea of religion being predominately a matter for the private domain has been challenged by minority faith groups, most vocally Muslims. Their ardent lobbying and activity has seen many of their concerns pushed onto policy and research agendas. One of the principle consequences of this has been the inclusion on the Religion Question in the 2001 Census of Population. By gaining a category in the most comprehensive data collection exercise in the country, Muslims have been firmly put on the map and officially recognised as a community in their own right.

A key concern for those campaigning for large scale data on religion was that ethnic groups whose adherents were overwhelmingly Muslim – namely Pakistanis and Bangladeshis – were found to be facing severe disadvantage on a number of measures. In addition the ethnically heterogeneous nature of Muslims meant that it was extremely difficult to create a 'community profile' for this faith group, given that many Muslims from ethnic and national backgrounds such as Arabs, Turks and Eastern Europeans are included within the ethnic category 'White Other'.

This study is based on research which looks at Muslims as a whole community from a sociological and social policy perspective. Drawing from a comprehensive review of studies on Muslims in Britain an insight into aspects of Muslim social life is provided. This is coupled with the analysis data from the 2001 National Census, supplemented by additional data sources; 1994 Fourth National Survey of Ethnic Minorities, 1999 Health Survey for England and the 2001 Citizenship Survey for England and Wales in order to depict the social position of Muslims as a faith community, rather than as ethnic subgroups, as has largely been the case when studying Muslims previously.

Creating a Community Profile

Muslims Groups and Disadvantage

As will be discussed in greater detail during Chapter One, Muslim communities have increasingly come into focus in recent times both due to their articulation of the importance of their faith in what have been commonly described as 'secular' societies and also because of local and global events involving Muslims. Islam has historically been viewed as suspect in Europe where there has been a legacy of anti-Muslim sentiment (Esposito 1999; Ballard 1996*b*). More recently the term 'Islamophobia' was coined to describe such hostility and Muslim-specific discrimination that has become ever apparent in the new wave of Muslim settlement post Second World War (Richardson 2004).

There is however another significant reason explaining why Muslims have become a focal point as a faith community and this is the substantial body of empirical data now available demonstrating that ethnic minority groups have differing socio-economic profiles and that the data consistently points to the higher levels of deprivation faced by Pakistanis and Bangladeshis. This is both in comparison to not only the White majority but also other South Asian ethnic groups, namely Indians and African Asians and when compared with other groups. Pakistanis and Bangladeshis of course are overwhelmingly Muslim and it is this stark divergence between Muslim and non-Muslim South Asians that has led sociologists and policy makers to explore data on Muslim communities.

One key source providing data demonstrating this is the Fourth National Survey of Ethnic Minorities (FNSEM) conducted in 1994. The findings from this survey showed clearly that the Muslim groups – Pakistani and Bangladeshi – exhibit the highest level of disadvantage; this was described by Modood et al. as 'a systematic pattern with particular groups being severely disadvantaged across a number of measures' (1997: 357).

The 1991 National Census found that nearly half of Pakistanis lived in cheap terraced accommodation and over 40 per cent of Bangladeshis lived in council or housing associated accommodation. These two groups had also been shown to have high proportions of overcrowded homes and accommodation without central heating. More recently arrived Muslim communities, such as Somali asylum seekers are similarly placed in areas of multiple deprivation. In a report published by Shelter, Garvie (2001) reported that 50 per cent of the 'bed-sits' in which asylum seekers resided were not fit for dwelling.

When looking at differential income and unemployment among ethnic groups a recent Cabinet Office report (2002) highlighted that Pakistani and Bangladeshi men are more likely to be unemployed than other Asian groups. This clearly impacts not only on the quality of housing as mentioned above but also the quality of life. The civil unrest in 2001 within certain Muslim communities highlighted how multiple social deprivation had led to deep alienation and frustration. Reports published after the 'riots' stressed that the wards most affected suffered from high levels of youth unemployment and inadequate youth facilities (Shadjareh 2001).

It is with this aspect of the condition of Muslims that this study is primarily concerned. The aim of looking at data on religious affiliation rather than ethnicity is to build a socio-economic profile of Muslims. Given what has already been demonstrated about Muslim groups, namely Pakistanis and Bangladeshis, academics, policy makers and Muslim organisations argued that data on religion would show that that Muslims are a disadvantaged community when compared with the larger British population.

Researching Communities

Empirical social research greatly enhances the understanding of the social processes and problems encountered by groups and individuals in society. Clarke (2001) describes the two broad types of social research as pure or basic research and applied or policy orientated research. The former is described as being discipline orientated, developing on the body of general knowledge for the understanding of human behaviour. He explains that 'Constructing, testing and refining theory is what basic research is all about' (p. 29).

The latter, it is argued, is not as concerned with theory building but rather with providing knowledge and information that can be used to 'illuminate social policy by providing an insight into contemporary social issues' (ibid.).

In this view applied social research is often conducted with the possibility of eventual practical use in mind. The research for this study falls into this latter category in that it is orientated towards fact finding or a descriptive effort using data to understand the social disadvantages affecting Muslims living in Britain. This work therefore is concerned with 'community profiling'.

During the 1980s and 1990s several associated techniques such as needs assessment, social audits and community consultation became more popular. Communities have also initiated and conducted profiles of themselves in order to demonstrate shortcomings of service provision or to raise awareness of specific and distinct elements within their community. The terms used here describe what appear to be similar operations; however, there are often differences in approaches and coverage. Hawtin et al. (1999) describe the term 'community profiling' to be the broadest in that 'it is used to refer to a diverse range of projects undertaken or initiated by different organisations' (p. 4). They define community profiling as '[A] comprehensive description of needs of a population that is defined or defines itself as a community' (p. 5).

What Makes a Community?

A key concern when wanting to discover what the Muslim profile is and how this differs from other groups is the assumed community element. Smith (2004) writes on the subject that 'Sociology has a long history of working with, deconstructing and at times rejecting the usefulness of the term community' (p. 185).

Hellyer (2005) describes the dangers of assuming a 'commonality' among Muslims simply because they describe themselves as such; he writes,

> Muslims [are not] an ethno-cultural group by virtue of being Muslim. Islam is not per se a culture rather it may give rise to cultures, or be a fundamental root of culture, but it is not, nor has it ever been a culture in and of itself. Hence whereas Islam as a faith spread across the world, the culture of the first Muslim community (Arabs of the Hijaz) did not … Thus the concept of an Islamic 'Identity' per se is problematic. (p. 27)

Despite this, to state that Islamic teaching does not provide a common thread throughout Muslim communities is unrealistic. The area of the family is one example, where marriage is the only sanctioned relationship for reproduction and formal marriage is therefore normative among all Muslim communities. It is not the objective of this study to demonstrate how an outcome can be or is directly a result of theological doctrine, but rather to demonstrate how those who chose to identify themselves as 'Muslim' or in this case chose to tick the 'Muslim' box compare with other faith affiliated groups residing in Britain. It is acknowledged here that Muslims are heterogeneous.

Hillery's (1955) study of communities led to 94 different types or definitions; however, Smith (2004) argues that these fall into three basic types. The first of these is defined by space and or by geographical reference. The second is described as being about solidarity which can be based on a reference point, giving them a shared identity or belonging. The third is to do with interaction and exchange and could therefore be about business relations and networks.

Muslims choosing to use their faith as a vehicle for political visibility and mobilisation fall into the second category of community, in which being a 'Muslim' provides solidarity and also, in this case, provides a nucleus for collective effort and deliberation.

Who Qualifies as a Muslim?

Elaborating on the conceptual difficulty raised about what makes a community leads to discussion regarding what qualities or characteristics individuals must demonstrate in order to qualify as members of a community. Such qualities are far more difficult to quantify for faith communities due to the practical difficulties which arise when attempting to measure levels of faith. On counting Muslims more specifically, Brown (2000) argues,

> While Muslim presence and Muslim identity might reasonably be discussed without explicit definition in a number of non-statistical contexts, clearly any attempt to count a population requires a precise determination of what constitutes membership of a group. (p. 88)

Ansari adds on this difficulty, 'The diverse nature of Muslim communities creates problems about how to define Muslims officially. For statistical purposes, family background has been thought to be most relevant' (2004: 12).

The debate regarding who should be counted as a Muslim involves the questions of whether Muslim identity should presume the profession and practice of Islam as a defence mechanism, religious doctrine

or whether an 'attachment' in a cultural or geographical sense is sufficient. A key issue which researchers need to understand when considering whether to count those who are Muslims 'religiously' is what
yardstick to use to measure religiosity and decide an individual is sufficiently practicing as a Muslim to be counted. At an individual level
the five fundamental tenets or 'five pillars' of Islam could be used.
Sanders (1997) explored these conceptual difficulties and produced
a religious index which inserted people into various positions on a
range, from inert origins in a faith to active worship. House (1997)
recognises that even those who are 'not practicing' or Muslims in the
latter sense, adopt the status of Muslim as a socio-political identity.
She calls these Muslims 'sociological Muslims'. In this view all debates
about who should and should not be categorised as Muslim appear
futile if an individual identifies himself or herself to be a Muslim.

Counting the attendance of religious institutions or places of worship as a indication of 'practicing' as with other faiths is particularly
problematic for Muslims as they are not compelled to perform prayers
in mosques with the exception of one Friday prayer *Juma* which is not
obligatory for Muslims women and children or for men facing practical difficulties in attending the congregational prayer. However, even
assuming it were possible to measure religious observance using such
means and criteria, it would almost certainly only capture a small proportion of those who would identify themselves as Muslims. Imple-
menting a broader definition allows Muslims to be defined and identified through other means such as data on country of birth or origin and ethnicity. Both perspectives have their supporters and from a
practical point of view the classification of Muslims based on the former would be more useful to policy makers and service providers as
it would be more likely to indicate practical needs such as dietary requirements. However for policy makers interested in group discrimination and exclusion the latter perspective could arguably be more
relevant.

Despite it being difficult to 'quantify' religiosity through practical
worship, there is evidence which demonstrates that religion plays a
much more significant role in the lives of many minority communities, when compared with their White counterparts. This is particularly true for those from South Asia. Modood et al. write about their
findings from the FNSEM in '*Ethnic minorities in Britain: Diversity and
Disadvantage*' (1997), 'The South Asians identification and prioritisa-
tion of religion is far from just a nominal one. Nearly all South Asians
said they have a religion, and 90 per cent said that religion was of
personal importance to them' (p. 306).

What is clear is that accurate figures on Muslims, as the second largest religious community, and the largest minority group in Britain, remained the subject of debate for many social scientists. Methods of calculation were often criticised but were the only vehicles available to those who sought such figures. The National Census was seen by those who campaigned for the religion question as being the only source from which an accurate figure could be produced, as Southworth (2001) argues in her work on classifying minority groups, the Census has an exceptional status of being regarded as an official provider of authoritative statistics, which form the baseline for many other data sources.

The Use of Official Categories for Researching Religious Communities

Census and other 'official' categories essentially create boundaries as well as legitimising communities according to Skerry (2001). It is not that this necessarily has a negative impact on society as he argues there is a need for suitable ordering of diverse parts that make up society. However, what he is asserting is that data derived from such categories are not objective and this should be acknowledged when conducting research on a community. In this view every category in the Census or in official surveys is the result of political judgements even if such judgements are not narrowly self-interested.

In this case, Muslims asserted an identity and the government responded with recognising their assertion to be classified as such. Yet Skerry, even with the acknowledgement that every group has the right to be identified as they wish, argues there are some conceptual flaws with this.

Firstly identities are in flux. Highlighted here is an important sociological argument that identity is constantly under construction (Rees and Butt 2004). One decade's 'Black' became another decade's 'Asian' which went on to become 'Pakistanis' and now 'Muslim'. Thernstorm (1992) argues that there are implications to the fact that categories in official surveys have become a matter of choice, a state of mind rather than a fact of genealogy. In this view it is not important whether a person looks Asian, but if they feel Asian they are categorised as such because they ticked the box. The same argument can be applied to Muslims. It cannot be assumed that if an individual chooses to tick a Muslim box she ascribes to certain characteristics.

Skerry also argues that it is often the case that individuals will insert themselves into the categories that they believe society perceives they should. If a group are rejected due to a facet of their identity, it is this particular aspect of themselves that they are most conscious of. What this leads to is the danger of viewing an individual or even a group as one dimensional, when in reality it is more realistic to speak of multiple 'identities'.

In many regards then this study is particularly experimental in that although research on the two Muslim ethnic groups demonstrated greater levels of disadvantage, it could not be said with any degree of certainty whether data on religion or rather using data specifically on Muslims (including those who are not Pakistanis and Bangladeshis) would demonstrate the same levels of disadvantage.

This is acknowledged and its implications are however that a group of people who have been presented as facing greater disadvantage can be examined using an additional variable which it is hoped will add greater insight to the debate.

Brown writes,

> The association between religion and social and economic outcomes remain poorly documented or understood, left largely to fairly crude inferences based on the presumed (but not measured) associations with ethnicity. (2000: 1037)

Peach also adds that 'religion is the new key to unravelling ethnic identity in the West' (2002: 255). There are of course fundamental flaws apparent already, even before any analysis is conducted, which limits greatly any analysis of Muslims in Britain. Although the Census data on Muslims provides data on 'all' Muslims rather than simply Bangladeshis and Pakistanis, it is not possible to explore divergence between all Muslim ethnic groups or in other words it is not possible to explore the heterogeneous nature of Muslims to any significant degree.

At present we appear to be stuck with two options when looking at data on Muslims:

- As an all enveloping 'Muslim' category or
- Across certain ethnic groups only (due to the limited ethnic categories available).

Studying data on ethnicity for Muslims is particularly problematic because there are only three commonly used ethnic categories in surveys which can be used for this purpose meaningfully. These are Pakistani, Bangladeshi and Indian (assuming in the case of religious affiliation is known). Other commonly used ethnic categories such as 'White' are particularly unhelpful because they have been demonstrated to include a huge array of Muslim ethnic and national groups, such indigenous Muslims who have converted to Islam, Eastern European Muslims, such as Bosnian refugees and even those from the Middle East.

It is fully acknowledged that this is a limitation which is unavoidable when conducting analysis for the purposes of this study, and it is therefore the former method of looking at Muslims as a whole group that the research for this book is primarily concerned with. However additional data sets have been employed (particularly the 1999 Health Survey for England) in order to provide some intra-Muslim analysis of the three South Asian groups mentioned above.

The Data

The 2001 National Census

Censuses have a long and significant history. The Babylonians and Chinese held them and their main function was for planning and monitoring military resources and taxation. The ancient Egyptians also used them for gathering information about their potential workforce and the Romans conducted censuses of their whole empire, which required members to return to their places of origin to be counted (ONS 2001). Although evidence of large scale data collection in England can be found from as far back as 1086 in the famous Domesday Book (2004), the first modern National Census for Britain took place in 1801. There has been a census every ten years since, with the exception of 1941 due to the Second World War. In addition there has been a quinquennial Census in 1966. The Census aims to provide a snapshot of the entire nation at a specific point in time which is known as 'Census day' and there is a legal obligation to complete and return the form. This makes it the most comprehensive data collection exercise in this country and it provides information about demographic, socio-economic and housing characteristics down to small geographical levels. The data is used extensively for many purposes and although this is mostly for government bodies to inform policy decisions and allocate recourses, it is also used by the private sectors to understand consumer profiles. Diamond writes, 'The Census is certainly the biggest and probably the most important data collection exercise carried out in the United Kingdom, as it is in most countries around the world' (1999: 9).

The question on religious affiliation for England and Wales asked

'What is your religion?'

there were seven options provided on the form and eight categories in the output data. These included a single Christian category for all Christian denominations. Even where a Christian denomination was stated in the 'write in' option, during the processing of the data it was grouped as part of the Christian category. In addition to this the other faith groups listed were: Muslim, Buddhist, Sikh, Hindu, Jewish and 'Any Other Religion' for those stating a religion which did not fall within these categories. There was also an output column in the tables for those who stated that they did not belong to any religion and as the question was voluntary, a column with data on those who refused to answer the question.

The type of questions as asked in Scotland and Northern Ireland differ in at least three main ways from that used in England and Wales. Firstly, they provide different options with regard to Christian denominations, there was lengthy debate surrounding the inclusion of Christian denominations in the England and Wales Census, however, it was regarded as being too expensive and unnecessary for the main purposes for collection of data on religion, namely to provide greater information on minority communities. Secondly, the questions in Northern Ireland and Scotland were asked in terms of belonging to a religion, 'What religion, religious denomination or body do you belong to?' for Scotland and 'Do you regard yourself as belonging to a particular religion?' and 'If yes, What religion, religious denomination or body do you belong to?' for Northern Ireland. In England and Wales the question is about 'what' the respondents religion is (a detailed discussion of the language and terminology used for the religion questions is provided in the next chapter as faith groups were consulted on this issue during the campaign for the question).

In addition, where only current religion is provided by the respondent in England and Wales, for Scotland there was an additional question asking 'What religion, religious denomination or body were you brought up in?' and in Northern Ireland if the respondent answered 'no' to the first question listed above they were asked 'What religion, religious denomination or body were you brought up in?' There are therefore important differences in the types of questions asked on religion and thus the type of data collected. It is primarily for this reason that this study looks at data for England and Wales and not the UK as a whole. The additional denominational and 'religion brought up in' would have raised important topics for discussion such as conversions to faiths for example. Also, uniformity of analysis would have been extremely difficult with some data having a single Christianity category and others having breakdowns of denominations for example.

Other Sources of Quantitative Data Used

In order to explore some areas further, particularly intra-Muslim differences on grounds of differing ethnicity, two additional sources of individual level data are utilised. These are the 1999 Health Survey for England (Department of Health) and the 2001 Home Office Citizenship Survey for England and Wales (Home Office Communities Research).

There are of course other sources of individual level data providing information on religion such as 1994 Fourth National Survey of Ethnic Minorities. It was obviously not possible to utilise all data sources for this project as there were time constraints and due to the fact that the FNSEM has already been given significant attention in previous studies and is referred to commonly when looking at minorities in a number of studies, it seemed more resourceful to utilise the existing findings. The 1999 Health Survey for England in contrast has not been provided with this amount of recognition and therefore a is resource which has not been employed as much as it might have been for research on faith groups. In addition the 2001 Home Office Citizenship Survey was conducted in the same year as the Census and has been used less for intra-Muslim analysis and more as a complimentary source of information to supplement the National Census data.

Themes Explored in the Book

When choosing areas to explore in relation to creating a profile for Muslims, a comprehensive review of previous studies was conducted to identify the principal themes to be considered in this book. The broad areas for empirical investigation covered are:

- Education (and the acquisition of what has been described as human capital).
- Family and roles.
- Socio-economic disadvantage.

As these are broad and distinct areas within themselves, a literature review of the position of both minority groups in general (for the purpose of 'measuring' success and disadvantage and comparisons between groups) and of Muslims within each broad area of investigation is required. This allows for the identification of key areas or issues within each topic in order to provide focus for exploration of the data. If such an exercise had not been performed for every topic, there was a danger of producing hundreds of tables, some of which may have been of interest and relevance for the study and others adding no additional insight to the position of Muslims within the topics chosen for investigation. In other words, the evaluation of previous studies on Muslims provides important indications of key areas for investigation using the data sources.

In reality because previous studies focussed on ethnicity rather than faith groups, the majority of former research drawn on to inform and provide background information for the themes is largely on Pakistanis and Bangladeshis. This is already something that has been commented on and of course has been a driving force for those campaigning for data on religious groups.

Before going on to explore the themes covered by this book, the next chapter provides a discussion of how Muslims have become politically visible in recent years as a 'faith community' and why the use of religious labels has become increasingly important for Muslim diasporas. In addition debates surrounding the ethical and historical misuse and the perceived need for such data on Muslims are also outlined. Chapter Two provides a background to the nature of Muslim communities in Britain, presenting a brief historical account of the 'three stages' of Muslim settlement including an overview of various Muslim communities, both 'hidden' such as Maghrebi, Arabs, Somalis and Turks, as well as those for whom large scale data is commonly available, such as Pakistanis and Bangladeshis. In addition, an overview of the demographic profile for Muslims as a whole, based on the findings of the Census, as well as geographical distributions will also be provided as an introduction to the more detailed focus for the themes, which are: Educational (Chapter Three), Families (Chapter Four) and Housing, Services and Disadvantage (Chapter Five). The book concludes with a discussion of main findings from the analysis, key policy implications and what the large-scale data demonstrates about Muslims that was previously unknown.

1

Becoming Visible

The year 2001 was significant for Muslims in Britain on three levels: the international, the national and the local. At the lower geographical level, in the summer of 2001 civil unrest occurred in four northern towns and cities: Oldham and Burnley in Lancashire; and Leeds and Bradford in West Yorkshire. Within discourse discussing 'race riots', religious affiliation was at the centre of the debate. The riots were viewed as clashes between Muslim youth and the police and were sparked by the far right's campaigns targeting Muslim communities. This is clearly demonstrated in this quote by Ansari, who writes,

> The activities of the British Nationalist Party (BNP) inflamed antagonism and mutual distrust between Muslim and White communities ... Muslim men of South Asian descent clashed with White extremists and police, highlighting the considerable discontent felt among some sections of the local Muslim communities. (Ansari 2000: 4)

On the national level Muslims had been firmly put on the map and officially recognised as a community in their own right. Religion, which had been viewed increasingly within the UK as being a matter for the private domain was not viewed as such by some minority faith groups. The proposed amendments to the Census Act had been passed through parliament and a category on religion publicly endorsed by the government through its use in the largest and most comprehensive data collection exercise in the UK: the National Census. Finally, after years of campaigning by Muslim groups, large scale data on Muslims in Britain would now be available. Weller writes that 'The inclusion of the Census questions on religion signals that religion – or at least some religions – are back on the agenda within public life in the UK' (2004: 5).

In 2001, globally, Muslims had now become more politicised than ever in recent history. The bombing of the Twin Towers in New York on 11 September 2001 increased anxieties about whether Islam was compatible with democracy and whether Muslims were able to affiliate with Islam and the Ummah (international Islamic community) whilst also remaining loyal citizens of non-Muslim nations. Concerns regarding citizenship from within Muslim communities were also increasingly apparent as Muslims were asked to defend their position and assert their commitment to their country of residence, an example being the poll conducted by MORI which indicated that 87 per cent of Muslims stated that they were loyal to Britain (*Time* 2001: 51)

An organisation called Growth from Knowledge (GFK NOP) conducted an opinion poll with approximately 1,000 British Muslims during spring 2006 and the results were presented as part of a British television channel documentary (*Dispatches* 2006). The results of the survey found that 42 per cent of Muslims aged 45 and above felt 'very strongly' that they belonged to Britain and Islam compared with 39 per cent of Muslims aged between 25–44 and 30 percent of Muslims aged between 18–24. However when asked the question:

'To what extent do you agree with the idea that Muslims should keep themselves separate from non-Muslims?'

94 per cent of respondents disagreed with 81 per cent strongly disagreeing. In addition, despite the younger generations being reported as preferring 'separation' when asked to respond to the following statement:

'I would prefer to have Muslim neighbours'

less second generation Muslims agreed (30 per cent) than first generation (39 per cent). Women were also more likely to agree than men (39 per cent and 32 per cent respectively) (Imaginate n.d.).

Anxieties between communities have also been increased by government initiatives such as the 'anti-terrorist' legislation which were viewed by large numbers of British Muslims as being unfair and discriminatory resulting in an innocent East London man being shot in the shoulder,[1] discussions about freedom of speech sparked by the depiction of the Prophet Muhammad as a terrorist by a Danish newspaper,[2] as well as debates surrounding acceptable levels of religiosity and symbolism in modern day Britain initiated by comments made by John Prescott, MP for Blackburn about his preference for Muslim women not to wear the veil or *nikkab* in his presence.[3]

From Private to Public

Prior to the 1970s culture and ethnic or national origin occupied the way in which Muslims participated in the public sphere and the indigenous majority and the institutions of wider society viewed them overwhelmingly in these terms and not primarily as members of a religious minority. However, Muslims have now been firmly placed on the map and their presence most certainly acknowledged but what processes occurred for these communities to be viewed progressively more so in terms of their religious affiliation rather than their ethnicity?

Weller argues that during the 1960s, proponents of the secularisation thesis believed that through a combination of technological advances, philosophical rationalism and the development of consumer society, religion would overwhelmingly be removed from the public into the private sphere, becoming akin to a 'leisure activity' (2004: 5). However, migrant groups had begun to add new fervour to religion in Britain in that they did not conform to this secularisation thesis and prior to being publicly acknowledged or endorsed, many of these new communities placed far greater importance on religious practice in their day to day lives than the indigenous majority.

> While only 5 per cent of Whites aged 16–34 said religion was very important to how they lived their lives, nearly a fifth of Caribbeans, more than a third of Indians and African Asians and two thirds of Pakistanis and Bangladeshis in that age group held that view. (Modood et al. 1997: 256)

As agendas widened minority communities began to assert their rights to religious observance in both the public and the private domain. Modood writes,

> Equality is not having to hide or apologise for one's origins, family or community but expect others to respect them and adapt public attitudes and arrangements so that the heritage they represent is encouraged rather than contemptuously expected to wither away. There seem, then, to be two distinct conceptions of equal citizenship, each based on different views of what is 'public' and 'private'. These two concepts of equality may be stated as follows:
>
>   – The rights to assimilate to the majority/dominant cultures in the public sphere; and toleration of difference in the private sphere;
>   – The right to have one's difference recognised and supported in both the public and the private sphere. (1997: 358)

For some groups the separation of religion from the public and private domains was particularly problematic. Muslims do not regard religion as compartmentalised and detached from other aspects of life but rather as a central reference point which permeates all aspects of their lives whether political, social and economic.

There were increasing concerns over whether their faith would eventually become so marginalised and acculturated by the dominant ethos of modern western cultures and whether integration, pluralism and economic advancement are too high a price if the Muslim belief system was part of the trade off.

In Yousif's critique of liberal democracy (2000) he argues that in Europe some religious minorities are more equal than others and that there are many examples of how Muslims are particularly marginalised by the state. Merry (2004) picks up on Yousif's critique and argues that,

> It is equally true that applications to establish Islamic places of worship and schools have met with considerable resistance, even in countries that openly support the freedom to establish denominational schooling … Yousif is right that Muslim communities must, in many instances, prove that their activities are aimed more at 'cultural preservation' and not

at explicitly religious objectives, seems an untenable double standard. (pp. 227–28)

The point made about separating or rather disguising the 'religious' element under the 'cultural' or 'ethnic' identity has become increasing challenging for Muslims who contest the notion that religion in the West, based on the liberal notion of freedom is constrained to a personal affair, distinct from the more 'rational' aspects of public life. In this view, the more secular structure of British society when compared with Muslim countries, far from providing affirmation for a religious worldview, has tended to portray it as progressively more irrelevant. Modood et al. write, 'Religion is perhaps the key area where the minority groups manifest a cultural dynamic which is at least partly at odds with native British trends' (1997: 356).

Why the Use of Religious Labels Has Become Increasingly Important for Muslim Diasporas

Religion and Identity

Modood et al. (1997) argue that minorities in the UK have been viewing themselves in much more defined ways than was previously thought. Discourse on race had been increasingly criticised for being too simplistic since the 1980s and it was acknowledged that many minority communities did not view themselves as falling under the umbrella term of 'Black', but asserted more specific ethnic labels. Many commentators have used the shift in language on race and identity to support the argument that identity is constantly under construction (Werbner 2003; Butt and Box 1998). Here it is argued that the identity asserted by members of a group at any given time is dependent on what is most functional in promoting the empowerment of that group as a minority in a majority setting. As Saeed et al. (1999) describes it, this as a 'mechanism which allows for the minority group to increase inter-group differentiation and to maintain its self-esteem' (p. 226).

Several other studies have demonstrated this. Self-identification surveys in particular have been useful in ascertaining how minorities view themselves. Hutnik's study in 1985 pioneered this type of self-reported identity among British Muslims. It was found that Muslim identity was listed by 80 per cent of the South Asian Muslims as an important identity item. Modood et al.'s (1997) research in the area supported these findings. Here, 83 per cent of Pakistanis mention religion as an important self-attribute. The study also indicated that 74 per cent of the sample asserted that religion was an important aspect of their lives.

Saeed et al. (1999) conducted self-identification surveys in Glasgow amongst second and third generation Pakistani Muslims. Their findings were consistent with the previous studies. The 'Muslim' and 'Pakistani' identities were the top two categories mentioned, with 'Muslim' (85 per cent) being chosen nearly three times as often as 'Pakistani' (30 per cent). This strengthens the argument that these young respondents were, indeed, identifying with their Muslim background, in the sense of belonging, rather than merely superficially tagging themselves in terms of 'my label is … ' (p. 831) Saeed et al. went on to write:

> Through our inclusion within some categories and exclusion from others (which involves both self-definition and definition by others), together with the values and emotional significance of these memberships, we define our social identity. A person emphasizing his/her Muslim identity wishes to share common ground with other Muslims, and also acknowledges (not necessarily willingly) that certain characteristics will be ascribed to him/her by non-Muslims. (1999: 831)

Ballard (1996a) describes the increasing self-identification of second and subsequent generations as Muslim, rather than Pakistani, Bangladeshi, Turkish or Somali, as a reaction to the external rejection, which they face from the White majority. First, because it is the Muslim aspect of their identity that they feel is under attack, and second, as described further below, that Islam is a more useful vehicle for political mobilisation.

The Shift Towards a Religious Identity: External Rejection

Maalouf (1998) explains that people often have the tendency to acknowledge themselves through the affiliation that is most attacked. So in the case of Muslims in Britain, their 'Muslimness' is attacked. Citizenship alone cannot encapsulate the notion of belonging; in a state that generally originates in ethnic bonding, new immigrants gravitate towards their own cultural and social groups.

In the UK this assertion of a more religious identity was facilitated primarily by the Rushdie affair (Mohammad 1999). The Rushdie affair, many academics argue, marked the beginning of the latest surge in Islamophobia in the West, particularly in Britain. Werbner describes this process,

> Until the publication of *The Satanic Verses* Muslims were a silent, apparently compliant and quiescent law abiding minority ... It was difficult to imagine their mobilisation as a united front. The global crisis which came to be known as the Rushdie affair, with the book burning in Bradford screened on TV world-wide, and the death sentence pronounced by the Ayatollah Khomeini causing a major international rupture between Iran and the West, visibilised this subterranean Muslim local-level politics into the public eye. A large demonstration in London mobilised Muslims, primarily South Asians, across the different sectarian and organisational divides. (2003: 905)

Khan (2000) and Ballard (1996*b*) describe how the reactions to *The Satanic Verses* by Muslims reinforced the view of Muslims and Islam among non-Muslims, as anti-Western and anti-democratic. It is argued by Ballard that far from holding an orthodox stance on Islam, most [UK] Muslims who came from South Asia practiced a much more 'Sufi' Islam, with most of these Muslims belonging to the Beralvi school of thought, which places greater emphasis on spirituality and devotional worship rather than a strict interpretation of theology and scriptures. Here, the Prophet Muhammed is held as a figure of devotional reverence. Ballard argued that *The Satanic Verses* was extremely hurtful to this community due to the way it portrayed the Prophet, mocking that which this community held so dear. In this view, the demonstrations were not about the 'fundamentalism' associated with those such as Khomeini, as the media so often portrayed the reaction.

Khan writes that the reactions to such prejudice by Muslims, who are interpreted as largely reflecting an ideological negation of the freedom of speech and all things common to democratic States, results in the construction of 'Muslims' as 'an alien minority with social and cultural values and belief systems diametrically opposed to those in the West' (2000: 30). He goes on to argue that such perceptions may have the effect of encouraging the majority of Muslims to remain more insular, resulting in the wider society having to face greater challenges in its relations with this community.

The Fourth National Survey of Ethnic Minorities (FNSEM), conducted in 1994, found that all ethnic groups under study believed that the most prejudice is directed at Asians and/or Muslims (Modood et al. 1997). The events of 11 September 2001 and, more recently, 7 July 2005 clearly further aggravated the relationship between the wider society and British Muslims. An opinion poll in *The Guardian* newspaper demonstrated the isolation that Muslims believe they are facing, with nearly 70 per cent stating that they felt 'the rest of society does not regard them as an integral part of life in Britain' (Kelso and Vasagar 2002). More recent literature (Modood 2003; Sheridan and Gillett 2005; Ahmed 2006; Adam and Burke 2006; Hopkins 2006) discussing debates surrounding identity vis-à-vis discrimination post 11 September 2001 and 7 July 2005.

The Commission on British Muslims and Islamophobia, established in 1996 by the Runnymede Trust, stressed the need for the government to legislate against religious discrimination, through an expansion of the coverage of the Race Relations Act (1976). The Commission argued that Islamophobia is comparable to the sectarianism of Northern Ireland and the anti-Semitism in Europe, and yet despite its presence and effects within society, there are insufficient legislative procedures to combat it. It has been argued that this lack of legislation in itself sends a message to Muslims, demonstrating that although there is now a wealth of research suggesting the damaging nature of Islamophobia within society, the government has been less than forthcoming in tackling the issue in any momentous way. However, legislation has now been enacted to cover religious discrimination and incitement to religious hatred.

Modood argues that 'Muslims (now) have the most extensive and developed discourses of unity, common circumstance and common victimhood among non-EU origin peoples in the EU' (2003: 101) There have been public demonstrations of frustration by young Asian Muslim men such as the northern riots in 2001. This has had a notable impact on how Muslims are not only perceived by wider society but also on how Muslims believe they are perceived. As Sheridan and Gillet (2005) explain, 'It is known that a major world event caused by one group can influence perceptions of other social groups' (p. 191).

Internal Empowerment

As well as constructing identities in response to external factors, identity is also constructed to suit the position of those who adopt it at any given time. European Muslims, who find themselves in the position of a minority, can opt for an 'interscholastic eclecticism' that consists of choosing the opinion of legal schools that appear to be the most appropriate to their own set of social issues and questions. An example of this is Ballard's argument that amongst British Muslims there has been a shift from the more 'Sufi' Islam, which was the Islam the majority of first generation Muslims practiced, to a neo-orthodox Islam, which has been adopted increasingly by the second and subsequent generations, and has also been an important factor in the development of a 'religious' identity rather than a 'cultural' identity. This is for two reasons. Firstly, this form of Islam places greater emphasis on a universal Islam and downplays cultural differences. In this view, for many Muslims, Islam provides a solution,

> Given that Islam is manifestly a sophisticated world religion, which is at the very least a match for Christianity, and better still its long historical role as Christianity's 'bête noir', it provides a wonderfully effective alter with which to identify, in response to White, European post-Christian denigration. (Ballard 1999b: 124)

Secondly, it served as a means of distancing the second and subsequent generations of British-born Muslims from the perceived 'backwardness' of the first generation, in turn equipping them with the necessary ammunition to 'fight their corner' on the domestic front (Ansari 2002).

Knott and Khokher (1993) found that many young South Asian Muslim women are conceptually establishing a firm distinction between 'religion' and 'culture', which were largely indistinguishable realms for their parents. Further, they are rejecting their parents' conformity to ethnic traditions, which are considered as emblematic of religiosity (such as manner of dress), while wholly embracing a Muslim identity in and of itself. Among these young women, Khokher et al. argue, is a necessary self-conscious exploration of religion, which was not relevant to their parents' generation.

Jacobson (1997) has also commented on how this gives second and subsequent generations greater bargaining power within their families and communities. Many young women who adopted the hijab and other Islamic symbols argued that parents found it increasingly difficult to refuse their daughters' requests to pursue their education and postpone marriage, as Islamically they had every right to do so.

Saint-Blancat (2002) also supports this view. She argues,

> The descendents of immigrants of Muslim origin are witnesses

par excellence of an active form of subjectivity, of autonomy
that they do not always risk acquiring. In evaluating their family and community past, they are helping to create a memory
that will also forge their own identity. They distance themselves from the stereotypes of host cultures that demand from
them a social and cultural conformity to the principle of individual and sexual emancipation, but also from fidelity to a
family genealogy, which they criticize even though they will
not tolerate its being disparaged. (p. 142)

The Identification with a Muslim Diaspora

As well as the recognition of a growing preference to be identified in
terms of religion amongst South Asian Muslims in Britain, it has been
argued that Muslim minorities in the West, whatever their ethnic origin, are increasingly presenting themselves as being part of a Muslim
diaspora, as well as, and in some cases instead of, an ethnic or national
diaspora. The concept of a united Muslim community within Islam,
known as 'the Ummah', has been discussed as being a contributing
factor in the mindset of many Muslims who identify themselves as
being part of a Muslim diaspora (Werbner 2003).

Saint-Blancat (2002) has written about this identification of European Muslims with a Muslim diaspora, arguing that the creation
of such a diaspora is one which various Muslim minority groups are
striving to adopt, as a result of the recognition that as minorities in
present day Europe they all share increasing hostility on the grounds
of one common denominator – Islam. It is argued, however, that the
Muslim disapora is not a result of the natural state of being, or a
concept which is easily applied without complications. Shuval (2000)
describes common definitions of diasporic communities as sharing
some of the following elements,

A history of dispersal, myths/memories of the homeland,
alienation in the host country, desire for eventual return
(which can be ambivalent, eschatological or utopian), ongoing support of the homeland, and a collective identity defined
by the above relationship. (p. 43)

Clearly Muslims in Europe do not share a common homeland, but
have origins in numerous countries, resulting in cultural heterogeneity. However, the association with a shared 'homeland' is not problematic for Vertovec (1999). When discussing approaches to diaspora,

he argues that an alternative definition is through common experience, such as discrimination and exclusion, and a shared common denominator, such as historical heritage or a contemporary world culture.

Saint-Blancat, however, argues that,

> The instrumental use of the morphological configuration of settlements in migration and the inter-polarity of relationships do not mean that a Birmingham Pakistani and a Strasbourg Turk feel they belong to the same diaspora. Only self-definition and interaction with the gaze of the other, in its turn creates a model for their identity. (2002: 141)

Therefore, in this view a single Muslim diaspora in Europe is reactionary and a result of the initial grouping together of communities by the discriminator and that these communities would perhaps not have otherwise viewed themselves as a unit or community in this way.

Strength in numbers is, of course, an important motivation for minority groups in attempting to unify with other minority groups, as demonstrated by minorities in Britain attempting to mobilise by uniting themselves under their common feature of 'non-Whiteness' in the 1980s. The attractiveness for Muslims, then, in uniting themselves with other Muslims by asserting this element of their identity, is that it serves to empower them due to the possibility of their minority status being transformed into a global counter-force (Khan 2000).

Further to this, a key source of alienation for migrant communities is the 'host' country's policy with regard to their countries of origin. Foreign policy impacting negatively, whether in reality or as perceived, on Muslim communities elsewhere can result in Muslim communities within the host country feeling detached and alienated from the State. Events that occur across the globe involving Muslims, such as 11 September 2001, the war in the Balkans and the war in Iraq, to name a few, are seen to affect Muslims everywhere, as the effect on 'a part of the whole'. Here, such events are viewed in a Muslim versus non-Muslim arena, which assists the process of cohesion amongst dispersed and internally divided Muslim communities, promoting a 'them' and 'us' dichotomy (Modood 2003; Werbner 2003).

Statistics on Religion

Using religion as a vehicle for political mobilisation within the public sphere resulted in data on religion being seen as an important symbolic recognition of Muslims as a faith community in their own right. The Muslim community actively campaigned for the inclusion of an official category for Muslims due to their ethnically diverse nature, acknowledging that there were many Muslims hidden in categories of ethnicity which were not indicators of a country of origin such as Pakistan and Bangladesh, for example many Britons of Turkish descent ticked 'White'. In addition as described in the Introduction, it was believed that data would assist with policy development to counter levels of deprivation found among Muslim communities.

The Campaign for Statistics on Religion

Before the campaign to include a question on religion in the 2001 National Census, Church organisations had raised the issue of a question on religion in the 1971 and the 1981 Censuses with little success. This was largely due to the fact that the case was raised, in both instances, too late in the census timetable to allow the necessary consultation to take place. In 1996, the 'Inner Cities Religious Council' argued that there had been a need expressed by various London Boroughs for data on religious groups in order to plan burial sites, community centres and education provision. In addition to the Religious Council, the British Board of Jews had also submitted a request for a question on religion to be included in the Census.

As a result the Religious Council formed a group where representatives of all the major faith groups in the UK, as well as smaller ones such as the Zoroastrian Trust Fund of Europe, Jain Samaj Europe and Baha'i Community of the United Kindgom, would collectively present a case for the collection of such data. The Census Office responded to the request by stating that there was insufficient support from agencies for the collection of data on religion in the Census, although they did acknowledge that such data should be collected by other sources. The 'Religious Affiliation Subgroup' was established in order to take the case forward, with Professor Leslie Francis as the group convenor. It was agreed by all the faith organisations consulted that religious 'belonging' rather than 'believing' or 'practising' should be measured if the question was to be included. This was due to the notion of belonging being the least personal of the three, as well as the opinion within academia that belonging is a useful predictor of other variables. Other national censuses were also consulted and were found to ask about religious belonging (such as Canada) rather than practical worship. In sum it was argued that religious belonging shapes the sociocultural aspects of religion and therefore was the most appropriate variable to suit the needs of the main census users.

One area which could not be decided on however by the sub group was sub-dividing religions. The Christian organisation felt that denominations should be recognisable from the census data, whereas other faith groups wanted to avoid this. The predecessors of the Muslim Council of Britain – the UK Action Committee on Islamic Affairs (UKACIA) wrote: 'From a Muslim point of view we do not believe there is a need to subdivide the faith, Islam or Muslim would suffice. For purposes of simplicity it would seem reasonable that faiths are not subdivided' (Sacranie 1996).

In 1997, as a result of the subgroup's campaigning the Office for National Statistics (ONS) agreed to include a question asking about religious affiliation in the 1997 Census Test. The ONS also invited the subgroup to join the 2001 Census religious affiliation subgroup, where Professor Francis remained as convenor. Despite the question being included in the Census Test, the subgroup needed to demonstrate that there would be sufficient use for the data by the main census users. As a result a series of consultations with various agencies and departments were conducted. The Department of the Environment, Transport and the Regions saw the information on religious affiliation as potentially useful for regeneration, housing and planning and particularly where services are delivered in partnership or consultation with the local community. The Department for Education and Employment felt there were a number of uses for such data including: the monitoring of education policy to ensure equity of opportunity and raise educational achievement, local environment information to put TEC performance into context, policy development in identifying disadvantage and priorities for action and for policy briefing on employment opportunities and racial disadvantage. The Department of Health stated that they would use information about religious affiliation for policy uses regarding elderly and health outcome indicators. The Home Office stated that the data was required for greater ethnic monitoring and the Race Relations Unit. Local Authorities in England and Wales stated that they would use information on religion for deprivation analysis, providing a statistical base for local surveys, profiling ethnic groups for resource allocation, identifying characteristics of refugees and other population groups, to assess whether local authorities are fulfilling their duties under the Race Relations Act (1976) and multicultural education.

The assessment of the business cases by the ONS for the inclusion of all new questions proposed appeared two thirds from the bottom of the list for priority topics. This raised concern and members of the subgroup felt the campaign needed to be more proactive. A draft White Paper including proposals for the new questions went through the Government Statistical Service Social Statistics Committee and then to three Registrars General for approval, before being submitted to Ministers. The White Paper was published in March 1999, which was the formal announcement of the Government's proposal.

The subgroup were able to include a statement in the White Paper stating that the faith communities of the UK unanimously supported a question on religious affiliation in the National Census. They argued that the information would assist with legislative requirements outlined in:

- Sub-sections of Section 11 of the Education Reform Act 1988 or part III of the Children Act 1989
- NHS and Community Care Act 1990
- Criminal Justice Act 1991
- Article 13 of the Amsterdam Treaty

The sub-group also argued that the information would provide benefits to the nation as far as being necessary for the monitoring of religious discrimination, assisting in providing adequate services in the area of health and community care, providing necessary information for local authorities for the break down of religion within schools, assisting with regeneration and local community partnerships, assisting the voluntary sector – as religious organisations themselves provide key services to the community.

The Government clearly saw the question on religious affiliation's main purpose as one that would compliment the question on ethnicity. Paragraph 64 of the White paper stated:

A question on religion is being proposed for inclusion in the 2001 Census in England, Wales and Northern Ireland. The topic is new to the Census and will help provide information which would supplement the output from the ethnicity question by identifying ethnic minority sub-groups, particularly those originating from the Indian sub-continent, in terms of religion.

The 2001 Census Religious Affiliation Group (RAG) was set up to follow on from the sub-group. RAG had its first meeting on 25 June

1998 and Professor Francis remained in his role as the group convenor. The three Muslim organisations who were now part of this alliance were the Islamic Foundation, UKACIA and the Muslim Council of Great Britain.[4] RAG saw their main task to be lobbying key Ministers to ensure their support for the question: 'There was agreement that it would now be appropriate for the group to make appropriate representations to politicians ahead of the publication of the White paper' (Francis 1998b) During the meeting itself this was re-iterated and noted that a list of useful political and religious contacts was needed.

Professor Francis contacted the Economic Secretary, Helen Liddell MP, requesting a meeting to allow a delegation from the group to discuss the question, however the request was refused. RAG went on to write letters requesting support from Ministers whose departments had a substantive interest in the issue. A delegation from the Muslim Council of Britain met the Home Secretary on the 15 June 1998 where the question was discussed and his support was sought. The Home Secretary agreed it was an important issue but noted that the structure of the Census questionnaire was still under construction.

Census Act 1920 Amendment

An additional barrier for the inclusion of a question on religious affiliation was the amendment of the Census Act 1920 which as it stood did not allow for the inclusion of a question on religion nor did it allow for voluntary questions to be asked in the national Census.

Professor Francis wrote to the Census Minister, Patricia Hewitt for assurance that if a religion question were to be recommended for inclusion in the census, interpretation of the Census Act 1920 would not stand in the way. Minister Hewitt's reply stated that, 'For a question on religion to be included in the next census of Great Britain, parliamentary time will have to be made for appropriate amendment to the census legislation' (Francis 1998a).

RAG were aware that this could pose serious difficulties for the question and that if appropriate time was not made available in parliament to amend the Census Act 1920 advocates of the question could be waiting another ten years before it materialised.

Professor Francis informed RAG members that he was,

> working on a strategy to get a Parliamentary Question tabled
> in the House of Lords to try to ensure that a shortage of

space in parliamentary timetable will not be used as an excuse for the legislation not to be changed, and ultimately for the religion question to not be asked. (Francis 1998*a*)

Lobbying for the inclusion of the question in the census was a priority at this stage in the campaign. The MCB wrote to Margaret Beckett, the President of the council and leader of the House of Commons, requesting the provision of time adequate for the amendment of the Census Act 1920,

> We understand that you will soon be drawing up the timetable for the next Parliamentary session. We seek your assurances that it is the Government's intention to make provisions for the parliamentary programme for the debate of passage of the Census amendment bill. (Sacranie 1999)

Other member organisations of RAG also forwarded letters urging time to be allocated for the discussion on the amendment of the Bill. The amendment to the Census Act 1920 was introduced in the House of Lords as a private members Bill by Lord Weatherall. The first reading of the Bill took place on the 16 December 1999 and the second reading took place on the 27 January 2000. Although those involved did 'not expect any difficulty in gaining approval in the House of Lords' (Sacranie 2000), this proved to not be the case at all. As a result of the debate around the question it was believed that the only way the Bill would be passed were if the question was voluntary.[5]

Although other peers argued that this would jeopardise quality of data obtained from the Census it was agreed that in order for the Bill to pass through to the 'other place' it would be necessary. It was also hoped that this would make it easier in the House of Commons, especially since it was already known that there would be opposition from two Conservative backbenchers. These Tory MP's, Eric Forth and David McLean, opposed the Bill on the general principle that legislation should not pass through the Commons without debate rather than any opposition to the Bill itself.

Member organisations of RAG pressed the Government to include the Bill in the Government's own legislative timetable. The Government agreed to this and the Bill passed through its final stages. The Bill received a Second reading on 21 June 2000. The main issues that were raised related to clarifying the voluntary nature of the question. The Bill passed through its third reading on the 26 June 2000 and received Royal assent on 28 June 2000.

Professor Francis wrote to the RAG members informing them of the news and his disappointment that although the Christian organisations had pushed for a sub-divided Christian category, it was not granted, however, '… to have a religious affiliation question included has been no small achievement' (Francis 2000c).

The part that Muslim organisations played in the inclusion of a religion question in the Census demonstrates their views on the importance of having data collected on religion. The reality of obtaining such data was no small feat and required the working together of all the main faith groups in the UK. At various stages of the campaign it seemed as though the question would not be included and it was only through the active lobbying by RAG that national level data on religion in Britain became a reality. Prior to the inclusion of a question on religion in the Census Muslim organisations argued that the importance the government placed on catering for the needs of British Muslims was clear. The government were reminded of this on many occasions during the campaign. The availability of 'hard facts', as was argued by the MCB, on British Muslims was a step in the right direction in recognising the needs of this community.

The campaign provides an example of the political process involved in getting a category 'officially' recognised. In this case it was not straight forward – the 'users' had to state whether such a category was worthy, as did the Census Office if it was to be considered at all. Parliament also had to decide whether it would not cause offence and in many respects this was a matter of subjective opinions. In reality it was not simply a matter of MCB or any other organisation wanting categories on religion to be available, but it had to be perceived as politically important to begin with to even be placed on the agenda.

Ethical Debates Surrounding the Collection of Large Scale Data on Religion

The possibility of large scale data collection on religion generated much debate and there were many who were vocally opposed to the prospect of the question on religious affiliation being included in the Census and other official government data collection exercises. Weller described how those who agreed with the collection of data on ethnicity did not necessarily do so for religion, which was viewed as 'an essentially private matter of choice, into which the State should not intrude' (Weller 2004: 10).

Southworth (1999) asks whether it is justifiable to categorise people in Censuses for the use of accumulating official statistics and whether it is a valuable and worthy means to an end. Here the main issues about the collection of statistics on groups, particularly minority groups, seem to be about government control over how people view themselves, since it is ultimately government bodies who decide on categories.

Another key issue in the debate is whether the risk of the wrong government, if it should ever come to power, using the information against the interest of some communities, is worth taking.

Zellick (1999) has argued that the state should not have asked a question regarding religious affiliation in the Census. He argues that it was 'an unprecedented exercise of State power' (p. 22) and could be judged as a manifest transgression of human rights. Here the main objection is that people should not be categorised on grounds of religion, due to its private and sensitive nature. Coleman (1999) supported this view and wrote 'religious faith is a private matter, not to be pried into by compulsory public enquiries' in a letter written by David Coleman to the Times, 12 January 1999.

Southworth states that the main issue with recording statistics on religion and ethnicity is the fact that so often in the past they have been used for negative purposes including the persecution of minorities. She argued against the possibility of including the religion question pre 2001 and stated that Britain needed to take note of the opposition in the rest of Europe to using categories of ethnicity and religion in official Census, given the historical weight associated with the creations of boundaries. The most well known of these is the use of the national Census in Germany by the Nazi's to identify where Jewish communities lived and even to identify where there may be one Jewish family or individual in a non-Jewish area, where they did not appear visible. In Edwin Black's 'IBM and the Holocaust' (2001) a detailed account of how the Census was used in order to identify Jews for deportation, ghettoisation, confiscation or even extermination is described. He writes,

> The Germans always had a list of Jewish names. Suddenly, a squadron of grim faced SS would burst into a city square and post a notice demanding those listed assemble the next day at the train station for deportation to the East. But how did the Nazis get the lists? The answer – IBM Germany Census operations and similar advanced people counting and registering technologies.

Black goes on to write,

Statisticians used their little known but powerful discipline
to identify the victims, project and rationalise the benefits of
their destruction, organise their persecution, and even audit
the efficiency of their genocide. (p. 3)

In addition to issues surrounding possibility of persecution, Southworth argues that some religious groups do not wish to be counted,
even though larger ones have been supportive, if not actively campaigning for the question to be included in the Census. Here it is argued that the views of minorities should be protected, for example
those orthodox groups who have theological objections to the collection of information on religion. The objections above seem less urgent
however, when reminded that the question on religious affiliation is
a voluntary one, therefore leaving it entirely up to the individual as to
whether they answer it or not.

Zellick's criticism goes beyond this however, as he has objections
to the question conceptually. He argues that the domain of religion
the question will capture will be on religious affiliation, even membership, and that religious bodies will already have this information
available to them. Therefore the additional information will be rendered useless. This was an objection that a Hindu spokesperson had
on the questions inclusion in the Census. He argued that religious
bodies should be allocated resources to conduct surveys of their own
communities to complement the statistics they already have. However
the main reason for this was that the spokesperson felt 'Some people
do not understand the term Hindu, and would not count themselves
as such ... (as a result) the Hindu community could be underesti-
mated' (Weller 1998: 7).

This was a concern then over the category itself and whether
Hindu could be interpreted too narrowly to include some groups.

Southworth also suggested that data on religious communities
could be gained through records of Church Attendance and that
other faith communities could undertake similar exercises. However,
what Southworth, Zellick and those arguing a similar case fail to
acknowledge is that not all faith groups place as great an emphasis on the attendance of a place of worship as Christianity does. As
Bodi (2000) explains in the case of Muslims, to use counts generated
through mosque attendance would exclude one half of the community, as women, by religious ordinance are not expected to worship
in a mosque. This would also exclude those who hold congregational
prayers outside mosques, which is also permissible in Islam.

Aspinall (2000) also challenged the point made by Zellick . He argues,

> Clearly, belonging to a group here in the 'Census sense' refers to the sharing of common sets of beliefs with a part of the population ... it is not the sociological sense of belonging that involves collective participation in social institutions and purposeful membership. (p. 587)

Individuals could claim to be affiliated to a faith group without necessarily participating in group worship, and therefore would not appear on the 'records'.

Some critics of the collection of statistics on religious groups, such as Southworth and Zellick , are also suspicious of the religious groups' motives for supporting the question on religious affiliation in the Census. Here it is argued that official recognition is likely to improve the image and profile of faith groups and religious organisations and enable them to better define their wider constituency and in turn become better equipped to access more funding from the bodies that distribute finances for social and charitable purposes. Coleman (1999) supported this view and argued that ethnic and religious minorities supported the inclusion of the categorising on grounds of ethnicity and religion in the Census in order to dispute over greater group related advantages and employ authority over and above that available to other citizens. He warns that this could lead to 'a new creeping statistical apartheid' (p. 17).

This aim is one religious groups would openly admit to, and do not view what they would describe as a fairer allocation of recourses, as something to be criticised. As the Inner Cities Religion Council has pointed out and the government has acknowledged, religious led organisations often provide valuable services at local community levels, and a reason the government supported the inclusion of the religion question is for the purpose of informing policy decisions and allocation of resources to communities that require them, whether the community identified itself as a faith community, an ethnic community or otherwise.

This view is in line with that of those such as Prewitt (1987) who argue that 'Being "measured" is to be politically noticed, and to be noticed is to have a claim on the nations resources... political visibility follows on the heels of statistical visibility' (p. 270).

The fact that the powers that be acknowledge your community is worth giving space to on a Census form means that you are important enough in their eyes to be recognised. Here the communities who are most likely to be persecuted and face varying forms of discrimination – namely the minority communities, were actively supportive of the inclusion of a question on religion, this was of course because they acknowledged the benefits of being counted. The fact also that the question is not compulsory allows those who wish to opt out of answering the question to do so. Such communities clearly feel that categorisation in this instance is not only justifiable but a necessity in order to gain recognition and in turn influence policy decisions about their communities.

Aspinall (2000) argued that the government's main reason for supporting the inclusion of the religion question was to enhance information on ethnicity, especially for those from the Indian subcontinent. Anthropologists such as Ballard (1994b) criticised the categories in the 1991 Census of 'Pakistani', 'Indian' and 'Bangladeshi' and stated that they needed to be more of an 'ethno-religious' nature. 'Punjabi Sikh' and 'Gujarathi Muslim', although both falling under the 'Indian' category have distinct dress, language, religions, food habits and so on. Such data could in turn provide baseline figures against which the government can monitor possible racial disadvantages and social exclusion and this is based on the widespread recognition that religion is an important element of ethnicity and a cultural marker of difference. Others such as Anthias and Yuval-Davis (1992) identify religion as one of the signifiers of an essential or 'natural' community of people.

Perceived Consequences of Becoming an Official Category

The campaign is an example par excellence of how Muslims have emerged as political group of actors, pushing their concerns on to policy and research agendas. For the first time demographics on the Muslim community across the length and breath of Britain are available. This information was seen as an imperative tool to counter discrimination and disadvantage faced my Muslims. In the Introduction arguments for why Muslims groups were described as the most socially and economically deprived of the minority groups in Britain are outlined. As argued earlier, one of the benefits of having statistics on groups is that they provide political visibility. This was exactly the intention of those such as the Muslim Council of Britain when campaigning for the inclusion of a question on religious affiliation.

The MCB produced a briefing paper outlining the need for data on Muslims in Britain in 2000, stating that,

> The inclusion of a religious affiliation question will send signals to the British Muslim community that their presence and contribution is recognised. The Muslim community will have hard facts that show that its needs are not being adequately met by the public services. (MCB 2000)

Many practical examples of how the Census data will assist in the provision of better services for the Muslim community were provided. In the area of education, the demographic distribution of Muslims will help indicate where provisions should be made for voluntary and single sex schools and where proper recognition should be given to the needs of faith groups in state maintained schools. It is also argued here that the housing needs of Muslims are distinct, based on extended families and care of the elderly. In the area of employment, there is a need for Muslims to be better represented in the public services, to reflect their population base in local communities; for business and commerce the Census will provide demographic data essential for planning the location of shops and niche services. In the area of health, there has already been a wealth of research literature demonstrating how religious differences can predict demands on medical resources and health care (Sheikh and Gatrad 2000). It is hoped that the Census data will provide information that can potentially challenge the extent to which Muslim are currently catered for, as in the view of many Muslims organisations this is at present woefully inadequate.

Although perhaps the Muslim Community has more to fear from the statistics getting into the wrong hands than other religious communities, due to the recent campaigns by far right parties such as the British Nationalist Party to target Muslims, this community clearly feels that the need outweighs any threat. The objections to the inclusion of categorising people in terms of religion and ethnicity were largely based on fear of persecution of those communities. Yet ironically it is due to discrimination already faced by some of these communities that the inclusion of these questions and such categorisation was supported so actively.

2

Muslim Communities:
Hidden and Seen

This chapter provides an initial overview of the demographic profile of Muslims in Britain before Chapters Four to Six present a more detailed exploration of some of the most prominent aspects of the Muslim community.

Section one provides a broad synopsis of the process of Muslim migration to Britain and discusses the prompts for certain communities and their settlement patterns. The migration of ethnic minority communities to Britain is already a well documented area, yet this is only the case for the larger more visible communities. When looking at the settlement process of those from the Middle East and Arab world for example the picture presented within the body of literature on migration remains vague, although there are some studies which look at specific communities such as Kucukcan's *'Politics of ethnicity, identity and religion: Turkish Muslims in Britain'* (1996). Therefore the latter part of this section provides brief overviews of various Muslim communities, both 'hidden' such as Maghrebi, Arabs, Somalis and Turks, as well as those for which large scale data is commonly available, such as Pakistanis and Bangladeshis.

The second section describes the attempts at quantifying the Muslim population in Britain prior to the 2001 National Census and as alternatives to the Census data (Brown 2000; Ansari 2004), which began relatively early on in their arrival to these shores. However it was not until the political visibility of Muslims became more apparent (as discussed in Chapter One) that attempts to quantify Muslims as a religious group, rather than ethnic communities became more prevalent. Difficulties in doing so were not simply tied in with locating data on faith groups, but also definitions and issues surrounding who should be counted as belonging to the Muslim 'community' as discussed during the Introduction.

Finally, the findings from the 2001 National Census will provide a geographical and demographic overview of Muslims in Britain. Key variables for which Muslims are particularly distinct as a group will be highlighted and then Muslims are compared with other faith groups present in Britain.

Brief Historical Account of the Three Stages of Settlement

Patterns of Muslim Settlement in Britain

During the first half of the twentieth century, Britain controlled parts of the Muslim world. As with other colonial powers there was an intake of immigrants from former colonies after the Second World War and for Britain the majority of Muslim migrants came from South Asia. Although there had been a Muslim presence in Britain prior to this (Sherif 2002) the Muslim community grew significantly from 1960 onwards. A clear demonstration of this is the rise in the number of mosques. In 1963 there were only 13 mosques registered in Britain. The number grew to 49 in 1970 and doubled in the space of five years to 99 in 1975, and again to 203 in 1980 and almost doubling yet again to 338 in 1985 (Vertovec 2002).

Ansari (2004) describes the large scale Muslim settlement to Britain as occurring in two broad phases: firstly from 1945 to the early 1970s and then the second phase from 1973 to the present. However it is argued here that it is more useful to have a three-fold division:

i)   1945 to approximately 1970 — which was characterised by the settlement of young male migrant workers.
ii) 1970 to approximately 1990 — where communities were formed as a result of wives joining husbands and British born children.

iii) 1990s onwards — characterised by settlement of young single men, asylum seekers and refugee communities rather than
economic migrants.

The first phase was to fulfil the needs of Britain's expansion of production which called for large numbers of migrant workers, many of
whom were Muslim. Ansari writes,

> Migration by Muslims since the Second World War helped to
> produce the heterogeneous mix of communities in contem-
> porary Britain. While the details vary from case to case, they
> were mainly influenced in their decision to migrate by sim-
> ilar combinations of factors encouraging them to leave their
> original homes and pull factors drawing them to the various
> opportunities on offer in Britain. (2004: 164)

The main pull factor for Muslim migrants in taking up undesirable
employment opportunities was the financial gain. The pay in Britain
for manual labour was up to 30 times greater than for equivalent jobs
in some of the countries of origin (Shaw 1988). However, it is clear
when considering events occurring prior to or during peaks of migration that poverty was not the main motive for uprooting and settling
overseas.

The partition of India and to a lesser extent Cyprus created a sense
of 'motion' among communities, which promoted the migration of
Muslims to Britain. For the majority of Pakistanis, originating from
Azad Jammu and Kashmir, the building of the Mangla dam in 1960
left some 250 villages submerged displacing 100,000 'Mirpuris' who
might previously have been cautious about migrating when offered
the opportunity by the British government to assist in rebuilding the
economy. Similarly the Bengali Muslims who moved from Sylhet to
Assam prior to partition did so to take up more advantageous land
tenure, however once Assam became a province in the new India
they returned to Syhlet as refugees finding themselves with little or no
other opportunities for economic betterment. Lewis (2002), in contrast, argues that migrants did not come from the poorest areas but
rather prosperous farming areas and places with a tradition of emigration.

Many of those who arrived initially as pioneers were joined by
members of their villages and *biraderi* or kin networks, who often
helped motivate prospective migrants to take the risks involved. This

process is often described as 'chain migration'. Ballard (2004) argues that the majority of migrants made their journeys to specific localities for settlement as a result of acquiring information of the opportunities within those towns and cities prior to migration. The knowledge of such opportunities was passed back to the villages left behind through channels of kinship, friends and clientship. Ballard writes, 'As a result what may seem at first sight to be mass migratory movements invariably turn out on closer inspection, to be grounded in a multitude of kin – and locality – specific processes of chain migration' (2004: 1). It is therefore not uncommon to find communities who resided in the same villages re-established in neighbourhoods within the UK.

Not surprisingly due to the availability of work in the industrial sectors, early pioneers headed for some of the main industrial conurbanations, and when joined by other migrants, Muslim communities began to emerge in areas such as Greater London, the South East, West Midlands, West Yorkshire and Lancashire in England, and in Scotland, central Clydeside, the ports of South Wales and in Northern Ireland the capital, Belfast.

In the early 1960s legislation, influenced by growing racial tensions, to halt the inflow of migrants paradoxically led to an enormous rush to 'beat the ban' and migrants saw this as a crucial period in which to take the decision to migrate and to bring over their families, wives and children. Once the legislation was in place the stream of migrants decreased although this was far from the end of Muslim settlement in Britain.

Bangladeshis continued to arrive into the 1970s but in addition to those from South Asia arriving primarily as economic migrants, a different type of migration phenomenon occurred from this period onwards. Those from the Middle East coming to Britain appeared to have a much more diverse profile, coming from various national and class backgrounds. There were Arabs who had taken advantage of their financial gain from the oil crisis of 1973–4 and invested in property and businesses in Britain seeing it as a safer option than their home countries, which were undergoing uncertain political developments and regime changes.

In addition there were Muslim professionals, also facing political unrest, who took advantage of employment opportunities in their fields in Britain. Ansari writes about this latter type of migrant,

> The needs that many of these migrants have striven to satisfy went beyond physical survival. Lack of material and

intellectual fulfilment and a sense of alienation from the operations of newly emerging society were often more important
in prompting these Muslims to migrate. (2004: 160)

The number of refugees began to grow as a result of ethno-religious
and communal conflict, famines and natural disasters. Refugees came
from areas such as Somalia and East Africa as well as the Middle East.
However from the 1990s there began a much more apparent arrival
of asylum seeker communities, which has resulted in a hostile culture
towards asylum seekers in the UK (Lewis 2005). Large applications
for asylum from Bosnia resulted due to civil unrest and the partition
of the former Yugoslavia. Of course these Muslims differed significantly from previous Muslim communities, firstly because they were
not economic migrants and therefore taking up positions within the
labour market was not their primary motivation for migrating, but
rather it was in order to flee from persecution. Secondly, this group
are ethnically European. There have been steady establishments of
other Muslim communities who have arrived as asylum seekers, including Kurds and Afghans for whom asylum applications steadily
rose by over a thousand per year from 1996 (675) to 2001 (8920),
and more recently Iraqis, for whom the number of asylum applicants
rose from 930 during 1995 to 14,570 for 2002[1] (Heath et al. 2004).
Koser (1998) reminds us that, 'It may not be accurate to distinguish so
straightforwardly between political and economic migrants because
of the need to recognise that almost all migrants in reality move for
mixed motivations, including social reasons' (p. 616).

Geographical Distributions

As described above Muslim settlement in Britain occurred periodi-
cally in that different communities arrived in higher concentrations
according to the pull–push factors facing them at any given time. This
has resulted in communities being formed along ethnic lines that have
come to be concentrated in different parts of Britain. Clearly chain
migration played a key role in the development of 'pockets' of communities and the reproduction of village and kin networks. These have
further been strengthened by transnational marriages where spouses
are often from the area of original migration (Ballard 2004).

Lewis (2002) argues that Muslim communities in Britain were extremely successful in reproducing many of their traditional cultural
and social norms, and this is similarly the case for Muslims from the
Middle East as it is for South Asians. Religion therefore initially had

little impact on their decisions to settle and the way they organised themselves in Britain.

Figures on ethnicity from the 1991 National Census demonstrated the extent to which communities were concentrated along ethnic lines. Over half of British Bangladeshis were found to live in Greater London and a quarter in Tower Hamlets alone. In comparison to the rest of the country, a smaller proportion of Pakistanis live in London, with their largest concentrations in certain industrial towns and cities in the West Midlands, Greater Manchester and West Yorkshire. It was also found that in Scotland the majority of the Muslim population is ethnically Pakistani with smaller communities of people from the Middle East in the larger cities. Like Bangladeshis, Turkish Cypriots are concentrated in London with 90 per cent of this ethnic group spread across several London boroughs. Muslims from the Middle East also have high concentrations in London with approximately 40 per cent residing in the area. There are also smaller communities concentrated in the South East, West Midlands and the North West, however over 25 per cent are dispersed across the rest of the country (Ansari 2004).

Hidden Communities

Recent research on ethnicity and racism has tended to focus on 'visible' groups such as Afro Caribbeans, Indians and Pakistanis, ignoring the less visible ones, such as Turks. Visibility is a complex concept with several dimensions. According to Modood (2004) there has been a long established social preoccupation in British culture with skin colour. Colour racism is an older form of racism with colonial discourse on Black or 'coloured' people describing them as less civilised, backwards and not of the same social standing as White people. This form of racism is heightened by the easy identification of the 'other' and by special concentration. However Modood argues that there has been a definite shift from simple colour racism to cultural racism with prejudice being fed by cultural distinctions such as food, clothing, different lifestyle choices and religion.

Somalis for example are visibly different due to their skin colour and also cultural markers such as dress. According to Modood's cultural racism, they fit the requirements of a group who are sufficiently culturally distinct. Yet wider society has not picked up on their activities as a community in the same way that it has the other visible minority groups mentioned above. Somalis are not readily recognised as a distinct ethnic group worthy of their own category in official statistics and are grouped under the heading of 'Black African'. Debates raised in earlier chapters regarding the importance of being recognised by the government as an official category, demonstrate how it can take decades for some groups, and until this happens Somalis, Turks, Eastern Europeans and other distinct Muslim groups, are likely to slip through the net when efforts to tackle issues such as discrimination and social disadvantage are explored.

This section draws attention to some of the larger Muslim groups who are often missing in research on Muslims in Britain. There are far less studies conducted on these communities and as a result there are fewer references made towards them during the discussion of data during the course of this book. However where possible, available studies on the communities described below will be addressed.

Somalis

The Somali Republic dates back to the 1960s but political instability, military government, conflict with neighbouring countries and civil war have devastated and divided the country (Dick 2002). Somalia was a land split into two; the northern Somaliland, a protectorate of the British and southern Somalia, by the Italians. In 1961, after the independence of Somalia the president of the successive government was assassinated in a coup d'état resulting in Major General Mohamed Siad Barre becoming head of state. In 1971, orthography of the Somali language was devised for the first time, followed by a nationwide literacy campaign. However the regime became increasingly repressive and Barre was seen by many as a dictator.

Harris writes 'When eight Muslim clerics opposed his reforms on women and the introduction of the roman script, he had them executed. These summary killings were by no means exceptional. Murder, rape and torture became commonplace' (2004: 19).

Some of the most brutal attacks were made on the former British north which precipitated the country's civil war. As a result, thousands of people were killed and millions displaced. Northern towns were heavily bombed and hundreds of thousands fled to neighbouring Ethiopia or overseas to Europe, America, South Asia and the Gulf States (Harris 2004).

There were Somalis in Britain prior to this conflict however, and the earlier generations of Somalis were seafarers, forming self contained communities since the nineteenth century. This earliest settlement reflects Britain's colonial ties with Somalia, recruiting Somalis to fight and serve in the royal navy before and during the First World

War and to work in the docklands areas such as Bristol, Cardiff and
South Shields. Khan and Jones write,

> This is thought to be the oldest African community in Lon-
> don. Whilst a lot of Somalis came to London as asylum seek-
> ers, fleeing civil unrest in their country ... there are records of
> Somalis in London dating back to 1914, when they were re-
> cruited to fight in the First World War and then settled in the
> capital. (2002:6)

The second phase of Somali migration to Britain came at the end of
the 1950s. The demand for seamen had declined but the economic
boom meant that there were opportunities for employment in industry. Communities grew in Sheffield and Manchester as whole families,
not just single men, settled in these areas.

The third phase of Somali settlement was not due to labour short-
age but due to political instability in Somalia. As a result the most
significant numbers of Somalis arrived in Britain as asylum seekers.
In general it is believed that 90–95 per cent of Somalis came to the
UK since the 1990s onwards (Khan and Jones 2002).

2001 Census country of birth data shows that there are 43,532
people born in Somalia, resident in UK, with the vast majority in England and Wales. There have been estimates in 1997 of 60,000, and in
1994 estimates ranged from 25,000 nationally to 65,000 in the capital
alone. Harris quotes an estimation provided by a Somali led women's
organisation (the Black Women's Health and Family Support located
in Bethnal Green) of 70,000 Somalis in London alone. On a whole the
calculations for Somalis in Britain without the presence of official data
are unsatisfactory. The largest concentrations of Somalis, after London, can be found in Sheffield, Manchester, Birmingham and Liver-
pool. The phenomenon of chain migration occurred for Somalis with
many opting to settle in areas where there were co-clan members.

Despite the length of residence in the UK their presence remains
largely overlooked by mainstream society. There are the occasional
articles on health, local crime or female genital mutilation. They are
marginalised by the media and as an ethnic minority community,
largely ignored. Most attempts to classify Somalis fail to take into
account their distinct position as the interface of two very different cultures. Subsumed within the category 'Black African' Somalis
do not share any culture, language, diet, dress and religious practice
with their near neighbours. As Muslims, Somalis worship at mosques

along side others from Asian and Arab countries but they do not share other aspects of their culture. The lack of sensitivity in monitoring categories has frequently resulted in the Somali community's needs being overlooked.

Religious identity appears to be significant for many British Somalis, despite the former Somali state being secular and many Somalis less than fervent in observing Islamic rituals. In the UK the culture is different so Islam offers a common denominator in constructing a specifically Somali identity. Results from a survey (Khan and Jones 2002) showed that when asked whether religion was important, on a scale of 1–7 (1 being very important and 7 not important at all) the overall mean score rating was 1.3, suggesting great importance attached to their Muslim faith.

Harris (2004) argues that through their dress and religious practice Somalis are readily identifiable as Muslims. Thus as well as discrimination and prejudice faced as asylum seekers and the colour racism described above, they also face Islamophobia, making Somalis vulnerable to multiple forms of discrimination.

Bosnians, Kosovars and Other Former Yugoslavs

The Federal Republic of Yugoslavia was made up of the Republic of Serbia (which included the autonomous province of Kosovo), the Republic of Croatia, Bosnia-Herzegovina, Slovenia, Macedonia and Montenegro. In the 1980s the relationship between the provinces in the Federation became increasingly strained resulting in genocide, war and the division of Yugoslavia.

Bosnia is now one of the successor states of the former Yugoslavia. In 1992 a Serb sniper shot two Bosnians taking part in peaceful demonstrations to support Bosnia-Herzegovinan independence. The conflict that followed killed thousands and destroyed Bosnian infrastructure and the economy. Although the country was multi-faith, with Christian, Muslims and Jews living and working together, it was the Muslim population that suffered the greatest persecution and who were the victims of genocide at the hands of the Serb authorities, led by the former Yugoslav president Slobodan Milosovic. Approximately 200,000 people died in the conflict leading to, and as a result of, the division of Yugoslavia. Two million people were made homeless and many were imprisoned in concentration camps or experienced serious injury.

A British Independent Television News (ITN) crew discovered one of the concentration camps on the 3 August 1992. Although the camp was closed many of the prisoners were transferred to other camps. Resettlement of ex-detainees from a number of concentration camps began in October 1992. At the time notorious camps in Omarska, Trnopolje, Batkovici, Manjaca and Dretelj were full, some of the the prisoners were badly tortured and starved and thousands of them killed (Masic 2003).

The conflict in the former Yugoslavia lasted for several years. Under pressure from UNHCR the British government agreed to accept a quota of refugees, along with 21 other countries worldwide. The first Bosnians refugees began to arrive in the UK in 1992 under a programme called *Governmental 1000*, transporting survivors of concentration camps overseas. The second group were evacuees who were injured during the war and came to the UK to receive medical treatment. The third group were those who escaped the conflict, lost their homes and became displaced (Kelly 2003). The majority of refugees were Muslims, although there were some Croats, Serbs and people from mixed heritage. Most Bosnians were given temporary leave to remain and were not able to travel as a result. The majority believed they would only remain away from their home country until the conflict ended and would return as soon as it was safe to do so; however this was not the case in reality.

There are Bosnian associations and organisations in most areas despite there being many rivalries and conflicts and little evidence of community (Kelly).

> In the case of refugees from Bosnia there was no chain migration, but the scattering of people according to the willingness of countries to accept them, taking little or no account of desires of the refugees themselves. This meant that they often went to places where they had few friends or family. (2003: 44)

Pre-departure waiting periods lasted from two to six months and many were separated from their immediate families. Most people did not know where they were being sent and on arrival to Britain their pre-war kin and friendship networks were nonexistent. Masic describes, 'There was no (immediate) community development … people did not try to organise themselves or get together to establish a group as there was not enough support' (2003: 22).

Although the majority of refugees were Muslims there was little collective organisation in Bosnia along ethnic or religious lines. Serbs, Croats and Muslims lived together and there were high proportions of mixed marriages. Therefore the persecution and genocide of Muslims on the grounds of religious affiliation meant that links between non-Muslims, which may have been close prior to the war, were unlikely to be re-established. As a result any community development that has occurred since their arrival in Britain is unlikely to include non-Muslims. On the flip side the establishment of a separate Muslim community was also difficult due to the lack of experience of Muslim mobilisation in the former Yugoslavia. In addition there were disagreements and fractions among the predominately Muslim Bosnian government and the Muslim lay person (Kelly 2003).

Organisations began to come into beings such as the Bosnia and Herzegovinan Refugee Community organisation called Ljiljan, in the North East of England. They organised social and cultural events, language classes, activities for children and the elderly (Masic 2003). However Kelly (2003) argues that the existence of community associations is not a reflection of the needs of community but instead an artificial construction responding to a social policy based on an assumption that communities exist. Therefore according to Kelly, what exist are not Bosnian communities but contingent communities.

Masic (2003) argues that the main issue with Bosnians not feeling settled or actively integrating into the wider community was their uncertain temporary status. They were not sure about how long they would remain in the UK, not only because they were waiting for the conflict to end but also because they knew there was a chance of the government asking them to leave at any given point.

Al-Ali et al. (2001) however argue that a large number of Bosnians socialise with other Bosnian refugees and that social visits were described as an essential part of their culture. Due to practical difficulties of geographical distributions and emotional instabilities, socialisation did not occur in the same way it did in Bosnia. They described how important language schools established to teach second generation Bosnian refugees and children their mother tongue were in helping to retain Bosnian culture. In 2001 there were already approximately ten schools established with 250 pupils aged 6–16 years.

Kosovars
Like Bosnians, Kosovars are new arrivals to Britain, almost half arriving during the 1990s as asylum seekers. The majority of Kosovars are ethnic Albanians and most Kosovars are Muslims with a minority of Catholics.

In 1999 the crisis in Kosovo was made obvious to the rest of the world after ten years of conflict in the former Yugoslavia. The people of Kosovo sought independence from the Republic of Serbia. Hundreds of thousands of ethnic Albanians from Kosovo (Kosovars) fled from Serb forces and genocide. This was a refugee crisis unparalleled in Europe since the Second World War.

Smart (2004) writes,

> Kosovars had been arriving in the UK in growing numbers since the 1990s. In addition, in April 1999 the UK government authorised an airlift of over four thousand Kosovars from camps on the border of Macedonia, under the Kosovo humanitarian evacuation programme. The rapid expansion of the Kosovar population, and the nature of the reception arrangements for the evacuees, meant that for many UK towns, their first contact with asylum seekers and refugees was with the arrival of the Kosovars. (p. 6)

As the conflict was resolved, Kosovar asylum seekers have returned at a faster rate than any other asylum seeker population and this rapid return has been one of the distinctive features of this population's experience in the UK. The period that many Kosovars remained in the UK was weeks or months rather than years, however many have remained, resulting in Kosovar communities in the UK. Of the approximately 2,000 Kosovars in Leeds, 200–300 people remain, in London although most Kosovars were sent to north London, they can now be found in many areas across the capital.

Asylum applications from the Federal Republic of Yugoslavia were the largest group of spontaneous arrivals for most of the period 1998 to 2000 (Smart 2004). The number of asylum applications peaked during 1999 reaching 11,465, with a total of 1,575 arrivals in the month of September alone.

Turkish Speaking Communities

Turkish Speaking Communities (TSCs) in Britain are comprised of three main groups: those from mainland Turkey, Turkish Cypriots and Kurds. TSCs have a long history of presence in the UK, having established a sizeable language community since the 1950s.

Turkish Cypriot communities in the UK can be traced to the 1920s. Numbers increased in the 1940s as young people came to work in specific trades such as catering, tailoring and in shoe making. In

1931 the Census provided the figure of 1,075 Cypriots in Britain, increasing to 10,343 by 1951 (Mehmet Ali 2001). In the 1960s the island became independent and as many Turkish Cypriots had been loyal to the colonial administration as civil servants, they were rewarded with British passports and a paid passage to Britain. The next large wave proceeded military occupation of Cyprus by Turkey which resulted in mass population exchanges and emigration.

The Turkish community in Britain began to appear in the 1970s. Their arrival coincided with stricter border controls across Europe following the recession of 1974 which was intensified by the oil crisis. Mehmet Ali writes 'Although the initial immigration to Europe was recorded as from the cities of Ankara, Istanbul and Izmir and from Western Turkey, the initial immigrants were from the countryside' (2001: 54). It is clear that the main 'pull' factor in Turkish migration was for economic betterment of people from largely rural areas.

Kurdish people form the largest nationality in the world without its own homeland. After the collapse of the Turkish Empire, Britain and France were responsible for the division of Turkish possessions and Kurds were denied self governance (Dick 2002). This resulted in Kurds having no land to call their own.

The first Kurdish refugees began to arrive in Britain in 1958. The number of Kurds entering Britain as asylum seekers increased due to the brutal regime in Iraq and the intensification of military operations against Kurdish fighters and civilians in south-east Turkey. The conflict resulted in many losing their homes and becoming displaced. The estimated death toll in the area is 30,000 (Mehmet Ali 2001).

The largest social presence of TSCS is in London. It is estimated that there are 80,000 Turks in the UK with 60,000 living in the capital according to estimates quoted by Enneli et al. (2005). Mehmet Ali (2001) in his paper on the migration of TSCS, quotes estimates of 180,000–200,000, including more recent arrivals of Turkish speaking Kurds and Roma from Cyprus. Some local authorities do collect statistics on TSCS, such as Hackney, Enfield, Southwark, Lewisham and Haringey. The majority of London's Turks are concentrated in Haringey, and make up 10 per cent of the borough's school children.

Although TSCS are Muslims they practice a more secularised Islam than the above mentioned groups and lack the political force and presence that can be found among other minority communities, both Muslim and non-Muslim. Religion was not found to be as important an identifier for TSCS as it was for other Muslim groups. 56 per cent expressed hybrid identities such as Turkish-Cypriot, Turkish and

British, Turkish Muslim. As a result it is argued that cultural visibility has not yet been developed due to less marked attachment to Islam (Enneli et al. 2005).

The Turkish community are far less distinctive from the wider population than Somalis, Pakistanis and Bangladeshis, in terms of their physical appearance. Mehmet Ali writes

> We now have third generation Cypriot Turkish young people, who have completed their whole education in this country yet the infrastructures to assess their needs and respond to them are negligible ... Although much has changed in terms of the vibrancy of the communities in their economic, cultural, social and political activities, highly visible in London, Turkish Speaking people are still made invisible. (2001: 87)

Arabs

The simplest definition of an Arab is someone from an Arab speaking community. Countries which classify themselves as Arab and belong to the League of Arab Nations are: Egypt, Libya, Tunisia, Algeria, Morocco, Mauritania, Sudan, Djibouti and Comoros in Africa. Asian Arab countries are Lebanon, Syria, Iraq, Palestine, Jordan, Saudi Arabia, Kuwait, United Arab Emirates, Bahrain, Qatar, Oman and Yemen.

There are approximately 500,000 Arabs in the UK originating from a wide spectrum of countries according to some estimations (Ermes 2002; Al-Jalili 2004). Others such as Bishtawi (1999) draw attention to the variations in statistics estimating anywhere between 70,000 to half a million. The absence of an Arab category within official statistics means that it is only possible to estimate figures. The 2001 Census country of birth data shows that there were 100,822 people born in the Middle East and 68,715 in North Africa. The main concentrations of Arabs can be found in Greater London, with estimates of 300,000 in the capital alone. Other significant Arab communities can be found in Manchester, Birmingham, Glasgow and Cardiff.

Arabs are arguably the longest-resident, non-European ethnic group in the British Isles. Their presence is largely a consequence of Britain's colonial past although it is known that the Romans brought Arab archers with them and assisted in establishing South Shields (Al-Jalili 2004). Others like Ermes (2002) argue that there is historical evidence that Arabs arrived in Britain prior to the Romans, to mine and export aluminium from places like Cornwall.

Al-Masyabi (2000) argues that Yemenis were the first substantial

Arab community in the UK and their presence can be traced back to 1885. Many Yemenis worked for the British Merchant Navy and gradually moved from the unsettling work of sea life to that of steel factories and foundries. Some married British women but others preferred to lead semi-single lives, having wives in Yemen but remaining in the UK themselves. Today the Yemeni community is estimated at 30–40,000 people in total with around 16 Yemeni organisations in Britain.

Traditional trading skills of Syrians and Lebanese brought them to Manchester where the famous Arab historian Albert Hourani was born. The Arab community began to grow after 1945 with the Palestinians, followed by Egyptians and Sudanese coming for professional progression. In the 1960 Moroccans seeking greater political liberty made their way to British shores, and political conflict has been a key 'push' factor in the continued migration of people from Arab countries to Britain.

Anti-Arab prejudice or *Orientalism* has long been a topic of focus within the academic study of colonialism. Well known Arab thinkers such as Edward Said and Rana Kabbani have both observed and written about the defamation and vilification of Arabs as the last socially and politically acceptable form of racism. There has been a legacy of conflict between the West and the Arab world, most famously represented by the Crusades. Al-Jalili writes,

> British Arabs are virtually invisible within British society as a group, apart from negative public stereotyping. They face discrimination in many aspects of life such as work, education etc; however given that the standard ethnic profiling forms which now feature so commonly do not contain 'Arab' as a separate entity, this is impossible to monitor. (2004: 2)

The London Civic Forum, recognising the marginalisation of Arabs as a community, conducted a consultation exercise and produced a document called 'the Arab Community in London'. The document provided several recommendations for policy development, these included: the increased representation of the Arab community at all levels of society; the recognition that Arabs have a long history of contributing to British society through science, art and finance; to ensure that Arabs are recognised as a community by being given a category in official data collection; and for literature produced by statutory agencies to be translated into Arabic.

Counting Muslims

Estimations of the Muslim Population in Britain Prior to the 2001 National Census

A key reason for Muslims campaigning for the inclusion of a question on religious affiliation in the 2001 Census was due to there being no agreed figure for Muslims in Britain. The size of the Muslim community in Britain has been debated since the influx to Britain after World War Two as described in the previous section.

There have been numerous attempts using various methods of calculation and sources (such as the ethnicity data from the 1991 Census) to estimate the figure of Muslims not only in Britain but in Europe also (Anwar 1993; Peach 1990; Wahhab 1989; Kettani 1986). Muslims are often stated to be the largest 'minority religious group' in Britain and various sources estimated the Muslim population at between 550,000 and 3,000,000. In the early 1990s, figures over 1.5 million were normally mentioned by Muslim organisations however the most common estimate of the Muslim population was one million.

Peach argues in his study (1990) that the figures for Muslims in Britain were often exaggerated. He argues that ever since events such as the Salman Rushdie affair, which highlighted the presence of Muslims as a faith community rather than solely as ethnic communities, there had been speculation on the size of the British Muslim community. Such conjecture was demonstrated in both in the popular media and within academia. Peach writes,

> The Independent, in a leading article on 9 January 1990, for example, estimated the Islamic population at between one and two million and calculated that Muslims formed between 2 and 4 per cent of the British electorate. These figures seem to represent media consensus, although there is no clear explanation of their provenance. (p. 414)

Heterogeneity and the Difficulties with Counting Muslims

Peach rightfully pointed out that there was no definitive or flawless method for providing a Muslim figure. Due to the heterogeneous nature of British Muslims it was particularly difficult to calculate their numbers; British Muslims, other than being Muslim, had no other common denominator with regards to identifiers such as ethnicity, region of origin or language. Despite this, the most common methods used to estimate the number of Muslims in Britain have been from minority groups' countries of birth and from data on ethnicity. This however, when using information provided by large surveys such as the PSI data and the Labour Force Surveys prior to the 1991 Census, only allowed for figures on Pakistani and Bangladeshi Muslims to a certain level of accuracy (Brown 2000).

Hai (1999) conducted research on the size of South Asian Muslims in Britain, and inferred a figure by taking into account the percentage of the country of origin for each ethnic group who are Muslims. Although he acknowledged that 98 per cent of the population of Pakistan are Muslims compared with 85 per cent of the population of Bangladesh and 11 per cent of the population of India, he argued that using percentages of Muslims in the country of origin to base estimations of percentages of Muslims within a particular ethnic group in the UK is defective. As Brown (2000) points out 'It may be inaccurate to presume that a population living in Europe will simply mirror the religious composition of the source country, even assuming the latter can be accurately ascertained' (p. 97).

When looking at specific geographical areas or regions from which migrants originated, Hai acknowledged this issue and took into consideration that the proportions of Muslims in such regions were higher than the national averages. Therefore, the area from which the majority of British Bangladeshis originate from, Sylhet, is likely to be closer to 90 per cent Muslim and Gujarat for Indians is estimated as having a Muslim population of around 20 per cent. Through understanding the cultural make up of South Asian Muslims, Hai was able to provide a more realistic calculation based on ethnic background.

Clearly any estimation on the number of Muslims in Britain derived by looking solely at South Asian Muslims will be flawed due to the fact that Muslims in Britain are of origins other than South Asia. This is made even more apparent by the fact that estimations for British Muslims based on South Asian figures alone could fall short by as much as 30 per cent. Modood estimated that South Asian Muslims make up two thirds of all Muslims in Britain, whereas others, such as Lewis have stated it was closer to 80 per cent.

Ansari (2004) argues that in addition to the South Asian Muslim figures, the 1991 Census found that the Turkish born population of Britain was 26,600, whereas others such as Kucukcan (1996) estimated it to be as high as 125,000 and there are various estimations for other ethnic groups such as Somalis and Moroccans (El-Solh 1992) and Yemenis (Halliday 1992) which are difficult to confirm using data on country of birth only. This is primarily due to the fact that they do not constitute their own ethnic categories in large scale surveys including the 2001 Census as discussed above (in 'Hidden Communities', on page 28).

Ansari argues that Muslims living in Britain from the Middle East pose further problems when estimating the total size of Muslims in Britain as their resident statuses are often ambiguous. Lewis (1994) also highlighted this issue writing,

> The large numbers of Arabs who have congregated in and around London are residents rather than part of cohesive communities. Their main country of residence and work remains the Middle East. The exceptions are communities of Egyptians (doctors, teachers and academics), Iraqis, Moroccans (hotel and catering staff), Palestinians (business people) and Yemenis (workers in manufacturing industries). (p. 14)

These latter exceptions that Lewis writes about have settled in Britain and therefore should be included in estimations.

Ansari's study *The Infidel Within* (2004), contained a comprehensive review of estimations from previous studies conducted by a number of researchers on identifiable Muslim communities, mainly using data on country of birth for head of household and ethnicity data for South Asians; he presents an approximate Muslim figure of 2 million.

An alternative means for collecting data on Muslims in Britain was to use self-assessed religious affiliation which is described by Brown as a 'direct observation' method (2000: 90). Where available, data from a direct question on religion derived from a small spatial unit is used to estimate certain demographic patterns and profiles for Muslims at a larger geographical level.

Peach and Vertovec (1997) described another method, also using religion more specifically but through organisations rather than measuring individuals directly. This was attempted by Holloway in 1985, using surveys of 314 registered British mosques. Holloway argued that on average, individual mosques served communities of around 1,000 Muslims and in total this gave an estimated figure of 300,000 Muslims. This method was clearly flawed due to its inclusion of registered mosques only.

Results from the Census

Overview of Results

The 2001 Census found there to be just over one and a half million Muslims in England and Wales. In addition, as demonstrated by

Table 2.1: Total Number and Percentages of People Within Each Faith Category for England and Wales.

	Population Count	Percentage
All people	52,041,912	100.00
Christian	37,338,486	71.75
No religion	7,709,167	14.81
Religion not stated	4,010,658	7.71
Muslim	1,546,625	2.97
Hindu	552,418	1.06
Sikh	329,356	0.63
Jewish	259,928	0.50
Any other religion	150,721	0.29
Buddhist	144,453	0.28

Source: Data from ONS (2001).

Table 2.1, 77 per cent of people in England and Wales reported belonging to a religion. The largest faith group is Christian with 72 per cent. This is followed by Muslim with just under 3 per cent, Hindus with 1 per cent and all other groups reported less than 1 per cent. Those with no religion make up 15 per cent of the population.

In Scotland 65 per cent of the populations stated that they were Christian. This was followed by 28 per cent of the population who answered 'No Religion'. Muslims formed the largest minority faith group in Scotland with 0.84 per cent, followed by 'other religion' with 0.53 per cent.

As mentioned earlier the Scottish Census produced output data which differed from that of England and Wales. One such table looks at whether the current religion of individuals is the same as that they were raised in or whether they have chosen a different or no faith at all. Muslims were the least likely to change their faith with 95 per cent of those who are currently Muslim being raised as Muslims, similar to the figures for Hindus and Sikhs (94 per cent and 91 per cent respectively) and compared with 88 per cent of Jews and 20 per cent for other religions not given their own category on the form.

Geography

Most noticeably the Census shows that there are Muslims in every local authority except the Isle of Scilly; however some local authorities have counts as low as 10 such as Berwick upon Tweed. Figure 2.1 shows the concentrations of Muslims by percentage for each local

Table 2.2: Local Authorities With the Highest Counts and Percentages of Muslims in England and Wales.

Local Authority	Muslim Count	Local Authority	Muslim Percentage
Birmingham	140,033	Tower Hamlets	36
Bradford	75,188	Newham	24
Tower Hamlets	71,389	Blackburn	19
Newham	59,293	Bradford	16
Kirkless	39,319	Waltham Forest	15

authority. Those in the darkest shades have the highest percentages.

The data showed some expected clusters in and around London, the West Midlands, Lancashire and West Yorkshire. However there are other areas highlighted, in terms of having communities higher than the national figure for Muslims, in the North East, for example, Middlesbrough and Newcastle, and at the opposite end of the country in the South West, Gloucester and Bristol. Areas such as these have remained largely outside the academic and public imagination when discussing Muslims in England and Wales.

The five local authorities with the highest proportions of Muslims are Tower Hamlets, Newham, Blackburn, Bradford, and Waltham Forest as shown in Table 2.2.

In Scotland nearly half of all Muslims live in Glasgow City (42 per cent). The next highest concentrated location is Edinburgh City, home to 16 per cent of the countries Muslims.

For researchers wanting to conduct field work on specific Muslim groups, the Census data will provide a good starting point in terms of identifying the possible geographical locations of certain groups.

Age

The Census data shows that Muslims have the youngest demographic profile as a faith group in England and Wales. Over 60 per cent of all Muslims are under the age of 30. At the opposite end of the scale Muslims have the lowest proportion of elderly people when compared will all groups.

Clearly, migration processes contribute to the age structures of groups in that the majority of migrants arrived as young adults and will have only recently approached retirement ages. Although this will also have been the case for other groups namely Sikhs and Hindus, as Ansari (2004) has argued, there has been a second and more recent

Figure 2.1: Map demonstrating the concentration of Muslims by percentage at Local Authority level for England, Scotland and Wales

Figure 2.2: Percentage of people under the age of 30 by religion in England and Wales.

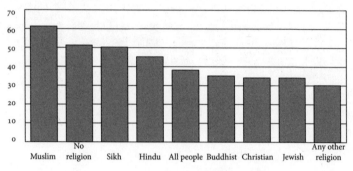

Source: taken from ONS (2001: Census table S149).

phase of Muslim migration which has not been mirrored by these other communities.

In addition, a key factor for the age structure of Muslims when comparing them to other migrant faith communities are trends in reproduction. As explored in Chapter Four on family formation, if Muslims have younger ages for the birth of their first child, and also have on average more children than other groups, this is likely to contribute significantly to the concentration of younger people within this population.

When looking at the concentrations of Muslims and the total population within each age band (from Census S149), the very youngest age bracket, 0–4, contains almost twice as many Muslims as there are for all people. There are more Muslims within every age bracket than for the total population up until the age of 40, where the percentages for Muslims decrease in comparison.

Sex

The gender distribution shows that there are on average more Muslim men than women. However there is not a significant difference for any of the groups as was apparent during earlier periods of migration, where there were greater proportions of men than women, particularly among Muslim groups. However as discussed above most men were joined by their wives and families by the early 1980s and this has provided a levelling out of the sexes in terms of proportions.

Ethnicity and Country of Birth

Figure 2.4 shows that 48 per cent of Muslims living in England and

Figure 2.3: Percentage of males and females by religion in England and Wales.

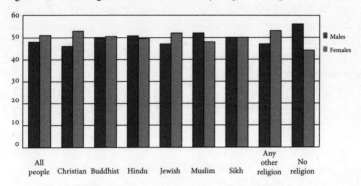

Source: taken from ONS (2001: table S103).

Figure 2.4: Percentage of people living in England and Wales born in the UK by religion.

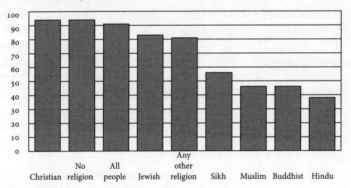

Source: taken from ONS (2001: table S150).

Wales were born in the UK. Despite being more concentrated in the younger age cohorts there are proportionately fewer Muslims born in the UK than Sikhs. This is likely to result from the settlement of more recent Muslim communities, not only Bangladeshis but others such as refugees from Eastern Europe for example, as discussed in the section above.

South Asians make up 68 per cent of Muslims in England and Wales. Other White make up the fourth largest ethnic category and Black African the fifth. It is possible to see at this juncture how the ethnic categories are particularly unhelpful when attempting to pinpoint specific Muslim communities other than the three South Asian groups. Other White and Other Asian for example could comprise of people from the Middle East, however Other White will also include those from Eastern Europe. Black African also covers an array of groups. In Scotland the majority of Muslims are of South Asian decent (approximately 80 per cent), with 67 per cent of Scottish Muslims coming from the Pakistani ethnic group alone.

Ethnic Geographical Distributions
The map showed areas in England and Wales with high concentrations of Muslims as a percentage of the total population of their local authority.

However when analysed as a percentage of the total number of Muslims, it is possible to find the largest Muslim communities. 25 per cent of all Muslims in England live in Inner London, and 22 per cent live in outer London. 10 per cent live in Greater Manchester, 15 per cent in the West Midlands and 11 per cent in West Yorkshire. Such areas provide insight into the ethnic of Muslims using the Census data.

For Muslims, London is the most ethnically diverse. Bangladeshis are the largest group among Muslims in Inner London and comparatively Pakistanis are much smaller, with there being proportionately slightly more White, Other White and Black African Muslims than Pakistani.

Outer London however shows a reverse with there being proportionately more Pakistanis, making up around a third and with only 8 per cent of Muslims being Bangladeshi. The figures for White, other White and Black African remain similar to their respective figures for Inner London.

Nearly 60 per cent of the Muslims in Greater Manchester are Pakistani. This is followed by 15 per cent for Bangladeshis. The third largest Muslim ethnic group here is Indian with 11 per cent. All other ethnic categories each make up 5 per cent and under.

There is a similar Muslim ethnic make up in the West Midlands, where the majority of Muslims are Pakistani (nearly 70 per cent) and this is followed by Bangladeshis with 14 per cent. Comparatively there is a much smaller Indian population of Muslim with 5 per cent. All other ethnic categories each report 5 per cent or less for this area also.

Three quarters of Muslims in West Yorkshire are Pakistani, compared with only 5 per cent Bangladeshi and 10 per cent Indian. Areas which demonstrated the highest concentrations of Indians when compared with all other Muslim ethnic groups were Gloucestershire and Warwickshire where over 40 per cent of Muslims in these counties are Indian. In terms of column percentage, rather than row percentage, Indians have high concentrations in Leicestershire and Lancashire also.

There were no counties in which Black Africans reported the highest percentage among Muslim, however Merseyside came close. Here 17 per cent of the Muslim community reported the White ethnic category which was the largest and 14 per cent Black African.

What the data shows most significantly is that apart from the counties with the largest percentages of Muslims (as detailed above), the ethnic make up of Muslims in other areas are diverse and by no means evenly distributed.

Chapter Summary

This chapter provided an overview of the demographic profile of Muslims based on some previous studies on Muslim migration and settlement patterns. An elaboration on some of the issues concerned specifically with counting Muslims was also provided as were examples of methods that have been employed to collect data on this faith group. An introduction to the findings from the 2001 National Census data has also been presented, providing an overview of key demographics prior to the exploration of the main topics (themed Chapters) for this book.

3

Educational Attainment

This chapter sets out to look at the 2001 National Census data on religion and educational qualifications. The main purpose of this is to ascertain whether: Muslims suffer from greater educational disadvantage than other faith groups. In doing so the educational attainment of Muslims and their participation in post-compulsory education will be explored by drawing on current research into differential educational attainment. The majority of research looking at differential educational success focuses largely on influences of ethnicity, gender and socio-economic status. Belonging to a religious community has received much less attention when attempting to explain differences. Therefore when discussing previous research conducted on students from minority communities and their success in gaining qualifications, there is a focus on differences between ethnic groups rather than religious groups. It is possible however to classify Pakistanis and Bangladeshis as Muslim communities, as the overwhelming majority of both ethnic groups are Muslims. It is of course not as straightforward to identify Muslims when looking at other commonly used ethnic classifications as described in Chapter One.

Section one will begin by exploring the differences in educational success between students who belong to minority groups and the

indigenous majority. Here the various explanations for these differences will be discussed as will research and literature specifically on
Muslims and education. Section two will explore the findings from
the analysis of the Census data on religious affiliation in order to examine the differential attainment of religious groups focusing particularly on Muslim attainment. Section three will discuss how far the
arguments looked at in section one can be used to explain the outcomes of the Census data analysis.

Differential Attainment Between Ethnic Groups

The subject of differential success in education of the various minority groups in Britain is a complex one. Findings on the achievement
of minority groups have often been contradictory. In this section an
outline of the core debates surrounding minority groups educational
attainment is provided. Here a demonstration of how the use of black
and white dichotomies and even broader ethnic grouping such as
Black, Asian and White masked an array of among non-White students.

The Problem with Broad Groups

The most comprehensive and influential policy studies on ethnic related differences in the 1980s were conducted by the ILEA Longitudi-
nal Literacy Survey (Mabey 1981); the Rampton Report (1981); the
Swann Committee (1985) and the ILEA Junior School Study: School
Matters (1988). The main findings regarding differential attainment
pointed towards the under achievement of Afro-Caribbean pupils in
comparison to White and Asian pupils. It appears that when broader
defining groups such as 'Asian' or 'Afro-Caribbean' are used Asian
pupils are seen to perform better than Afro-Caribbean pupils. However this was contrary to the experiences of many teachers and other
professionals working with these communities. It was clear that not
all Asian students were performing as well as such reports suggested.

The Fourth National Survey of Ethnic Minorities (FNSEM) conducted in 1994 made substantial progress towards providing a clearer
picture of how minority groups were performing. Data on approximately 5,000 people from six ethnic groups – African Asians, Indians,
African-Caribbeans, Chinese, Bangladeshis and Pakistanis were analysed when compared with to 3,000 people from the White majority.
It was found that the experience of minority groups is extremely diverse ranging from the 'highest achievers' to the most disadvantaged.
It was revealed that Indians, African Asians and Chinese groups had

similar or higher educational success to the indigenous White majority, whereas the performance of Pakistanis, Bangladeshis and Afro-
Caribbeans was lower. There were also findings to support that gender played a significant role in educational achievement within ethnic
groups.

Two measures of success were looked at; the first was whether people have 'no qualifications' and the second was whether people possessed degrees. The position of Chinese, African-Asian and Indian
with no qualification was found to be close to that of Whites, however comparatively, Pakistani, Caribbean and especially Bangladeshi
men were in a much worse position. Caribbean, African Asian and
particularly Chinese women were more likely to have a qualification
than White women. Pakistani and Bangladeshi women were found
to be as disproportionately without qualifications as their male counterparts. When exploring data on proportions of the various groups
with university degrees it was discovered that Caribbean men were the
least likely to have these qualifications followed by Bangladeshis and
Pakistanis. The position for Caribbean women was significantly better than their male counterparts yet the position of Chinese women
was described as 'outstanding' in comparison to all groups (Modood
et al. 1997).

Other studies have supported finding on the differential attainment of women and men in the same ethnic group and particular attention has been paid to the relatively high success of females
from Caribbean communities compared with their male counterparts. Gender has been found to be strongly associated with achievement regardless of ethnic background (Demie 2001; Ballard 1998).
Explanations for these differences will be discussed later during a discussion of explanations for diversity among ethnic groups.

Subsequent research also demonstrates the differences in educational success between Black African and Caribbean pupils. Demie
(2001) found when examining data on 5,832 pupils who were attending or had attended inner city schools in London, that African pupils
outperformed Caribbean pupils at key stage performance tests and
achieved a greater percentage of grades A–C in GCSE's. It was also
found that Caribbeans outperformed Bangladeshis at key stage 1 and
2 performance test, but not in attaining grades A–C at GCSE, for which
37 per cent of Bangladeshis compared to 25 per cent of Caribbean
pupils achieved these grades.

In his analysis of Universities and Colleges Admissions Service
(UCAS) data Ballard (1998) examined figures for seven ethnic groups

on A-level participation, A-level points scored, type of school at-tended/where A-levels were taken, chosen courses, entrance details and whether parents' social class was manual, non-manual or un-known. For all ethnic groups it was found that more women than men had A-levels, yet again for all groups there was a greater percentage of men in the highest points bracket. Bangladeshi women had the small-est participation rate compared to women from all other groups in the study. The largest gap between the sexes in the same ethnic group was found among Caribbeans, with participation for women close to dou-ble that of men. The smallest gender gap was found among Pakistanis with only a 1.5 per cent difference. Caribbean men had the lowest participation rate across all groups and sexes. Again substantial di-versity between ethnic groups was established. When looking at the higher end of the scale, Chinese participation rates were far greater than all the other groups. Indians had the second largest rates followed by Whites and Pakistanis and then Caribbeans, Black Africans and Bangladeshis. In addition the Chinese were found to have been the most likely to attend independent schools and Caribbeans the least.

Ethnic groups including Asians have a diverse educational profile despite the insistence of some researchers in using such broad cat-egories. Van Dyke (1998) conducted research on the progress and achievement of three ethnic minority groups (Asians, Africans and Caribbeans) and White students in two London universities in 1995. The project measured progression using retention rates of students for four courses at the end on the first year and the graduation rates for the same four courses. Enrolment onto a course did not neces-sarily mean completion of a course and therefore lead to obtaining a degree. Therefore the progression rates of those entering into subse-quent years of study were examined by Van Dyke. In doing so it was discovered that Asians were most likely to progress onto the second year and Caribbean the least likely. This was largely due to withdrawal from courses rather than other variables such as examination success.

There was no further breakdown of ethnicity amongst the Asian group. Significant differences were found in the graduation rates of all the ethnic groups. For the social science course 43 per cent of Caribbean students compared with 87 per cent of Asian students graduated. For the engineering course no African student completed the course in the normal time period compared to 63 per cent of the Asian students. Here Asians were identified as having the lowest drop out rates and the highest graduation rates when compared with the other three ethnic groups. Although for this study Asians clearly come out as the successful group in these terms, what could be extremely useful research, leaves the reader wondering who the 'Asians' actually were.

Other studies have shown the potential pitfalls of such broad grouping. Esmail et al. (1998) in their research into the representation of various ethnic groups in both medical professions and schools, argue that traditionally Asian applicants to medicine have been over represented when compared to the general population. However the ethnicity of the applicants to medical school in their study was predominately made up of applicants who classify themselves as Indian, with applicants who classify themselves as Bangladeshi, Pakistani and Afro-Caribbean being under represented when compared to their proportions in the general population. It is argued here that because of the large number of 'Asian' students in medical schools there is a perception that discrimination is not a factor in selection or examination success of students leaving the under representation of non Indian Asians largely unexplored.

As an OFSTED commissioned research report stated on the importance of acknowledging diversity among ethnic groups:

> If ethnic diversity is ignored, if differences in educational achievement and experiences are not examined, then considerable injustices will be sanctioned and enormous potential wasted. (Gillborn and Gipps 1996:14)

Therefore a key issue for the complexity and contradictions in findings on ethnic minority attainment have been the groupings or classifications used.

The Significance of the Breakdown of Broad Ethnic Labels for Muslims

As already mentioned the potential benefit of such information means that communities who would otherwise have faced increasing marginalisation in the education system, be they Caribbean males (for whom scores were increased when grouped together with females) or for Pakistani and Bangladeshis (who were presented as achieving as well as if not better than their White peers under the heading of Asian). The breakdown of such broad groups is especially useful for those interested in the achievement of Muslims.

If Asians are now increasingly being presented as polarised towards each end of the spectrum, it is at the lower end or rather the most disadvantaged end that those who are visibly classifiable as Muslim stand. As shown in the previous chapter the 2001 Census data demonstrated that 59 per cent of Muslims in England and Wales are Bangladeshi and Pakistani – this obviously means that Muslims will be included in the other ethnic groups being discussed, such as Indian and African but Muslims are also present in ethnic groups that are not commonly given their own classifications but collected under 'Other', 'Other non-European' or even 'Black African' for example. Studies of other minority communities, falling under these broad headings, have also pointed to underachievement among Muslim minority communities, emphasising the need for the exploration of Muslim achievement further.

Khan and Jones (2002) conducted a study of Somalis in Camden, where Somalis make up the single largest group among the borough's refugee school population. In 2000 only 3 out of 30 Somali boys entered for GCSE's attained 5 or more at grades A to C. The number of boys entered in 2002 was only 23 with 2 gaining 5 or more good GCSEs. Khan and Jones found that there was widespread perception among the community of underachievement in educational attainment and inequality of access to education. This was found to be the case for several reasons:

- Children having poor experience of school prior to arrival in the UK due to the collapse of education system in Somalia.
- Children being placed in streams according to their age rather than ability, resulting in less proficient children who came from Somalia being left behind and not given the opportunity to catch up.
- Poor literacy skills amongst mothers results in low parental ability to assist children with school work.
- Bulling and racism
- Stigmatisation as asylum seekers

A study by Enneli, Modood and Bradley (2005) found low educational achievement among young Turkish speaking people. Only 21 per cent of Turks, 13 per cent of Kurds and 14 per cent of Turkish Cypriots had five GCSEs at grade C or above. 38 per cent of young people from Turkish speaking communities (TSCs) had no qualifications at all. Language and literacy difficulties were found to be an issue as were high levels of truancy (50 per cent for boys, 15 per cent for girls). A quarter of Kurdish youth had been excluded from school at some point (the figure is lower for TSC as a whole at 18 per cent). Many young people from this community felt ignored and marginalised, one respondent from the study said 'Teachers like police, and always come late ... They only came when they hear very loud screams.'

Reasons for Differential Attainment for Minority Groups
It has been argued that the underachievement of some groups can be due to

> ... unintentional racism in schools, inappropriate curricula and teaching materials, differences in socio-economic conditions, prejudice on the part of some teachers, the discouraging effect of relatively poor employment prospects after leaving schools, lack of adequate support from schools and teachers due to lack of empathy towards cultural issues for some groups. (Foster 1993:521)

Whilst children of all non-White ethnicities or who belong to minority communities encounter prejudice why does it appear to be more detrimental to some rather than others?

Socio-Economic Status
Class background is clearly a major factor in educational success and the relationship between class background, cultural values and educational attainment has also been established through the analysis of large-scale surveys. The ethnic groups discussed above as having some of the poorest educational attainment come from communities, which are disadvantaged on most measures of socio-economic status. This has certainly been found to be the case for Pakistanis and Bangladeshis (Dale et al.).

Free school meal entitlement has often been used as a useful indicator of poverty for social scientists when others are not available (Demie 2001). ILEA findings show a negative correlation between free school meals and performance, the higher the proportion eligible for school meals the lower the performance in examination results. Such research has demonstrated that class affects educational attainment but class does not necessarily have the same affects across all ethnic groups. It has been found that the children of working class Pakistani parents are more likely to go on to pursue degrees at University than the children of working class Caribbean parents (Ballard 1998) and when controlling for class all ethnic minorities are more likely to remain in education post 16. This will be discussed in further detail in the next section when looking at Higher Education. Socio-economic status alone is therefore not sufficient on its own, when attempting to explain the diversity of educational success.

Stereotyping and Racial Harassment

In Foster's essay on defining equality for ethnically diverse schools he writes, 'One aspect of this (unequal treatment) would be to establish whether students from different ethnic groups enjoyed an equally safe and supportive learning environment' (1993: 526).

To demonstrate inequality we would need to show, for example, that certain ethnic groups were subject to a greater number or more severe acts of abuse, intimidation or violence, either from other students or teachers.

Gillborn (1998) argues that different groups encounter different forms of prejudice and that all ethnic minority groups may experience racism but they do not necessarily experience racism of the same degree. This is largely explained by those such as Modood et al. (1997) as resulting from a cultural racism rather than racism based on genealogy or biology. Here it is argued that different groups encounter different stereotypes. In a school setting pupils from Asian groups and Afro-Caribbean groups not only experience different stereotypes but these can be imposed and asserted in different ways, for example, through violence in the play ground by other students or expulsion by school staff.

There are numerous studies on why Afro-Caribbean's, particularly males, perform less well than some other ethnic groups. Gillborn (1998) argues that Afro-Caribbean students are frequently portrayed as conflicting with the behavioural requirements within the mainstream education system. He found, during two years of fieldwork, that Afro-Caribbean children of both sexes were disproportionately disciplined and criticised by teachers, and his research highlighted that Afro-Caribbean students were 4–6 times more likely to be excluded than their White peers.

Expulsion or suspension rates have been discussed by some as evidence of unequal treatment. Here it is argued that children from some backgrounds face harsher sanctions for equivalent behaviour because their cultural norms are interpreted as deviant. This could be perceived as a lack of respect for authority due to the way teachers or adults are addressed, which is viewed as legitimate within ones' culture but not within the dominant school culture.

Although it is has been widely established within the sociology of race and education that Caribbean boys occupy the lowest level of education achievement and experience the highest levels of exclusion from schools, Archer (2001) argues that this is also the case for Bangladeshi males despite much of the research indicating contrasting stereotypes of Asianchildren within schools. Mac an Ghaill (1988) is an example of such research. He found that Black males were seen to be of 'low ability' and potential discipline problems, whereas in contrast, Asians were seen as being 'technically minded'. Various qualitative research has demonstrated how patronising and negative stereotyping of Asian children within schools is widespread. It is argued that such behaviour by teachers is a result of their assumptions that Asian communities are excessively controlling with narrow and restrictive expectations for their children. This has also been supported by the findings from Wright (1992). Here it is argued that as Caribbean males are viewed as aggressive, gender specific stereotypes are also present for Asian girls. In Wright's study it was argued that Asian girls are seen as passive and almost docile with little enthusiasm for education and it was believed by teachers that this was largely due to parental expectations of their early arranged marriages (this will be discussed in further detail in the following section on differential parental expectations for the educational attainment of their children).

Bullying

It has also been argued that Asian pupils are the most likely to be bullied and victims of overt racial abuse within schools. Gillborn (1990) found such abuse to be a regular fact of life for most Asian pupils. He argues that studies have shown that even when teachers witness such acts they do not always act appropriately.

Eslea and Mukhtar (2000) conducted a study of Hindu, Indian Muslim and Pakistani children attending mosques and Temples in Lancashire and Asian and White children attending a Lancashire school. Here the children were asked about their experiences of school bullying. For the three Asian groups it was found that 57 per cent of boys and 43 per cent of girls had been bullied. Asian children experienced more bullying than White children. Bullying was at least as likely to occur by a member of another ethnic minority group as it was by a member of the White group, however bullying within the same ethnic group was rare. In this study a distinction between bullying because of racial or ethnic difference rather than for individual differences, such as wearing glasses for example, was emphasised.

A study by Boulton (1995) found that the nature of bullying was different for Asian and White children, 80 per cent of those Asian children bullied in his study had been taunted about their race or colour by White children. Eslea and Mukhtar concluded that the issue of bullying was not a straightforward White/non-White dichotomy but that just as non-Whites groups distinguish between themselves, as they are not a homogeneous group, not all non-White groups experience racially aggravated bullying in the same way. Craig (1999) suggested that the bullying experiences of Asian children varied depending on whether Asians are few or the largest minority group in a school. This theory is supported by the view that stereotypes for different groups vary depending on the ethnic make up of a school. Where Afro-Caribbean students make up the largest minority group, Asian students stereotypes can be relatively positive or they can be as discussed in a study by Parker-Jenkins (1992) virtually 'invisible' within the classroom. Where Asians are the largest minority groups however, there is evidence to suggest that, in the absence of Black students, the same basic stereotypes are expressed towards Asians in negative ways (Gillborn and Gipps 1996).

The results of stereotyping are that the educator sees children as having different aspirations and abilities intrinsic to their communities. The result of harassment is that children are forced to try to progress in an unsafe environment. Pupils facing negative stereotyping and racial harassment are therefore clearly not given the same learning opportunities as other children. Apart from the obvious disadvantage such lack of equality in the classroom can bring, research suggests that this background of difference and disadvantage for students from ethnic minority communities might result in low educational aspirations with a rejection of the formal educational system as a means of attainment.

Brah (1993) found that for many young Asian people in Leicester, when she conducted her fieldwork in the 80s, the education system produced a sense of marginalisation and alienation akin to that found amongst Black pupils. She argues that this creates a polarisation between those who feel disillusioned by the process and those who see success in the process as the only means of success in the world.

Human Capital

The origin of human capital goes back at least to 'The Wealth of Nations' (Smith 1776/1952) suggested that investment in physical capital through expenditure on machines might have parallels in investment in human capital through expenditure on education and training. Others have since developed this idea of humans as a potential form of capital and of learning and education as the means of investing in that capital (Schultz 1961; Becker 1964). The fundamental principle underpinning human capital theory is the belief that peoples learning capacities are of comparable value to other resources involved in the production of goods and services and as Coleman writes, 'Human capital is created by changes in persons that bring about skills and capabilities that make them able to act in new ways' (1988: 100). It is this ability to act in news ways to increase or generate financial capital or gain that is key.

Human capital theorists argue that the outcomes from investment in the accumulation of skill or in education is multifaceted and provides improvement on many levels not only measurable on the individual level in the form of improved performance, but at the organisational level in the form of improved productivity and profitability and even at societal level in the form of returns that benefit the entire society. Therefore in this view investment in education and training is a form of capital required for the development of individuals' organisations and communities (Brooks et al. 2004).

Human capital scholars have defined methods of quantifying returns to investment in education and training and the benefits although initially seen in terms of financial gain have far wider implications. McMahon (1991) argues that there should be three components of monetary return of human capital: the individual returns, the intergenerational benefits passed from one generation to their children, and dynamic returns that take account of earning trends over time. Private non-monetary benefits include health effects, enhancement of children's education, higher returns on financial assets, more efficient households purchasing, higher female labour participation rates, higher levels of part time employment after retirement, lifelong adaptation, continued learning, selective mating and non-monitory job satisfaction. Social non-monitory benefits to groups include lower fertility rates, lower population rates, better public health, democratisation, human rights, political stability and poverty reduction according to Little (2003).

Muslim Groups in the UK and Human Capital

It has been stated above that 'Muslim' groups (namely Pakistani and Bangladeshis) experience greater levels of disadvantage when compared with other minority groups. In explaining the different tra-jectories groups appear to have taken it has already been implied that human capital was key for some groups in that within generations a similar class profile was recreated despite downgrading on migration. Here, although financial capital was not present the eventual climb-ing up the ladder occurred because parents valued education, having come from urban areas with some formal qualifications. Although many of these qualifications were rendered practically worthless on entry into Britain, it meant that parents were able to not only assist their children with school work but also to instil in their children the value of human capital, because they themselves had come from an environment that valued education. Therefore although not neces-sarily visible through the accumulation of wealth, this idea fits with Bourdieu's (1997) in that within the family or even community 'cul-ture' education was seen as something to be actively pursued.

Although evidence demonstrates that all ethnic groups have made progress in terms of educational attainment and this is likely to be through access to free state education, particularly in that there were fewer with no qualifications, or qualifications below GCSE level, there were still twice as many Pakistanis and Bangladeshis in these cate-gories than Indians and African Asians (ONS 1991). The latter two groups were more likely to have had some form of formal schooling when compared with the former who are overwhelmingly migrants from rural farming communities.

Findings since the 1991 National Census have also supported this. Modood et al. (1997) found that Pakistanis and Bangladeshis, espe-cially women, were far less likely to have any qualifications at all com-pared with the White ethnic group and other South Asian groups in the study. Here too it was argued that educational attainment is a re-sult of both progress and disadvantage, most importantly in terms of progress it was found that the varied educational profiles of groups reflected those of their migrant generations.

In addition it was found that young men in all ethnic groups spoke English well; however, only about half of Pakistani and a quarter of Bangladeshi women aged 25–44 were at a competent level. A factor which affects the attainment of English fluency is marriages between South Asians born in the UK and spouses from the Indian sub-con-tinent. It is likely that the children of such marriages speak the South Asian language within the home and therefore have limited English prior to formal schooling.

Due to difficulties with language proficiency many minority chil-dren were unable to access the curriculum suitably so that educational attainment for groups with poorer English language skills, in this case the two Muslim groups, was found to be on average lower than for other ethnic groups. The fact that many of the parents of such children were uneducated meant that they had no first hand experience with the education system. (Halstead 2001)

In sum as Ansari writes,

Unskilled and with poor education, the majority of Muslim immigrants entered Britain at the bottom of the socioeconomic ladder. The economic position of the majority of Muslims has changed little since the 1960s. Many are still concentrated in semi skilled and unskilled sectors of industry. These communities experience unemployment, poor working conditions, poverty, poor and over crowded housing, poor health and low educational qualifications. (Ansari 2002: 9)

Criticisms of Human Capital

There are critics of theories of human capital and those who question whether the investment in terms of both time and money are worthwhile in every case. Even those who are well known advocates of the theory acknowledge the difficulties and impracticalities in measuring outcomes. Becker (1993) writes,

An investment on college education is subject to considerable risk, and is obviously extremely illiquid. Consequently, the gain from education should be compared with that of investment with equally large risk and illiquidity. (1993: 206)

Yet it is more in term of discrimination and ethnic penalties that education can be a doubly risky investment for some groups who are disadvantaged. Not only is there the risk in the investment of time, where perhaps taking a job (although low paying) would still generate much needed resources, but there is also the risk that discriminatory job markets may leave even those with qualifications in a position where they are having to take up jobs that they did not require any qualifications for in the initial instance. In other words orthodox economic theories and theories regarding the acquisition of human capital rely too heavily on a level playing field within the labour market (Loury 1981).

Even where the state is bearing the direct cost of education it is argued that not only the individual but the household bears the indirect cost in that they miss out on a potential financial contribution through the individuals hours spent in education rather than through making full use of their current earning potential, however low that may be.

Determination for Success and Family Expectations and Social Capital

An area that has been granted progressively more attention since the debate on 'social capital' began is the effect family encouragement has on the pursuit of and the attainment of educational qualifications. It is argued that of the various factors influencing achievement in school, household or family background is considered a single entity distinguished from schooling in its effects (Coleman 1988). It has already been stated that the socio-economic position of families can contribute to differential outcomes for individuals and these include greater financial capital. For those like Goldthorpe (1996), the financial provides the physical resources that can aid achievement. However it has been argued that human capital, even where there is little financial capital, is generally measured by parents' educational attainment or experience of the education system and provides the potential for intellectual development. However Coleman (1998) argues that social capital is more important in some regards than both financial and human capital, in that even where parents' years of schooling are low, higher levels of social capital compensate for those parents who have higher levels of human capital but little time to invest in ensuring their children attain the most emotional support and encouragement throughout their educational development. He provides examples of families where both parents have high levels of human capital, but because both parents are in full time employment their children do not benefit to the same degree as those who have more time spent with their parents.

Modood (2004) argues that there is one effect of social capital that appears to be particularly important for ethnic minority communities and that is its effect on the creation of human capital in the next generation. He argues that, 'The motor of the British South Asian and Chinese overcoming of disadvantage lies in migrant parents getting their children to internalise high educational ambitions and to enforce appropriate behaviour' (2004: 87).

In this view parents may have little relevant economic and human capital to transmit but successive human capital acquisition by their children may depend upon parent-child transmission of 'norms-laden and goals-directed identities'. He also argues that such cultural influence does not necessarily require the presence of concentrated tight knit communities and is more at the heart of ethnic minority social and cultural capital than geographical locations or community institutions. In this view beliefs and expectations about education/progress status may be transmitted from parents to children and may sufficiently motivate the latter to produce unexpectedly high educational outcomes.

Stereotypes regarding the value placed by parents from different communities on the education of their children have varied. As discussed above some teachers believed Asian students were unable to make their own choices regarding their future due to the authoritative nature of Asian families.

Several studies have found that ethnic minority parents and families support, encourage and even expect their children to pursue their education to a greater degree than White parents. Allen's (1998) study of a small sample of under-graduates found that respondents from ethnic minority communities were more likely to report family encouragement for the pursuit of qualifications than White respondents. Here it was found that 55 per cent of ethnic minority students had been 'strongly encouraged' to enter higher education by their families compared to 34 per cent of White students. 15 per cent of ethnic minority and 1 per cent of White students reported the influence of another relative had been 'very important' in their decision to enter higher education. This study gave no indication of significant differences between ethnic minority groups. A study of mature students by Gull (2001) found that even in ethnic minority families who had not been supportive initially, qualifications once obtained became a source of family pride.

Modood (2003) argues that for many ethnic minority groups encouragement does not only come in the form of parental engagement in school activities or assisting children with homework but rather in the form of high expectations and discipline. Here it is argued that these communities can seldom transfer skills and knowledge (due to lower levels of human capital) yet possess a strong sense that education is extremely valuable. Furthermore, some research suggests that the pursuit of qualifications for some ethnic groups is not only encouraged but is insisted upon by parents (Allen 1998).

Material resources play a significant part in educational success and as already commented upon; socio-economic status is linked with attainment of qualifications. Modood (2003) argues that there are findings that may suggest parents from ethnic minorities are more willing financially to invest in the education of their children, even where comparatively finances are sparse.

There are debates about underachievement surrounding gender. Some studies have suggested that there has been a lack of encouragement of Asian girls by parents due to the fear of their children being over exposed to undesirable influences and ways of thinking found in the host society. Here it is argued that once there is no obligation on parents for their children to attend school, there is a preference for them to be withdrawn. Ghuman (1997) writes, 'the home emphasises the collectivity (Biraderi) as opposed to the rugged individuality advocated by schools' (p. 23). Others such as Halstead (1991) have commented on the fact that Muslims' preference to single sex schools could be interpreted by some as these communities seeking a means of perpetuating traditional views of women's roles in society.

In Dale et al's (2002) study of Bangladeshi and Pakistani women in Oldham it was found that,

> Education was important for both girls and boys. Although responsibility for providing for the extended family is firmly located with boys – and this seemed to be accepted by both the boys and girls interviewed – this did not necessarily devalue the role of education for girls. Higher education was often portrayed by girls and parents as having intrinsic value. (p. 953)

Dale's finding are in line with higher education participation rates for women from these communities and as Ballard's study (1998) demonstrates, the greater participation of women in A-level courses than men for all groups including Pakistanis and Bangladeshis means the notion that Muslim parents are robustly opposed to the prospect of their daughters gaining advanced educational qualifications is in fact unsound at least nowadays.

Here it is argued that ethnic minority families and communities do value education and encourage their children in gaining qualifications. Although it has been traditionally assumed that some communities encourage their children more than others, evidence suggests that importance is placed on educational success even for those sections of minority groups such as Asian women, who in the past were thought to lack parental encouragement.

A variable used to demonstrate the determination to succeed by ethnic minorities is through their high rates of staying on in post-compulsory education. Some groups such as Pakistani and Bangladeshis are more likely to have to re-take exams in order to make the required grades for degree courses, and this in itself is argued to be evidence of such communities commitment to the pursuit of betterment through the attainment of qualifications (Taylor et al. 1991; Modood and Acland 1998; Ballard 1998; Dale 2002). As Gillborn argues ethnic origin has actually been found to be the single most important variable in determining the chances of staying on when controlling for all other variables.

Studies such as those conducted my Marks (2000) found that high participation rates in higher education for all ethnic minorities are much less related to class than for White groups. In this view White working class culture has traditionally considered higher education with a negative manner. In this view there is no stigma attached for minority groups in pursuing higher education and many parents of all class backgrounds view educational qualifications as a positive alternative to other avenues available to their children such as government training initiatives. Of course ethnic minorities do not have generations of working class culture and traditional occupations to pass on to their children as arguably White working class parents do. Racism may well be an additional push factor for ethnic minority students to remain in higher education, due to the belief that the labour market is highly selective and discriminatory.

Young people interviewed in Dale's (2002) study described their decision to remain in education and gain qualifications as the only route to success in the labour market. There was acknowledgement of the difficulties that would be faced even with qualifications due to having to compete with White people for jobs in a selective and discriminatory labour market. It was asserted by these young people that they would not only have to prove they were just as capable as White applicants but better in order to be given the same opportunities. Such views are supported by studies such as Cheng and Heath's (1993) who in their analysis of Labour Force Survey data found that, Indians, Pakistanis and Caribbeans in the service class were better qualified than their White peers, suggesting an 'ethnic penalty' as described in this chapter. These findings have been supported by subsequent research conducted by Allen (1998).

Although the visible minorities are broadly over-represented in higher education, they are currently much more heavily represented in the former polytechnics than they are in the longer established and prestigious universities. Therefore as Ballard (1998) has pointed out, even where they are disproportionately successful within the system as a whole, at an institutional level their status is still one of relative disadvantage.

It is clear from the research described above that ethnic minorities, do value educational qualifications; this can be demonstrated by participation in higher education. It is also worth noting that this level of attainment should be viewed against the lack of economic resources available to many of these communities, the fact that they have lower than average A-level grades for the courses they are applying and that for some communities such as Pakistanis and Bangladeshis, failing to obtain grades the first time does not stunt their determination for qualifications. Studies suggesting family expectations and students own perceptions of the importance of qualifications in combating racism within society further support this.

Language Ability

A child's inability to understand or communicate in English is undoubtedly a factor that could hinder the child's progress and his or her educational success. Kendall (1998) findings of how children who have English as a second language and are non-fluent in English have restricted access to the national curriculum and are severely disadvantaged, seem commonsensical. However the effect on educational attainment for children who cannot communicate in English or whose mother tongue is not English is not as simplistic as some have suggested. Starting school as a non-English speaker does not necessarily encumber a child for the rest of his or her educational career, nor does being bilingual. On the contrary there is evidence to suggest that such children are particularly swift when making progress with English, and therefore often catch up.

Research conducted by Demie (2001) on the significance of English language ability split children from ethnically mixed inner London schools into 5 classifications:

i) Bilingual learners who can engage in classroom activities using their mother tongue but need assistance to operate in English.
ii) Bilingual learners who can engage in all learning activities but whose written and or oral English shows English isn't their first language.
iii) Bilingual pupils who can engage successfully in both oral and written work but where further support is considered necessary for a number of reasons.

iv) Bilingual pupils need no additional support and can successfully engage with the curriculum.

v) Pupils who speak English only.

It was found that pupils who were not as long established in the
city; most of the African children particularly the Somali pupils and
other recent arrivers as refugees, were less fluent in English. Evidence
was found however that once these pupils become more proficient in
English their scores in their key stage exams matched and in some
cases were higher than the average scores for their LEA. Demie explains that the main reason for the Bangladeshi underachievement is
that at age seven about 90 per cent of Bangladeshi children were in the
early stages (1, 2 or 3) of English fluency. However by age 11, fewer
than 67 per cent of Bangladeshi children were in the early stages of fluency, while by the time they took GCSE's, the majority were reasonably
proficient in English. These figures demonstrate that once the disadvantage of language is overcome, it is possible for an ethnic group
to catch up with other groups who have outperformed them at the
early stages of education. In fact here it was found that Bangladeshis
outperformed Caribbean pupils at GCSE level, and Caribbeans are a
group who are often not bilingual. It was also argued that bilingual
pupils who were fully proficient in English were much more likely to
perform better on average compared to English only speakers. At Key
stage 1 it was found that Portuguese pupils had the lowest scores for
all ethnic groups in the LEA. This again adds to the evidence of English
proficiency being just as crucial as other causes of underachievement
faced by minority groups.

Section Summary

The different educational success of ethnic groups has been briefly
outlined. It has been argued that some minority groups are performing significantly better than others and that although all visible minorities face racism and discrimination some are more prone to group
specific negative stereotyping and racial harassment within schools.
Socio-economic status has also been found to play a significant role
in the educational success of ethnic groups and those ethnic groups
who have poorer attainment rates are found to be among the most
economically disadvantaged (Dale 2002). However the fact that many
students from such households are enthusiastic in pursuing their education post 16 suggests that the communities from which they come
greatly value educational qualifications and indicates the existence of

positive forms of social capital. The research suggests that the lack of success of these communities is not due to their lack of willingness and determination. The importance of language ability was also discussed and although many children whose mother tongue is not English do begin relatively disadvantaged, there is evidence to suggest that significant progress can be made in order to catch up with other children before it has a real effect – namely on GCSE's results. The key debates surrounding differences in attainment therefore seem to point towards socio-economic status, differential effects of cultural discrimination and social capital in the form of family encouragement and expectations as the main factors for the diversity in educational attainment.

Pakistanis and Bangladeshis have been the main reference groups when looking at the educational attainment of Muslims even though they only make up 59 per cent of Muslims in Britain. What we know about these ethnic groups with regards to educational attainment is that they are amongst the most socio-economically disadvantaged; they have the lowest educational success although this seems to vary at different stages of their education. Research suggests that these communities value education no less than any other and have as high expectations as parents from other ethnic groups. As Asians it is suggested that these groups face a racial discrimination within schools and a variety of damaging stereotypes depending on the ethnic make up of the school they attended. With the information derived through studies on ethnicity therefore, it can be asserted that Muslims in comparison to other minority groups are faring poorly in gaining qualifications despite their apparent commitment.

Issues Specific to Muslim Students

Academic research on education specifically of Muslims as a religious group, rather than ethnic groups, has focussed largely on state funded schools and women in education. Literature on the latter has largely explored the same issues discussed above when looking at Pakistani and Bangladeshi women in education. These are Muslim women's aspirations, the value placed on educational qualifications for women by Muslim communities and within Islam, single sex schools and obstacles faced by Muslim women within the education system. State funding of Muslim schools however is a subject that has largely been discussed in terms of religion specifically and an issue relevant to Muslims as a religious community rather than in terms of ethnicity.

State Funded Muslim Schools

Muslims have been portrayed as having somewhat definite practical needs within schools. Ghuman has commented on this, 'There can be a source of tension between home and school, particularly in Muslim communities, in the teaching of physical education and drama and over such matters as school uniform and dietary matters' (1997: 24).

Although of course the above could easily be true for other groups such as Hindus and Sikhs, Muslims have other needs such as provisions within schools for formal worship in the form of obligatory prayer. Others such as Parker-Jenkins (1992) have commented on the fact that some Muslim parents feel that Christian-orientated worship is unacceptable and exercise their right to withdraw their children. Others are simply frustrated at the belief that Christianity in schools is seen as superior to rather than equal to other faiths. Such issues raise important questions such as; to what extent can and should education reflect cultural differences in society and is it still possible to provide a common core curriculum adequate to meet the requirements of all children? There have been publicised examples of Muslim parents choosing to withdraw their children from schools entirely, invoking their right to educate their child outside the state education system, either with home tutoring or within the private education sector, including of course Muslim schools.

Those arguing for state funded Muslim schools assert that if British state funded schools cannot meet Muslim educational needs, then Muslims should have the right to their own state funded schools. Although there are currently some state funded Muslim schools, when initial applications for state funding were declined many viewed the decision as discriminatory due to the fact that Christian denominations and Jewish schools have been granted state funding (Molokotos Liederman 2000).

Opinions on state funded schools are divided. Those who support such initiatives based their arguments on multiculturalism and respect for diversity. Those who were against them felt that such schools would reinforce segregation, there was also concern over the equality women would have in such schools and since 11 September 2001, there have been debates around the compatibility of Islamic values and state values within schools.

The Swann Report (1985) recommended the avoidance of separate schools due to the belief that the presence of ethnic minority children are needed within states schools in order for White children to learn about minority communities and to eliminate prejudice. Advocates of faith schools however argue that such views are wholly unfair. In this view to use the group with less power, essentially to the detriment of that group (and in this case Muslim students) in order to provide a possible solution to prejudice (which essentially belongs to the group with more power, in this case non-Muslim students and staff) is irresponsible (Halstead 1991).

There have been vigourous debates within Muslim communities also surrounding separate schooling for Muslim children. Councillor Ajeeb, Bradford's first Asian Lord Mayor, spoke for some Muslims who disagreed with separate schooling during a speech in which he said 'what we want is accommodation for our cultural needs, especially in the education system' (cited in Cumper 1990:5). Taylor and Hagarty (1985) in their study on Cypriot Muslims in England found that members of this community, when the subject of separate schooling was discussed, voiced opposition, believing them to be counterproductive.

Many Muslims feel that various key arguments against state funded Muslim schools demonstrate the level of prejudice towards Muslims and Islam and myths surrounding the goals Muslims have for their community's educational welfare. A key criticism of Muslim schools is that they are monolithic and children who attend such schools will not appreciate or understand diversity. However as discussed by Johnson and Castelli (2002) in their research on Muslim schools in England, most were described as multi-ethnic and drawing children from a wide range of social and economic backgrounds. In addition it was argued that although such schools are mono-faith they portray diverse interpretations of Islam. Johnson and Castelli also point out in their study on faith schools that such establishments are increasingly gathering reputations for educational excellence. Many argue that if such schools facilitate the learning of children in a more productive manner they should be seen in terms of 'social solutions' and in this view faith schools should be regarded as a productive expression of a co-operative multi-cultural society.

Muslim Specific Discrimination in Schools

As discussed in the previous section, anxiety over Islamic values negating state school values are at the centre of the debate on separate Muslim schools. Concerns within schools however have also been articulated, over growing agitation of an increasingly more politicised and assertive Muslim community and students themselves

(Molokotos Liederman 2000). Researchers have pointed to how British Muslim young people are increasingly defining themselves in terms of their religion, as opposed, for example, to their parents country of birth (as discussed during pervious chapters, see Saeed 1999). Archer (2001) in her interviews with young Muslim men from various South Asian ethnic groups found that within every discussion group, all of the young men identified themselves first and foremost as 'Muslim'.

Archer (2001) argues that, increasingly, Muslim students are encountering very specific stereotyping in schools as a result of both a growing portrayal of Muslims as a problematic group in relation to 'the West' by the media and the assertion of Muslim identities by young Muslims. These stereotypes differ from those of Asian students as discussed earlier by some such as Mac an Ghaill (1988). Archer writes,

> It has been argued that Muslim young men are increasingly being constructed as militant and aggressive, intrinsically fundamentalist 'ultimate others' ... In contrast to the public discourse around Muslim masculinity, Asians young men have been conceptualised as effeminate, as more 'middle-class' and as behavers and achievers. (2001: 81)

It has been argued that expression of such identities among young Muslims is a means to articulate their space and belonging within a system which is increasingly viewing them as at the very least somehow associated with an undesirable world view. On this point Gilliat writes, 'The word reaction in many ways captures some of the attempts made by young Muslims to find a way of being British Muslims, especially where they feel their religious identity is under threat' (1995: 109).

It has already been suggested that although there are clearly differences in attainment for Muslim groups as discussed in the previous sections, it is very difficult to distinguish between Muslims and other South Asian groups, all being visibly of non-European origin. Ballard argues however that whilst Muslim Asians – Pakistani and Bangladeshis, have achieved much less upward mobility than Indians, it is difficult to prove that most members of the White majority would be able to distinguish a Muslim from a non-Muslim or be fully aware of what that would even mean. It is true that in larger society it would be extremely difficult for a lay person to distinguish between a

Indian Hindu and Pakistani Muslim on the street or in a public setting, but in a school setting were staff and pupils are more than aware
of the affiliation – indeed identity of perhaps their only non-White
students group, anti-Muslims stereotypes could well be adopted as argued above by Phoenix (1997) and Verma and Darby (1994), just as
numerous studies of Caribbean male pupils have found that teachers
adopt very group specific stereotypes for this ethnic sub group.

The presence of Islamophobia has not been as apparent as it has
in the last decade. It has been argued that although there is a long
and deep history of anti-Muslim sentiment in Europe, the most recent
wave of Islamophobia can be detected as re-emerging as a result of
key global and local events such as – the Rushdie affair, the Iranian
Revolution, the Gulf Wars, the Bradford and Oldham riots and the
bombing of the Twin Towers to name a few.

In the Fourth National Survey of Ethnic Minorities, members of a
White sample were asked whether or not they were prejudiced against
Asians, Muslims, Caribbeans and Chinese. 26 per cent admitted prejudice towards Asians, 25 per cent against Muslims, 20 per cent against
Caribbeans and 8 per cent against Chinese. When asked which religious or ethnic group faced the most prejudice, Muslims were given
the highest percentage for a religious groups and in the opinion of the
sample, were ten times more likely than Sikhs for (a group which is
arguable just as physically visible) to be indicated as facing the most
prejudice.

It has already been argued in this section that Muslims have been
viewed as a group who have very specific needs within schools and
have been portrayed as being vocal in asserting their rights within
the education system (Molokotos Lierderman 2000; Ghuman 1997).
It could be argued that Muslims are therefore viewed as being particularly demanding and difficult. Although there is little qualitative
research looking at teachers perceptions of Muslim communities, sociologists have commented on the attention Muslim educational matters have received in the media suggesting they are at the forefront of
debates surrounding religious communities and schools. Molokotos
Liederman writes,

> The schooling of Muslim children, particularly the display of
> their Islamic identity within the education system, has been
> perceived as problematic enough to become a focal point of
> the public and media attention and there have been contro-
> versial debates in the press. (2000: 368)

When discussing the differing discourses on Asian male students, more research on how males from the different Asian faith communities are viewed within schools is required. When Mac an Ghaill described technically minded Asian males was he describing Hindu or Muslim students or both? An explanation for the differences in discourse on Muslim males is that stereotypes have altered as a result of changes in perceptions within wider society. Perhaps in answering such questions, the area of differential educational attainment could gain an even clearer picture of whether some groups remain underachievers when compared to others, as a result of differential treatment within the education process.

Data Results

During this section the findings from the analysis of the 2001 Census data on educational qualifications of religious communities will be discussed. The data for England and Wales will be examined to gain a national overview.

Overview of Standard Tables Used in the Analysis

Census table s158 on 'Age and highest level of qualification by religion' is the main source of data for this analysis. This provides data on the following levels of qualifications for England and Wales:

0 No academic or professional qualifications
1 Level 1 — 1+ O-level passes, 1+ CSE/GCSE any grades, NVQ level 1, foundation GNVQ;
2 Level 2 — 5+ O-level passes, 5+ GSCES (A-C), School Certificate, 1+ A-levels /AS levels, NVQ level 2, Intermediate GNVQ;
3 Level 3 — 2+ A-Levels, 4+ AS levels, Higher school Certificate, NVQ level 3, Advanced GNVQ;
4 Level 4/5 — First degree, higher degree, NVQ levels 4&5, HNC, HND, Qualified teacher status, Medical doctor, Dentist, Nurse, Midwife, Health Visitor.

This, as indicated by the table's title, is broken down into age groups, but information on the highest levels on qualification by sex is not provided.

Table M299 'Nes SeC and highest level of qualification by religion' is used to supplement finding from the above table as it provides greater clarity in how levels of qualifications differ for Muslims and other religious groups when occupational class is also considered. It also provides an indication of discriminatory labour market practices or whether there appears to be an 'ethnic penalty' for some groups in attaining employment. Here it is argued that people from ethnic minorities with similar educational qualifications as those from the indigenous majority are often in lower occupational classes resulting from discriminatory recruitment practices.

For this table the qualification levels are represented by different numbers:

0 No academic or professional qualifications

1 Level 1 — 1+ O-level passes, 1+ CSE/GCSE any grades, NVQ level 1, foundation GNVQ;

2 Level 2 — 5+ O-level passes, 5+ GSCES (A-C), School Certificate, 1+ A-levels /AS levels, NVQ level 2, Intermediate GNVQ;

3 Level 3 — 2+ A-Levels, 4+ AS levels, Higher school Certificate, NVQ level 3, Advanced GNVQ;

4 First degree, higher degree, NVQ levels 4&5, HNC, HND, Qualified teacher status, Medical doctor, Dentist, Nurse, Midwife, Health visitor.

5 Other qualifications.

In addition to highest level of qualification, table M326 'Sex age and professional qualification by religion' will be explored in order to ascertain whether possession of such qualifications have proportionately increased by age cohort for minority faith groups in particular as possession of professional qualifications in particular are seen as an important means of attaining employment in discriminatory employment markets.

Data from the Standard tables 153 on 'Sex and age and economic activity by religions', 151 on 'Household composition by the religion of the household reference person' and 161 'Sex and communal establishment by resident type and religion' have also been analysed in order to provide information on percentages of males and females by religious group who are classed as students, and who are living in either educational establishment or all student households.

Participation rates in post-16 education by sex and religion will therefore be established and in doing so it is hoped that some indication of the highest level of qualification by sex can be achieved.

Highest Qualifications by Age
The Census data shows that Muslims have the highest percentage of

people under the age of thirty (62 per cent) and therefore have the highest percentage of people who would be of the ages most common for attending schools and higher education establishments. Whereas Muslims make up nearly 3 per cent of the population of England and Wales as a whole, Muslims make up over 5 per cent of all dependent children.

The Census provides information on highest qualification for those aged 16–74 years old and the age bands used below are the same as those used in the Census.

16–24 Years Old

The analysis of the data on qualifications for people in this age bracket found that 22 per cent of Muslims have 'no qualifications' compared with 16 per cent for all people. This figure is the highest percentage for all groups with no qualifications and is more than double that of Hindus and people classified under 'Any other religion' (see Figure 3.1).

When looking at qualification levels, Muslims have a higher concentration towards Level 1 and 2 qualifications. This group has the lowest percentage of people with level 3 qualifications, and although those with level 4/5 qualifications is lower than all other minority religions with 11 per cent, this is roughly half that for Hindus Buddhists and Jews, yet it mirrors the average national figure of 11 per cent. The Muslim figure is also higher than the figure for Christians of this age bracket, which is 10 per cent.

All the minority faith communities have higher percentages of people with qualifications classified as level 3 and 4/5 than the average national figure, with the exception of Muslims, who have similar or higher scores to Christians. The only level for which Muslims have the highest percentage of people across all faith groups is level 1.

25–34 Years Old

For this age bracket (see Figure 3.2) Muslims have the highest percentage of people with no qualifications. This is almost three times greater than the average national figure and over three times greater than Hindus. Across the qualification levels Muslims have lower percentages than the average national figure apart from at level 4/5 where, the percentage is again lower than all other minority faith groups, but higher than Christians and just under the average national figure. For Muslims in this age band there appears to be a polarisation between those with no qualifications and those with level 4/5 qualifications. This is not the case with any of the other faith groups.

Figure 3.1: Percentage of 16–24 year olds highest level of qualification by religion for England and Wales.

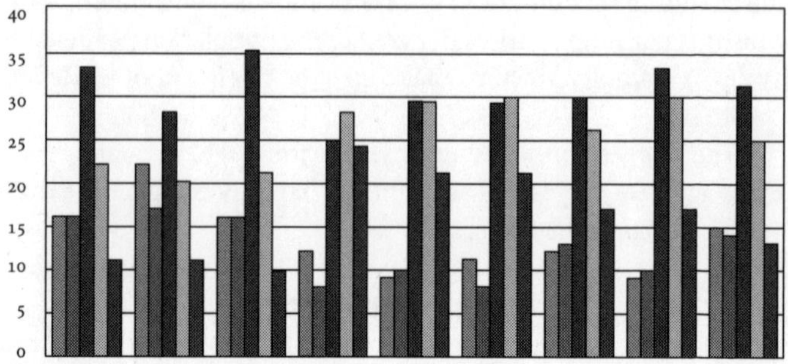

	All people	Muslim	Christian	Buddhist	Hindu	Jewish	Sikh	Other	None
■ none	16	22	16	12	9	11	12	9	15
■ level 1	16	17	16	8	10	8	13	10	14
■ level 2	33	28	35	25	29	29	30	33	31
▩ level 3	22	20	21	28	29	30	26	30	25
■ level 4/5	11	11	10	24	21	21	17	17	13

Source: taken from ONS (2001: Census table s158).

35–49 *Years Old*

As shown by Figure 3.3, Muslims within this age band have the highest percentage of people with no qualifications and at 47 per cent this is over double that of the average national figure. There is much less variation between groups with no qualification in this age band than with the previous one.

There appears to be polarisation for Muslims again within this age band, with the greater percentages being those with no qualifications and those with level 4/5. Muslims have a similar percentage of people with level 4/5 qualifications as the average national figure, but here the figure is not only higher than Christians but than Sikhs also. Sikhs too appear to show polarisation, as do Buddhists and Hindus. Muslims have the lowest percentage of people across levels 1, 2 and 3 and this is not surprisingly considering the percentage without any qualifications at all, and relatively high percentage at level 4/5.

50–74 *Years Old*

Here (see Figures 3.4, 3.5 and 3.6) for the first time Muslims have the second largest percentage, after Sikhs, of people with no qualifications, 53 per cent and 58 per cent respectively. For level 3 qualifications figures for Muslims, Hindus, Christians, Sikhs and nationally

Figure 3.2: Percentage of 25–34 year olds highest level of qualification by religion for England and Wales.

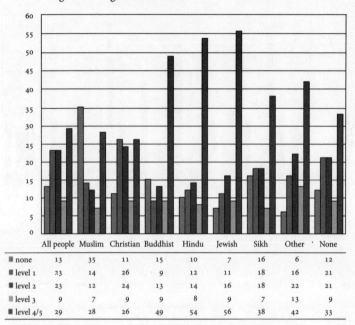

	All people	Muslim	Christian	Buddhist	Hindu	Jewish	Sikh	Other	None
▥ none	13	35	11	15	10	7	16	6	12
▦ level 1	23	14	26	9	12	11	18	16	21
▦ level 2	23	12	24	13	14	16	18	22	21
▨ level 3	9	7	9	9	8	9	7	13	9
▦ level 4/5	29	28	26	49	54	56	38	42	33

Source: taken from ONS (2001: Census table s158).

are similar and fall within 1.5 per cent of each other.

For level 4/5 Muslims have a higher percentage, as with the pervious age bracket as Sikhs, Christians and nationally and has greater variance than the previous age groups. Muslims have the lowest percentages with level 1 and 2 qualifications. This pattern is very similar for those aged 60–64 with the exception that Muslims have the highest percentage of people with no qualification, 64 per cent, but very closely followed by Sikhs, 63 per cent, and 65–74 year olds for whom the percentage of Muslims with no qualifications is 72 per cent and Sikhs 71 per cent.

Most strikingly the figures show that Muslims have the highest percentages of people with no qualifications. There is also polarisation between no qualification and level 4/5 qualifications within all Muslim age groups with the exception of the youngest (16–24). Amongst the eldest groups (60–74) Muslims and Sikhs have similar percentages of people with no qualifications. At 65–74 Muslims and Sikhs

Figure 3.3: Percentage of 35–49 year olds highest level of qualification By religion for England and Wales.

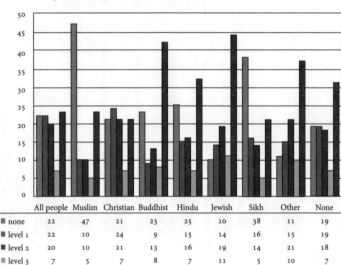

	All people	Muslim	Christian	Buddhist	Hindu	Jewish	Sikh	Other	None
▪ none	22	47	21	23	25	10	38	11	19
▪ level 1	22	10	24	9	15	14	16	15	19
▪ level 2	20	10	21	13	16	19	14	21	18
▪ level 3	7	5	7	8	7	11	5	10	7
▪ level 4/5	23	23	21	42	32	44	21	37	31

Source: taken from ONS (2001: table S158).

are roughly 10 per cent more likely to have no qualifications than Hindus, however for the 60–64 age bracket this increases to around 15 per cent. In the 50–59 age bracket, Muslims appear to have made slightly more progress than Sikhs, with Hindus still making good progress. However for 35–49 years olds, Muslims are 10 per cent more likely than Sikhs and over 20 per cent more likely than Hindus to be without a qualification. This gap widens even further for the 25–43 year olds, where the percentage of Muslims with no qualifications is over double that of Sikhs and over three times that of Hindus. The gap closes for the 16–24 year olds but only marginally. Therefore although all three groups have made progress and this is no doubt related to the availability of free State education in Britain, the rates of progress are far from similar.

However the figures could be interpreted another way. When looking at the relative progress made between Sikhs and Muslims from the age band 50–59 and 35–49, the percentage for Muslims with no qualifications decreased by 6 per cent compared to 21 per cent for Sikhs, then for the next age band, 13 per cent and 22 per cent respectively, and then for the youngest age band 13 per cent and 3 per cent

Figure 3.4: Percentage of 50–59 year olds highest level of qualification by religion for England and Wales.

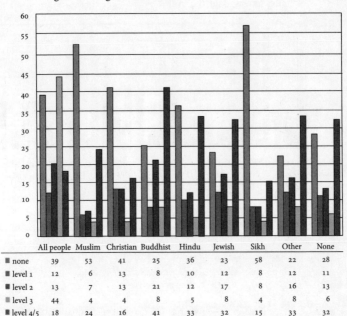

	All people	Muslim	Christian	Buddhist	Hindu	Jewish	Sikh	Other	None
none	39	53	41	25	36	23	58	22	28
level 1	12	6	13	8	10	12	8	12	11
level 2	13	7	13	21	12	17	8	16	13
level 3	44	4	4	8	5	8	4	8	6
level 4/5	18	24	16	41	33	32	15	33	32

Source: taken from ONS (2001: Census table S158).

respectively. Therefore it could be argued that Muslims are catching up in terms of making progress but this could also be overly optimistic as there are no data available to suggest that the percentage decrease for Muslims will continue to be large enough to make any significant headway.

The Scottish Census results on qualifications and attainment where similar to those for England and Wales, with one noticeable exception. Sikhs, not Muslims were found to be the group with the highest proportion of people with no qualifications (42 per cent) followed by Muslims (39 per cent). At a guess the larger proportion of Muslims from South Asian backgrounds in Scotland compared with England and Wales suggests that a larger proportion of Muslims in Scotland have had a similar period of settlement to Sikhs and Hindus. In England and Wales however, the higher proportions of new Muslim communities is likely to impact by increasing the figure for Muslims without qualifications.

Figure 3.5: Percentage of 60–64 year olds highest level of qualification by religion for England and Wales.

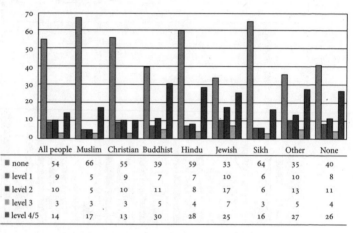

	All people	Muslim	Christian	Buddhist	Hindu	Jewish	Sikh	Other	None
▨ none	54	66	55	39	59	33	64	35	40
▨ level 1	9	5	9	7	7	10	6	10	8
▨ level 2	10	5	10	11	8	17	6	13	11
▨ level 3	3	3	3	5	4	7	3	5	4
▨ level 4/5	14	17	13	30	28	25	16	27	26

Source: taken from ONS *(2001: Census table S158).*

Figure 3.6: Percentage of 65–74 year olds highest level of qualification by religion for England and Wales.

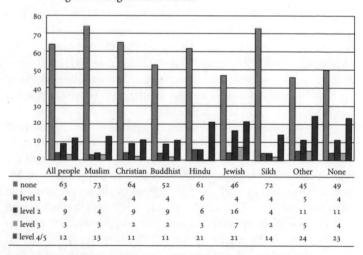

	All people	Muslim	Christian	Buddhist	Hindu	Jewish	Sikh	Other	None
▨ none	63	73	64	52	61	46	72	45	49
▨ level 1	4	3	4	4	6	4	4	5	4
▨ level 2	9	4	9	9	6	16	4	11	11
▨ level 3	3	3	2	2	3	7	2	5	4
▨ level 4/5	12	13	11	11	21	21	14	24	23

Source: taken from ONS *(2001: Census table S158).*

Figure 3.7: Map showing concentration of Muslims by percentage aged 16–24 with no qualifications by Local Authority for England and Wales

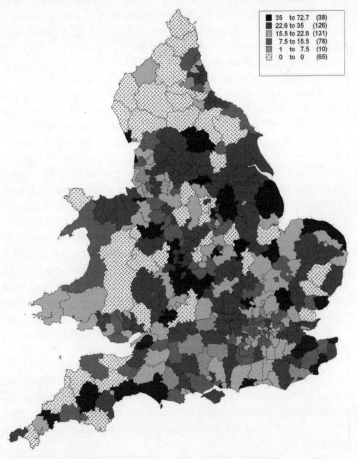

■	35 to 72.7	(38)
■	22.6 to 35	(126)
▨	15.5 to 22.6	(131)
▨	7.5 to 15.5	(78)
▨	1 to 7.5	(10)
▨	0 to 0	(65)

Local authorities represented by 'zero' on the map contained 15 or less Muslims of the age of 16–24. Any percentages derived from such small counts resulted in outliers, and these percentages were not mapped for this reason.

Highest Qualification by Occupational Class

The Census shows that Muslims have the highest proportion of people in the lowest occupational class, which is 'never worked or long term unemployed' and the lowest proportion of people in the highest occupational class, 'higher managerial and professional occupations'

Within the highest class, Muslims have the highest proportion of people with no qualifications, 6 per cent compared with 4 per cent nationally and for Sikhs, 5 per cent of Christians in this class, 2 per cent of Buddhist, Jewish, no religion and other religions and only 1 per cent of Hindus. Muslims do not have the highest proportion of people with no qualifications for those in intermediate occupations however, with 8 per cent compared with 11 per cent of all people and 13 per cent of Christians. For small employers and own account workers, Muslims have the highest proportion of people with no qualification with 42 per cent compared with 29 per cent nationally and the lowest 15 per cent for those with other religions.

Muslims have the highest proportion of people in lower supervisory and technical occupations with no qualifications also, with 32 per cent compared with 25 per cent nationally. For the occupational classes, semi-routine and routine occupations, Sikhs then Muslims have the highest proportion of people with no qualifications (40 per cent and 39 per cent). For routine occupations Sikhs, Hindus and then Muslims have the highest proportions of people with no qualifications. For those who have never worked or are long term unemployed, Muslims have the highest proportion of people with no qualifications with 67 per cent compared with 60 per cent nationally.

It is not surprising that Sikhs and Hindus have higher proportion of people with no qualifications in routine and semi-routine occupations as they have higher proportions of people in the higher occupational classes and therefore those without qualification would be more likely to enter such occupations. Therefore a better measure of occupational class success would be through the measurement of higher qualifications such as degrees and equivalent attainment as measured by level 5.

There are proportionately more people from minority religions, including Muslims with level 5 qualifications in the higher managerial occupation class than the figure for Christians and the national figure. Hindus have the highest percentage of people in this class with degrees and equivalent qualifications with 87 per cent followed by Buddhists with 81 per cent and Muslims with 79 per cent. For lower managerial occupations all minority faith groups again have higher proportions of people with level 5 qualifications when compared with the national figure and Christians. Here Buddhists, Hindus, those with other religions and then Muslims have the highest percentage (63 per cent, 58 per cent, 54 per cent and 53 per cent compared with 42 per cent nationally).

For those in Intermediate occupations Buddhists, Hindus and then Muslims have the highest proportion of people with level 5 qualifications (41 per cent, 34 per cent and 31 per cent). Again all minority faith groups have higher proportions of people with level 5 qualifications than Christians and all people (12 per cent and 15 per cent). This pattern continues for all other occupational classes also. All minority faith groups have higher proportions of people with level 5 qualifications when compared to the national figure and the proportion of Christians in small employers and own account workers, lower supervisory and technical occupations, semi-routine and routine occupations and even for those who have never worked or are long term unemployed. Consistently Christians have the lowest proportions with level 5 qualifications and Muslims rank towards the middle.

What is evident even from this first glance at the data is that Muslims have higher if not the highest proportion of people with no qualifications regardless of occupational class. At the other end of the scale however Christians not Muslims have the lowest proportions of people with level 5 qualifications.

All minority faith groups have higher proportions of people with level 5 qualifications that the national figure and those with no religion also regardless of occupational class. Although it is difficult to comment as to whether the higher proportions of people with higher level qualifications in lower occupational classes is a result of unfair labour market and recruitment practices the figures are in keeping with previous research discussing ethnic penalties. Hindus and Buddhists appear to be most affected by this in that they have the highest proportions of people with level 5 qualifications in all occupational classes and this is particularly apparent amongst the never worked and long term unemployed in which 22 per cent of Hindus compared with 8 per cent of all people have higher qualifications.

Professional Qualifications

Muslims as a group and Muslims males and females when compared with males and females from other groups are least likely to be in possession of professional qualifications (see Figure 3.8). However the data provided by table M326 provides figures for the attainment of

Figure 3.8: Percentage of people with Professional qualifications by religion and sex for England and Wales.

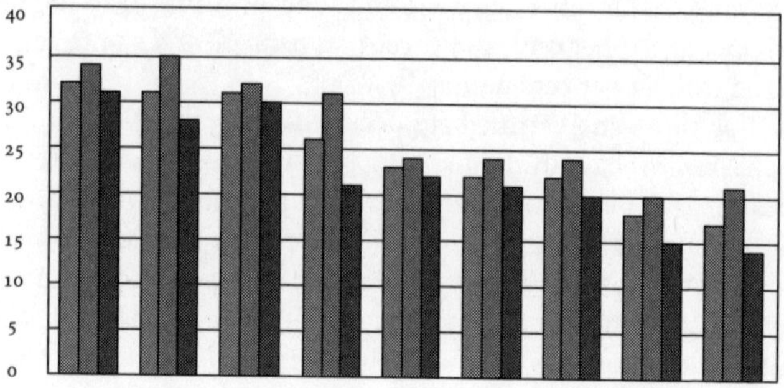

	Other	Jewish	Buddhish	Hindu	No religion	All people	Christian	Sikh	Muslim
▨ All	32	31	31	26	23	22	22	18	17
▨ Male	34	35	32	31	24	24	24	20	21
▨ Female	31	28	30	21	22	21	20	15	14

Source: taken from ONS (2001: M326).

professional qualifications by age cohort and it is therefore possible to see whether the proportion of Muslims has increased in the younger cohorts due to longer periods of settlement.

The analysis shows some increase in the possession of professional qualifications by age cohort for Muslims. However Sikhs appear to have started off at a more disadvantaged position with regards to the possession of such qualifications and have superseded Muslims in the youngest age cohort. The increase for Muslims appears to parallel the increase for all people nationally.

Students in Post 16 Education
The data for this table are split into two age brackets 16–24 and over 25. It is also broken down by sex.

16–24 Year Olds
The largest percentage of people in this age group who are classified as students are Buddhists, of whom 70 per cent are students. Hindus follow with 65 per cent, Muslims have the fifth highest-ranking percentage with 52 per cent compared with 41 per cent nationally. For males in this age group Buddhist followed by Hindus and then Jews have the highest percentages. Muslims rank fifth highest again, with 57 per cent of Muslims males classified as students compared to 40 per

cent nationally. For females, Buddhists again followed by Hindus and then Jews have the highest percentages for students. Muslim females rank sixth with 47 per cent compared to 42 per cent nationally. For Hindus, Jews, Muslims, Sikhs and people with no religion, there are greater percentages of male students than female. The largest gender gap however is found among Muslims for whom there are 10 per cent less women students than men in this age group.

25 Years Old and Over
The largest percentage of students for this age bracket are Buddhists at 7 per cent, Muslims have the second largest percentage of students at 4 per cent and this figure is more than four times the national figure. The third highest is for people of 'any other religion' at 3 per cent.

For males Buddhists have the highest percentage again at just over 6 per cent, Muslim males follow at 5 per cent, this is nearly five times greater than the national figure for men of this age group. The ranking is the same for women in that Buddhist yet again have the highest percentage, at nearly 7 per cent and Muslims the second highest at nearly 4 per cent, this is just over three times greater than the national figure.

Student Residence
The Census table on communal establishments provides figures for percentages of faith groups living in educational establishments, including halls of residence. Muslims as a group have the sixth highest percentage for living in such an establishment. This figure was double that for Christians who have the lowest percentage, Buddhists, followed by Sikhs have the highest.

For men, Muslims rank seventh highest, but surprisingly for women Muslims rank fourth. For both men and women living in educational establishment Buddhist, followed by Sikhs again have the highest percentage. For people living in all student households Buddhists have the highest percentages again, with 1.7 of all Buddhist households being such. This is followed by Hindus, people with no religion and then fourth, by Muslims, with 0.8 per cent of all Muslims households being student households, this compares with 0.4 per cent nationally. The data for all student households is not broken down by sex.

Summary of Key Findings
Muslims have higher participation rates in post-compulsory education for both males and females when compared with the national

average. Although for the younger age bracket the percentage of Muslims is lower than other minority religions and ranks fifth, the participation rates do not match the outcome. If Muslims had the lowest participation rate and also the highest percentage of people without qualifications this would appear to be a meaningful outcome, however this is not the case. Those with no religion have the lowest participation rates in post 16 education yet Muslims are still more likely, than people with no religion to report having no qualification (21 per cent compared with 14 per cent). What is also worth noting is that Muslims for this age bracket have the highest percentage of level 1 qualifications, these are qualifications obtained at the age of 16.

Further participation in post-16 education does not appear to reap as many results for this group as it does for the other groups. One explanation would be in keeping with the view that Muslim groups, such as Pakistani and Bangladeshis are most likely to have to re-take exams to gain qualifications. Here, although remaining in education, a high percentage are re-sitting the exams that others have already passed.

Therefore whilst others are now pursuing level 3 and even 4/5 qualifications, Muslims are still catching up and working towards the level 1 and 2 qualifications they missed whilst at school. Modood (1998), Dale (2002) and Ballard (1998) have all suggested that although some groups remain in education for longer some of this time is spent compensating for poor grades obtained earlier. Therefore gaining a level 1 or 2 qualification may require one or more years in further education.

In the previous section, arguments for the determination of some groups to succeed despite poorer results through continuing to pursue qualifications were discussed. The data on Muslim participation in education after the age of 25 is consistent with the argument. As shown, Muslims have the second largest percentage of students over the age of 25 for both men and women. An explanation for the relatively high percentages of Muslims in education over the age of 25 may also be that this group has higher rates of returnees, which has also been previously suggested by Modood (1998).

The figure for Muslim womens' participation is smaller than men in both age bands, as is the case for other groups. However for the ages of 16–24 Muslims, as already discussed have the largest gap between the sexes. Although this could be taken as evidence of less emphasis being placed by Muslims on the women's pursuit of qualifications, it should be noted that the figures for Muslim women are still higher than for women nationally, as well as Christian women and women with no religion.

Discussion

During this section there will be a discussion of the how applicable the arguments outlined in section one are in explaining the outcomes of the Census analysis. There has already been some discussion during the previous section, focusing around the different outcomes for gender and also the differences in progression in gaining qualifications between Muslims and Sikhs, who appear to start from a very similar position.

Diversity, Ethnicity and Class

When discussing broad groupings in section one it was argued that this is problematic and an array of diversity is missed as a result. It was also discussed how far from having a single educational profile, Asians are found to be polarised towards both end of the spectrum, and this is largely as a result of Bangladeshi and Pakistanis worse performance than Indians. A polarisation towards no qualification and level 4/5 qualifications has been found among Muslim for some age cohorts. Knowing that Muslims are ethnically diverse, ethnicity may well play a significant part in the polarisation found.

Multivariate analysis of the Health Survey for England data does show a clear difference in the proportions of people with qualifications for the three Muslim South Asian groups. The results show a step like gradient for the ethnic groups with Indian Muslims at the higher end and Bangladeshis at the lower. This is also the case when comparing males and females from each group.

In addition Indian males are marginally less likely to have obtained their qualifications in Britain when compared with Pakistani males. Bangladeshi males are also slightly more likely to have obtained their qualifications in Britain, when compared with Indian and Pakistani males. However the vast majority of Bangladeshi women with qualifications obtained them in Britain. This analysis is significant when discussing the possession of human capital on migration. Those who are less likely to have obtained their qualifications in Britain are more likely to have done so in their countries of origin prior to migration and as already stated, human capital is particularly relevant when discussing trajectories.

It is also possible however that the differences may be due to period of settlement rather than ethnicity. When considering the effect different socio-economic status may play on the differential educational attainment among Muslims, a similar kind of class polarisation is not apparent. There is a high concentration toward the lower end of the scale – 'never worked and long term unemployed' and 'unclassifiable' for Muslims.

Therefore it is difficult to ascertain whether socio-economic status alone can explain the polarisation among Muslims found when looking at highest qualifications. One association that is evident however is that Muslims have the highest proportion of people without qualifications and highest concentrations of people in the lowest socio-economic classification. Against this backdrop it is extraordinary that Muslims have a higher percentage of people with level 4/5 qualifications than the national average and other groups such as Christians, who in comparison have a more optimistic socio-economic profile.

A key element in the discussion of differential educational attainment of minority groups is in the form of parental expectations on their children's pursuit of qualifications and students from particular communities' drive for educational success. Muslim participation in post-16 education, for 16–24 year olds, ranks fifth. The figure for Muslims students here is over 10 per cent less than for Hindus and 6 per cent less than that of Sikhs, yet it is still higher than those with no religion, Christians and the average national figure. This may suggest that Muslims are less determined than other minority groups such as Hindus and Sikhs, due to their participation rate being lower. However as discussed in the previous section, the percentage of Muslim students is the second highest for those over 25 years of age. An explanations for this is that Muslims of this age band have either returned to education or are still 'catching up' to other groups, who have already gained their qualifications and thus are no longer within the education system. However even if this is the case for the majority of post 25 year old Muslim students, it does provide evidence for drive and determination to gain those qualifications.

Language Ability

Kendall (1998) commented on the potential hindrance low English language proficiency can have on a child's educational success. The Census provides data on country of birth for religious groups and although being born outside the UK does not necessarily imply low proficiency of English it could provide some indication of the percentage of people who may not have English as their first language. As demonstrated in the previous chapter, 46 per cent of Muslims are born in the

UK, this figure is the same as Buddhists, but less than Sikhs, for whom 56 per cent were born in UK. Hindus have the smallest percentage of people who are born in the UK, and it could be argued that as one of the most successful groups that birth overseas does not appear to have had a particularly negative effect. The Census data on country of birth does not provide a breakdown by age cohort and for this reason it is extremely difficult to know how many Muslims of school age English language proficiency could effect.

A more useful measure of language proficiency and its potential effects on attainment of qualifications is ability to read and write English. The 1999 Health Survey for England provides data on English language proficiency and reading ability. Analysis shows that both Muslim males and females are second least likely, after Buddhists, to be able to read English.

Islamophobia in Schools

During section one it was argued that Muslims are increasingly encountering stereotypes specific to Islam and Muslims. Although as suggested more qualitative research within schools focusing on teachers and students perceptions of Islam and Muslims and how this can affect Muslim children is required. Also as discussed previously, the most recent wave of anti-Muslim sentiments can be linked to a series of global and local events involving Muslims, which have occurred mostly in the last decade. Although it is likely that Muslim students are exposed to extremely damaging stereotyping within schools since this recent phase of Islamophobia, it is questionable whether such stereotypes were commonplace in schools resulting in the severe disparity in success seen for the older cohorts, particularly the 25–34 year olds.

During the discussion of literature on Muslims and education the subject of state funded Muslim schools was examined. Advocates of separate Muslim schools argue that such schools are the only means of ensuring Muslim students are provided with the educational environment needed for them to succeed. The data from the Census is consistent with the arguments in that it clearly demonstrates proportionally more Muslims leaving the education system with no qualifications when compared with all other groups and the national figures. If schools cannot boost the morale of Muslim children and demonstrate through measures such as attainment of qualifications that they are meeting the educational needs of Muslims, the debate for separate schooling will only be strengthened and justified, especially where shown to produce more successful results in comparison.

Minority Communities and Social Trajectories

In terms of human capital, the analysis of the Census data shows that the qualification level of successive generations dramatically increased as schooling improved – the younger age groups are always better qualified than their parents irrespective of religion, ethnicity and socio-economic position. However the data also shows that the speed of this improvement is not the same for all religious groups. Muslims in particular are behind in the qualifications race and the question of whether Muslims are catching up or falling further behind needs some additional exploration.

Cross (1989) has argued that there is an 'Asian trajectory' which includes upward mobility by educational attainment, self-employment and entry into professional occupations. In this view it is erroneous to divide Asians into two brackets – successful and disadvantaged, as the latter are likely only to have less longevity of residence in Britain, looking at families and communities not just individuals, or have suffered temporary setbacks as a result of economic restructuring (Modood 2003). Here it is argued that those successful today – namely Indians were disadvantaged yesterday, and so it will be for other Asians – namely Pakistanis and Bangladeshis, who are disadvantaged today. The closure of industries upon which many first generation Muslims were reliant on for employment was certainly a setback for those in areas such as Oldham and Bradford.

Other factors – particularly discrimination affecting Muslims specifically – however suggests that the Asian trajectory theory oversimplifies barriers these communities face. In this view Muslims cannot necessarily progress in a similar way to other Asians as they face quite specific barriers. The Census data do appear to suggest that the gap between Muslims and Sikhs is beginning to close and the economic setbacks discussed above could be used to explain why Muslims appeared to fall behind Sikhs, even though initially they began in similar positions. Of course Muslims are not only of South Asian ethnic origin and newer Muslim communities in the form of Somalis and other refugees mean that whilst Sikhs and Hindus are relatively settled and established communities, Muslims as a community have substantial elements who are currently going through a process of settlement. This would fit in with the trajectory theory as it suggest that once Muslims have had a similar period of settlement they will progress as other minority communities have.

Data on participation does suggest Muslim women are less likely than men to be students. Greater participation of women from other religious groups could have contributed to the process of upward mobility for those groups. The Asian trajectory theory goes a long way in explaining the differences in mobility, yet it does not adequately provide discussion of issues surrounding isolation and discrimination faced by Muslims in the current climate. In this view 'Asian trajectory' as discussed here over-homogenises Asians and perhaps even Muslims.

Conclusion

The Census data in many respects confirm previous research on the educational success of Muslims, (namely Pakistanis and Bangladeshis) in that the educational attainment of this group is poorer than other minority groups. Analysis of the data could support the view that racial discrimination does not affect Hindus and Sikhs and Muslims in the same way, as Hindus and Sikhs are faring particularly well in comparison and discrimination is not as significant a barrier in the upward mobility, yet certainly for Hindus data shows higher levels of human capital among the older generations and this too clearly has impacts on success.

Although Muslims have the highest percentages with no qualifications, the data show that this group also has higher percentages of people with level 4/5 qualifications, than all people and the largest faith group, Christians. This coupled with the higher rates in participation in post-compulsory education supports the arguments discussed above that family educational expectations and determination of Muslims is greater than for the indigenous majority.

The main explanations for the relatively poor educational attainment discussed within this section are that although Muslims and Sikhs started at a very similar position, economic setbacks facing areas with high concentrations of Muslims hindered the economic mobility for this faith group. Secondly the educational participation of Muslim women, although now very similar to that of men, was not at the same rate as for Hindu and Sikh women. Despite these setbacks Muslims have expectations for their children's success as do other minority communities, but shorter periods of settlement for some Muslims communities has contributed to their slower progress within the education system.

Muslims children also have very specific needs, and schools may not always be willing to cater for these, having potentially detrimental

affects on the morale of these students. Although racism may have affected all Asian groups similarly this is no longer the case and Muslims
are disproportionately affected by discrimination due to recent surges
of Islamophobia (Sheridan et al. 2002). Differential levels of discrimination however can only explain differences to an extent, whilst of
course it has become more apparent due to recent global events that
Islam and Muslims have become far more politicised than any other
faith group, this can not be argued with any conviction to have resulted in greater levels of discrimination for Muslim over any other
group within British institutions twenty or even ten years ago. Therefore acquisition of human capital, economic geography, period of settlement as well as gender participation have also contributed to the
positions for the various communities to date.

Clearly more qualitative research is required to try to make sense
of the extent to which Islamophobia is prevalent in schools and
whether this plays a role in the high percentage of Muslim children
leaving school at 16 without any qualifications.

An area which will no doubt gain more attention as a consequence
of recent events and initiatives prompted by the anti-terrorist activity not only within the United Kingdom but globally, are sociological
concepts such as deviance and moral panics and how these impact on
the construction of masculinity and effects of 'self-fulfilling prophecies' on youth within Muslim communities.

4

Muslim Household Composition

There is growing recognition within social science regarding religious affiliation as an important determinant of economic and demographic behaviour, including the choice of marital partner, entry into cohabitation and marriage, divorce, fertility, employment of women outside the home, education and even wealth are influenced by religious affiliation. Lehrer writes, 'I argue that religious affiliation matters because it has an impact on the perceived cost and perceived benefit of various interrelated decisions people make over the life cycle' (2004).

As discussed in Chapter One affiliating to a faith group is not an indication of the religiosity of an individual and does not assume a certain base line level of observance. The term 'religious affiliation' is very much a sociological one in that it focuses on group membership, identity and self-definition rather than a yardstick to measure levels of spiritual practice.

As well as using data on religious affiliation to explore whether Muslims as a faith community are more disadvantaged than other communities on a number of measures, this thesis also sets out to ascertain what Muslim social networks look like (this is linked to some of the theory already discussed above particularly social capital).

When looking at social networks – the family as the smallest social network is explored.

Families, Intimate Relationships and Individuality

The increase in extramarital fertility in Britain is consistent with the notion that there has been a decline in traditional family values and increased emphasis on individual autonomy. From a sociological perspective changes in family and personal relationships are a consequence of post industrialisation which has led to the detraditionalisation and individualisation of social life.

According to Parsons (1956) as the economy became increasing differentiated from family and the need for a specialised mobile labour force grew, isolated nuclear families were freed from obligations of extended family and were, as a result in a better position for adaptation to the requirements of industrial society. In this view the family evolved from fulfilling the purpose of economic production and consumption, within rural settings, to performing the less distinct role of socialising children and stabilising adults within boundaries. Consequently the family was perceived as the key to social cohesion with the structure exemplifying the moral well-being of modern society. Goode (1963) argued that family members gained the most in limiting their commitments to the nuclear family unit. In Goode's view wider kin networks were most common in upper class families as a result of the power and influence that can be gained through maintaining family connections. In contrast working class networks were seen as offering few incentives to sustain their existence. Willmott and Young (1975) challenged such views with empirical finding on working class families, arguing that mothers in particular played a meditating role, maintaining three generations of families which were characterised by a system of mutual aid and support. Kinship networks were viewed as increasingly less significant and as a result attention was reduced within sociology, although recently revived by social capital theorists (Gillies 2003).

Some theorist argued that the extent social change influenced the family had been overestimated and provided empirical finding to suggest that diversity and plurality had long been a feature of the family (Laslett 1972; Anderson 1971). Others criticised the notion of the nuclear family as presented by functionalists for other reasons and the most systematic and widespread challenge to the ideology of family came from feminist theorists. The primary arguments from such theorists were that family structures are not natural, inevitable or necessary and that the family has a central role in the reproduction of patriarchy and capitalism (Oakley 1972; Mitchell 1971).

These critical evaluations of the modern family surfaced in the context of increasing divorce, cohabitation and extramarital fertility rates, which led many to predict the eventual collapse of the nuclear family as an institution (Berrington 2004). Amid the debate on family, studies such as *'The symmetrical family'* by Willmott and Young (1975) claimed that married couples were moving towards a more egalitarian partnership characterised by a relationship of sharing and negotiation. From this a more optimistic approach to rising divorce and separation rates was taken and this was now seen to reflect choice and quality of marriage and partnership rather than a weakening of the ideal of marriage. Consequently, with the ideal of compassionate marriage came the notion that intimacy is achieved and sustained rather than simply ascribed through marital status. Here it is argued that relationships are individualised and negotiated interactions as opposed to prior models of set familial roles and obligation. For Jamieson (1998) the term intimacy has come to mean a specific kind of association characterised by openness, mutual benefit and the expression of feelings.

Giddens (1991, 1992) argued that people are progressively liberated from the roles and restrictions associated with traditional social ties. Relationships are evaluated and conducted from a position of self-awareness and are sought on mutual intimate connections and maintained on the basis of mutual knowledge and understanding. Such 'pure relationships' are entered into for their own sake and reproduction is now an area where plurality of choice prevails. In this view couples have become the core of the family with intimacy and love becoming the new lynchpins as the economic role of the family has weakened.

Choice has led to a diverse array of family formation, with no 'standardised' model being the most commonly accepted. However the premise of de-traditionalisation has also been widely criticised and questions about the extent to which expectations and certainties characterised with the past existed and also the extent to which traditions and beliefs on family formation have been shed are questioned. In addition it is argued that the nuclear type family unit is still the most common, idealised and aspired to (Heelas et al. 1996).

Post-Modern Family and Muslim Communities

As a result of this shift from social obligations to negotiated intimacies it has been argued that society has become more individualistic and as a result actors take more risks. According to Beck and Beck-

Gernsheim (2002) a key factor of modernity is that individuals face greater uncertainty are forced to make themselves the centre of their planning and conduct in their lives.

Van de Kaa (1987) and Lesthaneghe (1995) argued that the process of individualisation was heavily influenced by the rejection of religious institutions and teachings in favour of personal autonomy. Their literature highlights the influences of the growing economic independence of women and of technological advances of contraception in producing family change. Lehrer (2004) in a more recent study noted the significant influence religion can still have on family formation for those who do adhere to doctrine. He writes,

> Religion affects marital stability because the faith to which an individual belongs has had an influence on the perceived costs of marital dissolution. Because virtually all religions are pro family, affiliation with any faith should have a stabilizing influence, although the effect may be more pronounced in some cases than others. (Lehrer 2004: 709)

Since Muslim communities have not rejected religious teachings in the same way and are argued to be more patriarchal than society as a whole (Macey 1999; Ballard 1990) it would follow that there is a greater trend towards family formation, gendered roles and less emphasis on individual autonomy.

Data from the FNSEM found that South Asians, especially Pakistanis and Bangladeshis were characterised by parental authority and large numbers of children, who were more likely to have been conceived within marriage. It was also found that these groups were more inclined than others to live in households containing grandparents or adult children. This is clearly in divergence with some of the theory above, particularly Goode's view that working class or less advantaged families have weaker links with extended family members.

Against this backdrop the main objective of this chapter is to explore how Muslim families and households differ from other faith groups. In doing research on Muslim family structure will carried out in order to explore whether there is a preference for certain family formations on the part of Muslims and Muslim ethnic groups such as Pakistanis and Bangladeshis. A discussion of the literature on both Muslim family structure and other minority groups in Britain will be provided for purposes of comparison – primarily to ascertain the extent to which Muslim family formation is distinct from other minority groups as well as the indigenous majority.

When discussing the above mentioned areas, the 2001 National Census for England and Wales will be analysed in order to provide clarity for several key points that have commonly been forwarded in literature and previous studies on Muslim families and households. These will be highlighted throughout the chapter.

In addition to the analysis of the Census data, multivariate analysis of the 1999 Health Survey for England and to a lesser degree the 2001 Home Office Citizenship Survey for England and Wales will also be discussed in order to provide insight into Muslim intra-group patterns as well as greater exploration of themes within the Census, where pertinent. The aim of this analysis therefore is to provide greater clarity and exploration of Muslim family formation using data specifically on Muslims, rather than primarily on ethnicity, as is the case for the majority of literature cited in this chapter.

Preferences and Family 'Types'

Research in the area of family has largely been concerned with describing the overall picture and examining differing trends in household structure and family units, such as lone parenthood, post divorced families, step families, homosexual families, long term partnership without formal marriages and the effects on different family types for children (Edwards et al. 2003).

Within discussions surrounding contemporary family life, ethnicity and to a lesser extent religion have also been identified as being important variables in the diversity of household structure in modern day Britain. Becher and Husain (2003) write,

> Cultural norms about the family have an important effect on the way in which family life is organised. For example, the concept of what a 'family' is; perceived roles for parents and children; expectations of proper behaviour; ideas of what constitutes successful parenting; these kinds of beliefs differ across different time and places, and are reflected in varying family structures and child rearing practices. Thus families of non-European origin may draw on different sets of beliefs and value systems, and therefore differ from 'majority' British families in important ways. (p. 21)

The family as an institution is of significant importance for Muslim communities, just as marriage is normative for Muslims (Hassouneh-Phillip 2001). O'Brien and Husain (2000) argues that due to the many influences and factors at play for Muslims living in a non-Muslim setting it is difficult to speak of a single Muslim family type. Here it is argued that sociocultural norms regarding family structures in countries of origin are influenced not only by family models and laws in the country of residence but also by socio-economic restraints and other external factors such as housing size. Islamic tradition does however provide definitions of what a family is and in the simplest sense a family consists of members related by a direct bloodline or marital relationship. This does not therefore exclude the idea of the contemporary nuclear family unit, and is open to the possibility of various family types, including polygamous or extended families (O'Brien and Husain 2000; Basit 1997; Ballard 1990).

Despite this there appears to be a greater trend towards what researches such as Berthoud and Robson (2003) describe as the 'traditional' family type for Muslim groups, as well as amongst South Asians more generally. In his study of early motherhood and disadvantage, using the Labour Force Surveys from 1992–2000, Berthoud and Robson describe three types of family and how they are more common amongst some ethnic communities than others. He describes Black Caribbean communities as showing greater levels of 'Modern individualism' which is characterised by low rates of marriage and high rates of child bearing independently of marriage. Some similarities between Caribbeans and Black Africans were found within this family type and in particular the figure for lone mothers was similar.

The 'Old fashioned family', which refers to the similarity of family formation of White women in the 1950s and 1960s is more common amongst South Asians and virtually all members of these communities in the study with a partner were in formal marriages. The most noticeable difference amongst the groups however is that Pakistani and Bangladeshi women were least likely of all groups to have their children outside of a formal marriage. These two groups also have the highest proportion of people entering into marriages and having their first child at a younger age and as will be discussed in the next section, fertility rates for Pakistani and Bangladeshi women are greater than for other South Asian groups.

According to Berthoud and Robson's analysis, White communities were somewhere in between these two family types and even though Bangladeshi women have higher rates of teenage births when compared to White women, they are most likely to be in a marriage at the time of their birth.

This finding is in keeping with earlier research conducted by the Fourth National Survey of Ethnic Minorities (FNSEM) in which none of the Pakistani and Bangladeshi women in the study reported they were single when they conceived, not even those in their teens and early twenties (Modood et al. 1997). In this view, family formation patterns of ethnic minority groups are often different from the dominant culture, as people from different cultures bring with them the norms of their place of origin. The migration of people with varied cultural and religious backgrounds in the United Kingdom has necessarily diversified the types of family formation that are considered 'morally appropriate'. Mistry (2000) argues that this is especially the case for South Asian migrants who come from societies where religion and its practice is a natural part of life and religious observance permeates daily routine, particularly within the domestic domain.

Other authors have produced similar descriptions to the Berthoud's 'Old fashioned family' when studying Muslim families in particular. Here it is argued that the clash between so-called Western and Muslim values is most apparent in family structuring around traditional gender roles. Parker-Jenkins (1992) writes,

Cultural diversity in Western societies has provided ample opportunity for teaching to reflect different perspectives on the family. Yet for many Muslims this approach appears as a competing perspective which challenges and undermines their own identity. (p. 270)

In reality however actual spousal relationships within Muslim communities are based on traditional family roles common to most capitalist societies, that of the male breadwinner and the female nurturer and child-rearer (Mistry 2000; O'Brien and Husain 2000; Hassouneh-Phillip 2001).

Although the old fashioned or traditional family type is found amongst other South Asian communities, in her study of South Asian Muslim and Hindu mothers, Mistry (2000) found that Muslim women were living in more traditional families and had more traditional and restricted roles within the family than Hindu women. Such marked gender roles are associated more often with Muslims and Ballard argues that this is primarily related to the concept of *izzat* or family honour as well as Islamic teachings on *purdah* or segregation. This will be discussed in greater detail when looking at households composition. The FNSEM also found significant differences between Pakistani/Bangladeshi women and Indian/African Asian women in this regard.

Pels (2000) however, in his study of Moroccan Muslims living in the Netherlands, argues that there is evidence to suggest that such 'traditional' family formations are slowly shifting for Muslims and other minorities in Europe. Here it is argued that in Europe, modifications in the gender power balance are taking place for minority communities, but the sociological reasons are different to the ethnic majority. In this view, due to factors such as high unemployment, not only for women but also for men, there is a direct effect on the power balance of the father/husband as breadwinner. This will be examined further when exploring Muslim and extended families.

Complex Households and Co-Residence Cohesion

A household is defined as all individuals collectively sharing the same accommodation. From each household, information on the links between its members is used to define family units. A family unit can be either a single person or a couple with or without children, the children being defined both through their links with the adults and through their ages and marital status.

The majority of Households in Britain consist of one family (Beishon and Berthoud 1997). According to analysis of the Fourth National Survey of Ethnic Minorities, the most common forms of complex household is when adult children live with one or two parents. Three fifths of single White adults without children live with their parents compared with four fifths of South Asians.

In addition it was found that two thirds of elder South Asians live with an adult child. High levels of co-residence cohesion generally were found among South Asians compared with the lowest rates of living with parents among migrant Caribbeans. Amongst all ethnic groups, Pakistanis and Bangladeshi were found to have the highest proportion of large and complex households.

A key factor explaining the higher proportion of South Asian communities having a greater proportion of complex households is that traditionally, within these cultures, parents are responsible for the support and maintenance of children until a daughter is married and a son becomes self-supporting. Age, as is the case in most European societies, is not a criterion for child maintenance (O'Brien and Husain 2000). Ballard's research supports this view as he argues that marriage is the usual way in which young Muslim women, in particular, establish their independence from their parental authority (2004).

Dale and Heath's (1994) analysis of the 1991 Sample of Anonymised Records found that within ethnic groups South Asian women consistently have the highest proportions for living with their parents. This would support the arguments that South Asians women are more likely to remain with their parents until married as by the mid thirties the difference between Black, White and South Asian women is reduced. By the ages of 34/35 only a small proportion of women are living with parents; 4 per cent White, 6 per cent Black and 3 per cent South Asian.

The FNSEM found that among the few White and Black couples that lived with one set of parents, the women's parents were chosen more often than the men's. However in the case of South Asians it is found to be the reverse. In O'Neale's (2000) study of service provisions for ethnic minority families, she found a high proportion of South Asian couples and their children living in the same houses as the parents of the bridegroom on marriage.

Dale and Heath's analysis shows that the vast majority of South Asian men and women who have formed their own family unit within a parental home are living with a parent of the husband, 89 per cent of men are sons of the 'household head', whereas 90 per cent of women are the daughter-in-law.

This finding is in keeping with Ballard's study (1990) of the differential marriage patterns of Punjabi Muslims and Sikhs. Here it is argued that all Punjabis regardless of religion follow the basic kinship conventions, which are patrilineal descent and patri-virilocal residence. Although this particular study is of Punjabis, this has also been a popular convention for other South Asian groups (with the exception of some southern Indian and Tamil communities). There is also evidence that such preferences have remained stronger in Britain amongst Muslim communities in particular as they are likely to be less acculturated (Mistry 2000), and this will be explored to a greater degree in a later section.

Marriage Patterns and Childbirth

The FNSEM found that amongst the population as a whole, men and women now marry later than before. In addition, a higher percentage of marriages end in separation and divorce, although many re-marry. Jamieson's study on the sociology of intimate relations (1998) explains this as resulting from a shift towards greater emphasis on personal fulfilment within our society. Cohabitation is an example of this new form of partnership and it has increased as a preferred option, taking on three main forms; short term partnership, a prelude to marriage and a long term alternative to marriage.

As discussed in the section above there are differing trends in family formation according to ethnicity and where relevant, religious belief. This is also reflected in the rates of formal marriage and alternative forms of partnership such as cohabiting. The FNSEM survey found that people of Caribbean origin are much more likely to have remained single than Whites or South Asians, although one third of Chinese people in the study were also single. Nearly three quarters of South Asians were in formal marriages compared to three fifths of Whites and Chinese and only two fifths of Caribbeans. Unsurprisingly cohabitation, separation and divorce were more common among the Caribbean and White communities than South Asians.

Higher proportions of marriage amongst the two Muslim groups (Pakistanis and Bangladeshis) are in keeping with Islamic tradition as Sherif (1999) writes, 'Throughout the Islamic world, marriage is at the heart of social and religious life' (p. 619).

Hassouneh-Phillips (2000) argues that although Muslims are culturally diverse and come from a variety of backgrounds, in her study, for Muslim women in particular, marriage is viewed as normative behaviour for Muslims. She argues that women are often socialised to look forward to marriage from an early age and that it is these socialisation processes that shape Muslim women's perceptions of marriage over time. A key factor in the importance placed on marriage is that it is the only sanctioned form of sexual activity under Islamic law. Groups such as Pakistanis and Bangladeshis according to Hassouneh-Phillips Muslims are encouraged to marry earlier and this appears to correspond with findings on age and marriage of Muslim (Dale and Heath 1994).

Age of Marriage

In the FNSEM amongst younger people, aged 20–24, Pakistanis and Bangladeshis have the highest rate of formal marriage and this was 7 times higher than the figure for Caribbeans, who had the lowest rate. Of the South Asian groups under 25, African Asians were the least likely to be in such a partnership. When exploring differences in age for men and women, Pakistani, Bangladeshi and Indian men tend to marry 1–3 years later than their counterpart women.

Berrington's (1994) study also found that Pakistani and Bangladeshi women have significantly higher rates of marriage amongst certain age groups. Her findings show for 25–29 year old women, 90 per cent of Pakistani and Bangladeshi women were married compared to 60 per cent of White women.

Dale and Heath's (1994) analysis also found that among South Asian women marriage rates are higher at young ages and increased to about 88 per cent by ages 34/35, which is substantially higher than the figure for White women. In contrast to White and Black women, cohabitation for South Asian women is negligible for all ages. Cohabitation is higher for South Asian men, but still considerably lower than other groups, never exceeding 4 per cent. Of the very small numbers of cohabiting South Asians, over half of women are living with non-Asian men and over two thirds of men with non-Asian women.

When educational qualifications are taken into account the age of marriage alters. Dale and Heath found that amongst South Asian women aged between 21–24 and 25–29 clear differences were evident in the proportions who were married amongst those with and without higher educational qualifications.

The proportion of women aged 25–29 with higher qualifications who were married was only slightly lower amongst White women than their South Asian counterparts (although once cohabitation is included White women have a much higher level of partnership). Higher qualifications therefore appeared to delay marriage amongst South Asian women during their 20s, although this cross-sectional data suggests that by the early 30s they had caught up with South Asian women without higher qualifications. In contrast, Black women with higher educational qualifications in the 25–29 age group were more likely to be married than those without (32 per cent compared to 21 per cent), the figure is higher still for Black women aged 30–35 at 40 per cent. Unfortunately Dale and Heath's study does not provide detailed ethnic breakdowns and hence Pakistanis and Bangladeshis were grouped with other South Asian communities.

Arranged Marriages

In Modood's et al.'s (1997), study it was reported that the majority of South Asians over the age of 35 had their spouses chosen for them by their parents. Arranged marriages were most common among Pakistanis and Bangladeshis, the majority of Sikhs (56 per cent) were also married in this way, but to a lesser extent the Hindus (36 per cent), followed by the African Asians, who were the least likely to have had this form of marriage. When socio-economic status was also taken into account, it appeared, however, to be more common for Indian and African Asians of 'lower classes' than for Pakistanis and Bangladeshis, for whom class was shown not to be a determining factor.

Pankaj's study (2001) conducted in Scotland, suggests that it would be most accurate to say that marriages are initiated through parental proposals rather than arranged marriages in the 'traditional' sense. However, the study found that among Pakistani respondents marriages arranged by parents were still the most common, and it is argued that there was clear evidence of negotiation. Another study which suggested arranged marriages are still prevalent for Muslims is that conducted by Hennink et al. (1999). In their study of second generation South Asian teenage girls, the majority of Hindu respondent (75 per cent) reported that they did not expect to have an arranged marriage, on the other end of the scale however, 85 per cent of Muslim girls reported that they were expecting to have arranged marriages. Sikh girls also had a high figure reporting such expectations (75 per cent).

Due to Islamic conventions of purdah, dating is frowned upon by many Muslim communities. Arranged marriages have and continue to be an important means of finding a spouse for Muslims. However Hassouneh-Phillip's study on Muslim marriage found that this strategy is most likely to be successful in Muslim countries where the families who are involved in arranging marriages have typically known each other for many years. Her research found arranged marriages to be increasingly problematic for those in non-Muslim settings, where Muslim women are married to men who their family and friends may have only known for a short period of time.

Ouis's (2004) study of marriage strategies among young Muslims in Europe found that many young Muslims felt disillusioned with traditional methods for finding a husband or wife and lacked confidence in their parent's abilities to allocate the most suitable spouse. However according to Ouis the majority Muslims in her study did not approve of the 'western' means of obtaining a spouse either. She argues that alternative methods for finding spouses will need to be established and will inevitably become more popular as increasingly, young Muslims are finding it difficult to obtain a partner. This study suggests that young Muslims still have views regarding family life that Berthoud has described as 'old fashioned', yet they are also open to non traditional avenues such as the internet, for attaining marriage partners.

Consanguinity

When discussing consanguinity in the context of ethnic minority groups, it is often seen as a Muslim phenomenon, in contrast to arranged marriages which are often viewed more in terms of being a South Asian preference. The main reason for viewing consanguinity in this way is that for some South Asians groups the practice is not permissible under religious doctrine. As Ballard describes, traditionally in the sub-continent marriage rules prohibited the union of men and women within the same kin group. After conversion to Islam, however, Muslims appeared to have completely abandoned the rule of clan exogamy. This has resulted not only in marrying within the same clan group but also a preference amongst some Muslim groups to marry people as closely related as permissible under Islamic law.

Becher and Husain (2003) describe why consanguinity is a preference for some Muslims,

> In Muslim communities, marriages to first cousins are seen as particularly desirable; they are considered safe because the respective partner's families already know each other well. Cousin marriages are also seen as a way of strengthening links with the extended family and keeping families and family finances together. (p. 29)

Modood et al.'s study found that this type of marriage was more popular amongst some ethnic groups than others. Here it was found that 54 per cent of Pakistanis and Indian Muslims married cousins. However, only 15 per cent of Bangladeshi and African Asians, in this study reported being married to a cousin. The figure was higher still for younger sections of the community as amongst second generation Pakistanis, where 64 per cent were married to their cousins. Those such as Ballard have explained high figures amongst some groups as a result of greater emphasis being placed on retaining kinship ties and 'Biraderi' honour. This will be explored further in the section on extended family.

Separation, Divorce and Lone Parent Households

In Becher and Husain's study of Muslim and Hindus families it is asserted that South Asians are less likely than other groups to live in lone parent families and 90 per cent of South Asian children aged 0–14 live with both biological parents. This is because, 'Divorce figures are relatively low amongst British South Asian and Hindu and Muslim families. In these communities the proportion of people who have divorced or separated is less than half that recorded among White people' (p. 31).

However Pankaj (2001) found that the rate of marital discord is increasing among South Asian communities. Shah-Kazemi (2001) produced a report on the practicalities of 'untying the knot' for Muslims in which he exposed some of the problems faced by Muslim women in Britain when seeking divorce. He highlighted the fact that there is currently no system of liaison between the legal profession and religious and community groups and that this is something that clearly needs to be addressed as increasingly marriages are ending in divorce.

Ballard's study (2004) on transnational marriage and kinship networks also argues that arranged marriages have been producing difficulties from relatively early on in settlement to the UK,

> It was not long before the resulting marriages began to display an alarming tendency to go wrong. It was not so much that they all went wrong, but the fact that a significant number of such couples clearly found it difficult to reach a satisfactory *modus vivendi* and that in some cases this led to the outright collapse of the union, was enough to set alarm bells ringing, most especially amongst young people themselves. (p. 13)

The report by the DWP found that one of the key reasons Black and South Asian lone parents in the study had no contact with the non-resident parent was because he or she was living abroad and had never returned or entered the UK. This is more likely to be an issue for lone parents of ethnic minority background than those from the indigenous population. This could suggest that the marriages are still intact but the distance of separation creates lone parents families in some cases, or rather for analytical tidiness these couples are classed as separated. The FNSEM found that 1–2 per cent of people were living apart in this way in most ethnic groups but the figure rose to 6 per cent for Pakistanis and Bangladeshis, in other words these two Muslim groups are 3 times more likely to have spouses living abroad.

Chambaz's (2001) study of lone parent families in Europe describes the difficulties in defining lone parent families in the context of different cultures.

Some lone parents may be more inclined to share their accommodation or household with other family members. Chambaz describes these as 'included' lone parent families. The important point to note here is that the 'real' rate of lone parenthood among some communities may be masked. For example in a research conducted by the Department for Work and PensionsDWP (Pettigrew 2002) it was found that many of the South Asian lone parents relied on support from

their families more than other groups and in similar ways to those described in Chambaz's study of Spanish lone parents who had higher
rates of co-residence with other family members.

Pettigrew's study also found that lone parents had differing profiles according to ethnicity. Black lone parents in the sample were less
likely to have been married and more likely to have children by different fathers than South Asian lone parents who are most likely to be
divorced or separated with children conceived in a formal marriage.
This is in keeping with findings from the FNSEM in which 47 per cent
of never married Caribbean women had dependent children.

Fertility

Berthoud et al.'s (1997) analysis of people claiming child benefit found
that women in Britain appeared to be having fewer children and
uses this as evidence of a decline in fertility rates. The number of
families claiming child benefit with 5 or more children in 1965 was
232,000 families, compared with 77,000 families in 1995. Here it was
argued that the decrease in larger families resulted in the issue of overcrowded households being pushed to the back of public policy discussion. However, although this may be the case when considering
the total population, according to the analysis of the FNSEM all ethnic
groups contained more children than the White group.

Qualitative research has suggested that most ethnic minority origin mothers value the role of a mother, seeing it as an important part
of their sex-role identity (Ochieng 2002). For some ethnic groups the
figure for the average number of children is higher than others, the
greatest of which are amongst Pakistani and Bangladeshi families. An
exceptionally high proportion of Bangladeshi and Pakistani women
still had dependant children in their 50s and 60s. This suggests that
many continued to bear children well into their 40s. Younger ages
of first birth and older ages of last birth was the main reason for the
higher numbers of children for these women.

Berthoud et al.'s study indicated that White women and Indian
women have similar fertility rates. Indian women tend to marry
later than Pakistani and Bangladeshi women and consequently have
smaller families and later first births. Berthoud's analysis of the
Labour Force Survey found that over 40 per cent of Bangladeshis
had a first birth as a teen, compared with only 9 per cent of Indian
women and 14 per cent of White and African women. Only 19 per
cent of Pakistani and 15 per cent of Bangladeshis had a first birth after the age of 27, compared to almost 40 per cent of White women

and African women, and approximately 30 per cent of Indian and
Caribbean women. Around 60 per cent of White women who were
formerly teenage mothers were married or cohabiting at the time of
the survey, this compares to only 25 per cent Caribbean women who
had their first child as a teen and were married or living with a partner,
and 50 per cent of African women.

There appears to be some evidence to suggest that higher levels
of education correlates with smaller numbers of children for Muslim
groups, namely Pakistanis and Bangladeshis. In Pels's study of Muslim families in the Netherlands, parents from second and subsequent
generations with a higher level of educational attainment generally
had fewer children.

Dale and Heath's (1994) analysis found that as with marriage, the
higher a South Asian woman's educational attainment was the later
she would marry and it follows, as discussed previously, because the
majority of South Asian women are in formal marriages when they
have their first child, the age of first birth would also be later than
those women with lower or no qualifications.

In the study of Hindu and Muslim mothers, Mistry (2000) showed
that Muslim mothers and grandmothers were younger than their
Hindu counterparts, less likely to be in paid employment and came
from less acculturated families. As acculturation is often associated
with level of education, this younger age of the Muslim women in the
study was likely to reflect their levels of education also.

Areas of Further Exploration

During this section on marriage and childbirth it has been argued
through the exploration of previous literature that formal marriage
for Muslims is the normative state for having children. It has been
argued that Muslims have higher rates of formal marriage and the
highest rates for bearing children in this type of partnership across
all groups. In addition Muslims are most likely to marry at younger
ages when compared with other groups. Arranged marriages, as the
case for other South Asian communities, have been identified as an
important means for attaining a spouse, and figures in Modood et
al. (1997) study found this to be higher for Muslims, when compared
to Sikhs and Hindus.

Consanguinity, although argued to be more common among
Muslims than other groups, is clearly not a preference for all Muslim
communities and there were demonstrations of intra-Muslim variations according to ethnicity.

The Muslim groups, namely Pakistanis and Bangladeshis, were identified as having the highest proportions of couples with the largest numbers of children. This is associated with early marriage and age of first birth among these women. Although when educational attainment was also included in the analysis, there is found to be a correlation between higher qualifications and fewer children, later ages of marriage and first birth for these women. Although the studies cited ' here only identified these two Muslim groups, it is argued that due to the emphasis placed on traditional gender roles and marriage being normative for Muslims, Islam is associated with larger families.

It is possible to explore further some of these key themes emerging from the literature reviewed in this section by analysing data which specifically quantifies Muslims. A discussion of the findings from the Census and other sources will now be provided in order to attempt to clarifying the trends among Muslims in family formation and fertility rates.

Do Muslims Have Greater Rates of Marriage and the Lowest Rates of Cohabitation and Lone Parent Households?

The 2001 Census table S151 on family composition shows that almost half of all Muslim households are described in the Census as married couple households (ONS 2001)[1]. This compares with 54 per cent of Hindus and 52 per cent of Sikhs. The national figure for this type of household is 37 per cent. Muslims are therefore the third most likely to report this household type which is essentially a 'nuclear' family type household.

When broken down by age however, analysis of the 1999 Health Survey for England shows that for those reporting to be either currently married or ever married, of people aged 16–24 Muslims are more likely to be married than Sikh and Hindus. Of this age cohort 34 per cent of Muslims were currently or had been married compared with 21.5 per cent of Sikhs, 7 per cent of Hindus and 3 per cent of Christians.

For those aged 25–34, 93 per cent of Muslims compared with 84 per cent of Sikhs, 79 per cent of Hindus and 44 per cent of Christians reported this marital status. Analysis of the next age cohort, 35–44, shows that the proportions of people who had been married for Hindus, Sikhs and Muslims are very similar with all three groups reporting close to 98 per cent. This compares with 72 per cent of Christians in this age category. The proportions of married people in all other age cohorts remain smaller than these three groups. It is clear from the analysis that Muslims do have higher rates of marriage amongst the younger age cohorts compared to all other faith groups.

Census table s151 also demonstrates that Hindus, Sikhs and then Muslims have the lowest proportion of cohabiting couple households (2 per cent, 2 per cent and 3 per cent respectively). These figures are lower than those for other groups. The highest proportion of people living in cohabiting couple households is for those with no religion with 16 per cent and the national figure for cohabiting couple households is half this figure.

The Health Survey shows that for Hindus and Sikhs cohabiting is a younger life style choice. 6 per cent of Sikhs in the 16–24 year old age cohort and 5.5 per cent in the 25–34 age cohort described themselves as cohabiters, however there were no cohabiters for all other age cohorts. For Hindus the proportions were smaller, never exceeding 2 per cent and were absent from ages 44 onwards. Muslims however, although reporting the smallest proportions and never higher than 1.5 per cent, reported cohabiters up until the age of 64. The data clearly shows that religion is explicitly a factor in choosing to engage in this form of partnership.

Figure 4.1 demonstrates that when quantified by religion Muslims have the highest proportion of lone parent households when compared with all other groups. It has already been discussed how a household can comprise of more than one family unit and when looking at the figures for lone parent families rather than households, the percentage of lone parents increases for all groups including Muslims. There is an important shift however. Muslims no longer have the highest proportion of lone parent families, although with 18 per cent they still have a higher percentage than the national average.

This figure appears to contradict some of the studies looked at earlier such as Becher and Husain (2003) who argue that separation and divorce is lower than average for both Muslim and Hindu families. However the lone parent figures for Muslims need not be a result of divorce or the break up of marriages. It is likely that other cultural factors could be at play. Possible areas for greater examination when attempting to make sense of these figures are:

- *Geographical distance due to:* Spouses awaiting residence in the United Kingdom, living or working overseas. As already mentioned in this chapter the FNSEM found that Pakistanis and Bangladeshis were at least 3 times more likely to be living away from a partner in this way. This was not a result the break down of marital relations, however for analytical

Figure 4.1: Percentage of lone parent households by religion in England and Wales.

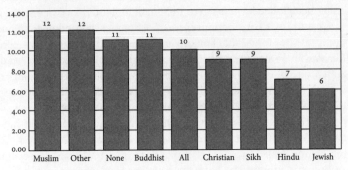

Source: taken from ONS (2001: table S151).

Figure 4.2: Percentage of lone parent families by religion in England and Wales.

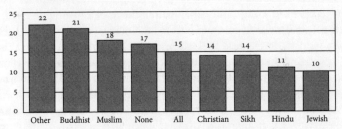

Source: taken from ONS (2001: table S151).

neatness these couples are often categorised as 'separated'.
- *Polygamy:* In some schools of Islamic jurisprudence it is permissible for Muslim men to marry up to four wives. In a recent publication Muslim community leaders stated that as many as 4,000 Muslim men in Britain could have entered into multiple marriages (AP 2004). In reality this will mean that only one of the wives would be recognised as such under English civil law even though accepted as such within the Muslim community by under going the religious or 'nikkah' ceremony only.

An often overlooked characteristic of one of the Muslim communities in Britain, however, goes a long way in explaining what could be a key factor in high proportions of lone parents. Harris (2004) explains, 'The great increase in the Somali population in the UK was made up of women and children. Some came to join their husbands, but a great many were single women with children – their men had either been killed or had stayed in Somali to fight' (p. 23).

A study by Khan and Jones (2002) of Somalis in London confirms this also. They found that Somali families were often headed by single females. In Somalia the father was the breadwinner and family head. Stereotypically, in the UK, he is unemployed, his role is marginalised and his manliness is challenged. In some cases, the father may be in the UK but not living with the family to maximise benefits. They argued that some single mothers still receive support from their husbands, but this is not always the case. It is apparent from the finding demonstrated by study that marriage was considered important among this community, however many married women were bringing up families on their own.

The findings from the data are clearly in keeping with some of the conclusions reached from the studies discussed earlier in this section. The three predominantly South Asian groups appeared to be similar in terms of marriage and cohabitation; however Muslims showed a clear trend towards entering into formal marriages at younger ages, as found to be the case by Dale and Heath (1994) and FNSEM. The surveys under study have limited data on divorce and it is not possible to discuss divorce and legal separation to any meaningful level/extent.

The finding on higher proportions of lone parent families among Muslims, when compared with Hindus, Sikhs and the national average however, is an area which has not appeared previously in literature on Muslim family formation and requires further exploration which is beyond the scope of this chapter.

Do Muslims Have More Children?

Muslims have the highest proportion of children, and the Census illustrates that 34 per cent of Muslims are aged 0–15. Although Muslims make up 3 per cent of the total population of England and Wales, Muslim dependent children make up 5 per cent of all dependent children in England and Wales. In other words, one child in every twenty in England and Wales is a Muslim.

Figure 4.3 shows data from commissioned Census table M293. 63 per cent of Muslims households contain dependent children and this is the highest percentage of households with dependent children for all groups and double the proportion of households containing dependent children nationally. In addition table 151 on household composition demonstrates that proportionately Muslims have the highest percentages for two or more children in every household

Figure 4.3: Percentage of households containing dependent children by religion for England and Wales.

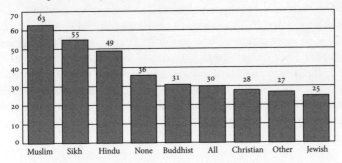

Source: taken from ONS (2001: table M293).

type apart from cohabiting couple households (although Muslims still have a higher percentage with two or more children in such households compared with Hindus and Sikhs and Jews).

The Health Survey demonstrates that Muslims also had the highest percentage of three or more children per households when compared with all other groups. In addition Muslim women were proportionately more likely to be pregnant at the time of the survey than women from any other group, although closely followed by Sikh women (5.5 per cent and 5 per cent respectively). The percentage of Christian women who reported being pregnant at the time of the survey was just over 3 per cent.

Census table M287 also demonstrates that Muslims also have the highest proportion of households with three or more infants (aged 0–4 years old). 23 per cent of Muslims had three or more children in this age range compared with 7 per cent of all people, 5 per cent of Hindus and 9 per cent of Sikhs.

Muslims therefore do have the highest proportion of households with the largest numbers of children. Of course the fact that Muslims are younger in comparison to other groups means that they are more likely to be of child-bearing age, and as a consequence more likely to have children. Therefore part of the higher fertility rates is age related.

Intra-Muslim Differences

There is however a difference in the average number of children for the different ethnic groups. Indian Muslims are the most likely of all three groups to have no children and at 46 per cent this is closer to all other faith groups than the Muslim figure. In comparison 31 per cent Pakistanis and 19 per cent of Bangladeshis reported no children households. Muslims were found to have larger proportions of households with three or more children, and 30 per cent of Muslims households were described as such. 18 per cent of Indian households had three or more children compared with 26 per cent of Pakistani and 30 per cent of Bangladeshi.

The data shows that Muslims explicitly have higher fertility rates when compared with all groups, however there are apparent differences according to ethnicity among Muslims. The significantly higher proportion of children and young people among Muslims requires consideration by service providers.

Extended Family Explored

At the beginning of the chapter, during the subsection on community cohesion and co-residence it was argued that certain ethnic groups stress family relationships and recognise obligations to relatives beyond the nuclear family more than others (Ballard 1994; Shaw 2000; Bose 2000). It has already been discussed that Muslims and South Asian groups place greater emphasis on parental responsibility towards their children which goes beyond age and even self-sufficiency in the case of unmarried daughters. Beishon and Berthoud's study (1997) contains interview based evidence which supports such assertions.

As well as obligations towards children, it is expected that parents will be taken care of by their adult children and even grandchildren when they become elderly. Consequently, in traditional families in Muslim countries, elders are rarely to be found living on their own, let alone in institutions for old people. Ballard (1990) argues that children are exposed to close relationships with extended family members and kin from a young age,

> They are taken to all functions and ceremonies and due to this kind of socialisation, the children internalise the values of the parents at an early age and, thus learn to behave in accordance with the ethos of the family. Among some Muslim groups in particular, due to the practice of consanguinity most kin members are related to each other several times over by entirely different routes. (p. 231)

Traits described here by Ballard are characteristics of positive social capital. They provide bonding capital and also provide what Coleman (1988) describes as 'closure'. In addition the description here of family members being related to each other several times over is a particularly robust form of multiplex relationships also discussed as being a useful method for the generation of social capital.

Zokaei and Phillips (2000) argue that recognition of kin obligations is of particular importance for Muslim groups due to the altruism that is encouraged in Islam,

> Religious teachings and ideology are the most important normative sources in many societies and often address codes of behavior in the private and public sphere of social life. It (altruism) is a collective concept and it's a result of collective commitments that members bring to a structure. (p. 26)

In Abd al'Ali (1977) comprehensive writings on family structure in Islam, he argues that family relationships within Islam are guided by the concept of 'ihsan', which is to treat others with mutual kindness, compassion and charity. In addition O'Brien and Husain (2000) write 'Specifically, religion connects people; it symbolizes core values of that collective and enables its members to feel a profound sense of belonging' (p. 1).

In their study of Muslim communities, Zokaei and Phillips also argue that in reality a significant level of competitiveness exists amongst Muslims; however within kin groups he did find a definite sense of altruism. Ballard has argued that an important maintainer of altruistic behaviour within extended families is the concept of *izzat* or respect. Here it is argued that to neglect obligations towards extended family, within traditional Muslim families from South Asia, would result in the loss of *izzat*, which Ballard (1990) describes as a crucial aspect of human dignity. Therefore the 'norm' which in this case is a sense of expected responsibility towards kin is effectively sanctioned by the threat to the individual's honour or integrity.

This is supported by O'Neale who writes,

> Thus as opposed to western ideology the honour, and welfare of the family which could include the extended family are considered to be more important than the feelings of 'selfish' interests of an individual ... Young women are more closely protected and are perceived as the epitome of family honour. (p. 13)

Such altruistic behaviour is at any rate an ideal as perceived by families of South Asian origin, and more notably Muslims, according to these authors. The concept of *izzat* is important for other South Asian groups also, however, if Muslims are less acculturated and do place greater emphasis on duty towards family members due to religious doctrine, it is reasonable to construe that this concept holds greater importance for Muslim South Asians.

It has already been discussed that Muslims and South Asian groups place greater emphasis on parental responsibility towards their children. For many parents from these communities, with responsibility comes control. Primary socialisation of children particularly in a non-Muslim setting is a means by which concepts regarding family, culture and religion are embedded in the psyche of the individual from a young age. However there are elements of Muslim children's lives and experiences which can not be as easily influenced and controlled by parents, especially with regards to interaction with the larger community via educational establishments. Zokaei and Phillips write, 'Interaction between Western values and Islamic values is often seen as potentially disruptive and as something which requires constant vigilance by the parents to keep their children in control' (2000: 49).

However, other studies have shown that many Muslims were of the opinion that imposing strict behavioural requirements on children will only lead to rebellion and this was the majority view of both younger and older Muslims in Basit's study (1997). Whether or not the acceptance of a laxer imposition of cultural codes of behaviour on children will necessarily result in a shift in the importance of duty towards family has been raised, particularly in a setting where the dominant attitudes towards kinship ties are conflicting.

Extended Family in Decline

Post industrialisation has seen the nuclear family become more common and the expected family unit in many societies. Organisations such as UNESCO and UNICEF propagate specific models of parenting and examples of 'the happy nuclear family' (Pels 2000: 35). The preference for nuclear families in Europe and Britain has led researchers to question how long the extended family type will be a preference for minority communities.

It has already been suggested that the 'traditional' gender roles within some of these communities, and in particular amongst Muslims, could be undergoing change for sociological reasons, other than simply emulating the majority community. There appears to be a vocal debate on whether or not preferences for 'extended family' is in decline amongst minorities who come from cultures for which it is the preference.

Researchers such as Othieno (1998) have argued that the extended family has survived the process of westernisation into what is now the second or third generation of many minority ethnic families living in Britain. In this view issues such as socio-economic status and persistence of discrimination have encouraged the survival of these structures.

Others such as Pels (2000) however have queried such opinions. Pels argues that the functionality of extended families for minority communities has declined on migration. In this view mutual dependency and solidarity were central values overruling the private interests of the individual, thus enabling families to survive in a society without a collective social security system. If based on these needs it would appear that the purpose extended families serve elsewhere is not as important in countries such as Britain.

Ochieng's (2002) research contests the argument that extended families are no longer functional. In this study it was found the lone parent mothers who are active participants in an extended-family system have greater opportunity for self-improvement, work and peer contact than do other lone mothers. In most cases in the study, it appeared that the elders donate rather than receive services. Though the area still requires further exploration, the presence of extended family in child care remains important.

In addition to whether the extended family type is functional within western societies, attitudes and preferences of younger Muslims and family formation have been explored. Inevitably as a result of migration, one immediate change has been the distancing of kinship and in-law relations in the countries of origin.

Zokaei and Phillips have argued that the lack of visible relationships between parents and grandparents has affected the socialisation of second generation Muslims in that they have no experience of caring for elders to refer to. In this study although all young married people interviewed had maintained close relations with their families, they were also conscious that the emerging gap between generations, particularly between first and third generations, would have some impact upon the lives of older people.

Quasi Extended/Joint Family

Research by Blakemore (2000) has identified that among the ageing population, due to the nuclear family model becoming more prevalent and family space more constrained, it is anticipated that there will be an increase in the number of elderly Muslims living alone or in need of care. While it is usually assumed that minority families take care of their own, this may no longer be true for future generations. This raises issues of an ageing Muslim population whose specific requirements need to be addressed in a systematic and holistic manner.

Stopes-Roe et al.'s (1990) study on family unit preferences of second and subsequent generation South Asians also highlighted this issue. Their research suggested that attitudes towards extended families were changing and two thirds of women expressed a preference for nuclear families. One third of fathers and three fifths of mothers reported preferences towards this type of family unit also.[2]

Shaw (2000) however, found that whilst young British Muslims gave the impression of being thoroughly westernised in the sense of being fluent English speakers or holders of educational and professional qualifications, they were often still committed to cultural distinctiveness and upholding their community's moral and religious identity.

Although this in itself does not necessarily mean that extended families would be the preferred type for such young Muslims what is worth noting is that the commitment to community cohesion and cultural distinctiveness are still of importance. Therefore, it seems more realistic to acknowledge that extended families may be shifting somewhat in their appearance and organisation, however kinship ties and altruism towards family still holds importance for Muslims in all the studies cited here.

Basit (1997) developed the theory of the 'Quasi-joint family'. Although most of the subjects in Basit's study lived in nuclear families, many had relatives living on the same street or in close walking distance. This has also been noted by Barkat-E-Khuda (1985) and Shaw (1988, 2000). This appeared to be more practical due to structural constraints also, and so, whilst the families had their privacy due to either personal preference or smaller housing, they still had the support of the extended family nearby, if needed. Ballard's work also supports this view, as he argues that even in South Asia, once a conjugal pair is established with offspring, it is common for them to seek greater autonomy within the joint family by partially separating themselves from it and this is not therefore an unusual or unexpected event. He writes,

> Even though the principle of co-residence is much celebrated, closer inspection soon reveals that so long as family members continue to act as if they were still members of single cooperative households even though they live apart on a day to day

basis, the underlying of the group is not regarded as having been seriously compromised. (p. 4)

Ahmad (2000) points out that there is heterogeneity and are various definitions of extended family. Although a much used concept in relation to most ethnic minority communities, he argues that it remains poorly understood. Therefore the existence of an extended family need not imply complex households, just as conversely a one family household may actively be part of a quasi extended or joint family specifically in areas such as decision making with regards to finances and child rearing.

Areas for Exploration

Muslims families although varied in type have been described as having greater preferences towards a 'traditional' family type, in that there are clearly defined roles within the family structure for all its members.

In addition to marked gender roles, children and parents have roles which encourage responsibility and loyalty to a much greater degree when compared to families among the indigenous population. This is demonstrated through parental responsibilities to care for children well into adulthood if unmarried, and in the case of sons, until they are financially independent. There is also a strong emphasis on care and maintenance of elderly parents by adult children, once they have become established.

Although emphasis is traditionally placed on the importance and maintenance of kinship ties by other minority groups, namely South Asians, arguments to do with levels of acculturation and altruism encouraged in religious texts has been highlighted to infer that such households are more common for Muslims.

However Pels (2000) has argued that preferences for extended families will inevitably be replaced for single family units or the nuclear family. Others like Shaw and Ahmed argue that extended families need not be characterised by the existence of a complex household and due to space restraints and preferences for more personal privacy, this is likely to be more the case than not.

Yet there are still preferences for kin to live in close proximity to each other and share many aspects of daily routine. Here, it is argued that greater research on how 'extended families' are reinventing themselves in Britain is required in order to adequately understand preferences towards extended families for some communities.

Attitudes towards these roles and responsibilities within family

structures can not be measured through Census data analysis, however, the preferences in terms of proportions of such households can
be measured when exploring trends for Muslims specifically and it
is therefore possible to infer from this whether Muslims have greater
preferences towards certain family type when compared with other
groups. The key themes summarised in this section will now be explored using the data available.

Do Muslims Show Greater Signs of Traditional Gender Roles and Less Acculturation?

A running theme throughout the chapter when discussing Muslim
families has been the defined roles which family members adopt.
Within this it has been argued that Muslim women are likely to take
on the role of wife and mother (both accepting formal marriages as
normative and having higher and longer sustained periods of reproduction) and that this is influenced by acculturation (Mistry 2000)
and educational attainment (Dale and Heath 1994).

There are several indicators for acculturation available from the
data under study. The 2001 National Census (s153) provides data on
economic activity, broken down by sex and provides data on reasons
for inactivity.

Although both Muslims men and women have the highest rates
for economic inactivity, Muslim women are nearly twice as likely to be
so than both Muslim men and all women (70 per cent, 36 per cent and
41 per cent aged 16–75, respectively). As already stated Muslims have
slightly lower married couple households, higher cohabiting couple
households and higher proportions of one parent households as Sikhs
and Hindus. If this were an indication of how Muslims are slightly
less inclined towards 'traditional' family types, economic inactivity
may be an indication of gender specific roles within these communities. 41 per cent of Sikh and Hindu women are economically inactive
compared with 26 per cent of Hindu men and 27 per cent of Sikh
men. Hindu, Sikhs and all women are therefore 1.6 times more likely
to be economically inactive compared to their male counterparts. This
compares with Muslim women who are twice as likely to be economically inactive compared to Muslim men. Therefore in absolute terms
and in terms of male female ratios, Muslim women are more likely
than any other group to be economically inactive.

The 1999 Health Survey for England asked whether or not women
from each group had ever been in paid employment or been self-
employed. 75 per cent of Muslim women in this sample answered 'no'

compared with 45 per cent of Hindu and 35.5 per cent of Sikh women. 12.5 per cent of Christian women. English language proficiency could not only be used as an indication of acculturation of those from minority groups, but also a prerequisite to most employment. Muslim women were least likely to report English as a spoken language, when compared with women from other faith groups. 73 per cent of Muslim women could speak English compared with 76 per cent of Buddhist, 81 per cent of Sikh and 90 per cent of Hindu women.

A more specific indicator of gender roles however is that of caring or looking after the home. The Census data shows that 18 per cent of Muslims are looking after home or family compared with 7 per cent nationally (aged 16–74). Muslims have the highest percentage of people in this category. When broken down by sex, both Muslim men and women (3 per cent and 34 per cent) are three times more likely than all men and all women to be caring for the home and family (1 per cent and 12 per cent).

When broken down by sex and age however, Muslim women aged 16–24 are 5 times more likely to be looking after the family or home than women of this age group nationally and have the highest percentage of women in this category across the all faith groups. For women aged 25–74 Muslim women also have the highest percentage looking after family and home at 29 per cent, this is nearly three times greater than the national figure for women of this age range.

Here again Muslim women have the highest proportion across all groups looking after the family or home and a third of all Muslim women aged 16–74 are in this category. This clearly indicates a significantly greater preference or trend for women from this community.

The 1999 Health Survey for England asked men and women whether they had engaged in housework in the four weeks prior to the survey being conducted. Muslim men were the least likely to report partaking in any housework within the time period stated with 46 per cent compared with 68 per cent of Sikh and Hindu men. 82 per cent of Christian men reported doing housework in the four weeks prior to the survey.

The data does reveal that Muslims do show a greater trend towards what would be commonly referred to as traditional gender roles, in so far as a smaller proportion of Muslim women are economically active and therefore leaving the 'bread winning' largely to men. Of course the high proportion of female economic inactivity could be seen to reflect the high proportion of economic inactivity for Muslims as a whole, however as stated Muslim women are twice as likely to be economically inactive compared with women from all other faith groups who are 1.6 times more likely to be so than their male counterparts.

Higher proportions of both Muslim men and women reported looking after the home and family, however when broken down by age Muslim women when compared with other women had greater female/male ratios for looking after the family and home compared to the other groups. In addition a question on housework asked in the Health Survey demonstrated that Muslim men were least likely to have reported doing any housework in the month prior to the survey. Muslims therefore do appear to show greater differentiated roles, with regards to female nurture/home keeper rather than bread winner or contributors to 'bread winning'.

Intra-Muslim Differences

When looking at these indicators by ethnicity among Muslims the Health Survey revealed that Bangladeshi women were less likely to have qualifications than Pakistani and Indian women (60 per cent compared with 50 per cent and 45 per cent). Women from this group are also less likely to be in employment compared with Pakistani and Indian Muslim women (14 per cent compared with 17 per cent and 26 per cent). A higher proportion of Indian Muslim women spoke English (86 per cent) and this was followed by Pakistani Muslim women (75 per cent). Bangladeshi women were least likely of the three to report English as a spoken language (52 per cent).

Bangladeshi men were least likely (38 per cent) to report having done any housework in the past four weeks, 52 per cent of Pakistani, 45 per cent of Indian men reported doing housework.

With regards to acculturation and gender roles there appears to be a clear step like gradient with Indian Muslim women being most likely to hold educational qualifications and able to speak and read English and Bangladeshi women least likely. However the question regarding housework demonstrated that Pakistanis and Indians were closer with reference to male participation, whereas in terms of household size and number of children, Pakistanis appeared to be closer to Bangladeshis.

Do Muslims Have the Smallest Proportion of Elderly People Living Independently?

During this section it has been argued that Muslims, to a greater extent than other groups maintain a sense of responsibility towards parents and even grandparents, as adults. This tied in closely with arguments about extended families, altruism and even honour. The 2001 National Census data can be used to explore some of the themes discussed here.

When looking at care and maintenance of the elderly, Census table s151 shows that Muslims have the lowest proportion of single pensioner households at 2 per cent, compared with 3 per cent for Hindus and Sikhs and 14 per cent of all people. For households made up of pensioners only, Muslims also have the lowest proportion of such households for all groups. This is more than twice as unlikely as Sikhs and nearly three times as unlikely as Hindus. Muslims are also the least likely to reside in a care home for the elderly according to Census table s161. Just over 1 per cent of Muslims are in nursing homes compared with 17 per cent of all people.

These findings are clearly in keeping with the arguments previously discussed in this chapter. Muslims (as shown in Chapter Two) are particularly concentrated in the younger age cohorts and have proportionately smaller numbers of elderly or those of pensioner age.

Do Muslims Have Higher Proportions of Large and Complex Households Than Other Groups?

Although Muslims are not the least likely to have one person households, the figure is still considerably lower than that for all people at 30 per cent. The findings discussed in the section on marriage and childbirth demonstrate that Muslims have the highest proportions of children and the literature discussing extended family households suggests that Muslims would be the most likely to report large and complex households when compared with all other groups.

A commissioned Census table (M295) provides information on household size or in other words the number of people residing in a household. The average Muslim household size is 4 compared to 2 nationally. Muslims have the highest average household size closely followed by Sikhs. Muslims are least likely to have two person households, with only 15.5 per cent compared with one third of all households nationally. At the higher end of the scale Muslims have the highest proportion of households with 6 or more people compared with all other groups, with 18 per cent. Muslims and Sikhs are the only two groups to report 11 person and 12 or more person households, although both these are less than 1 per cent of all Sikh and Muslim households.

In addition the 2001 Citizenship Survey for England and Wales

Figure 4.4: Percentage within each household size by religion for England and
          Wales.

	All HRP	Muslim	Christian	Buddhist	Hindu	Sikh	Jewish	Other	None
1	30.0	14.7	30.0	35.7	14.2	12.7	36.1	38.3	28.9
2	34.2	15.5	35.5	27.3	21.4	17.0	32.4	30.1	31.9
3	15.5	16.5	15.3	16.3	21.0	17.7	12.4	14.5	17.0
4	13.4	18.8	13.1	13.2	24.8	24.4	11.5	10.7	14.8
5	4.9	16.3	4.5	5.4	12.2	16.7	4.8	3.9	5.3
6	1.4	9.7	1.2	1.5	4.5	7.3	1.7	1.2	1.5
7	0.3	4.0	0.2	0.4	1.2	2.5	0.4	0.3	0.3
8	0.1	2.2	0.1	0.2	0.4	0.9	0.2	0.1	0.1
9	-	1.2	-	-	0.2	0.4	0.2	-	-
10	-	0.7	-	-	0.1	0.3	0.1	-	-
11	-	0.2	-	-	-	0.1	-	-	-
12+	-	0.2	-	-	-	0.1	-	-	-

Source: taken from ONS (2001: table M295).

found that Muslims reported the highest proportion of 'large households' when compared with all other groups with 32 per cent of Muslim households falling within this category.

Exploring the total number of adults in a household can provide
an indication of complex households. The two adult household type
is characteristic of a nuclear family. Where there are more than two
adults in a household, the household could therefore be a complex
household.

The 1999 Health Survey for England demonstrated that two adult
households were the household type with the greatest percentage for
all groups; however there was a significant difference in the percentage size for some groups. 49 per cent of Christians reported two adult
households compared with Muslims who had the second lowest percentage across the groups with 38 per cent. This was closely followed
by Sikhs with 39 per cent and Hindus had the lowest figure with 35 per
cent. At the higher end of the scale, Muslims had the highest proportion of people reporting 6 or more adult households with 8.5 per cent.

The 2001 Citizenship Survey for England and Wales looked at
household types and provided data on whether a household was not a
'family' households, in other words whether the household consisted
of unrelated people. Sikhs were least likely to report this type of household with 8 per cent according to the survey. Muslims and Hindus
followed as second least likely to report such households, both with

15 per cent.

When looking at joint families however the citizenship survey provides data on households containing two family units and three or more family units. Proportionately there were more Muslim households containing two family units when compared with other groups with 8.5 per cent and this was closely followed with Sikhs and Hindus both with 8 per cent. For three or more family unit households, Sikhs have the highest proportion with 1.3 per cent and this is closely followed with Muslims and Hindus with 1 per cent. All other groups had proportions close to 0 per cent reporting such households.

According the Census figures, Muslims after Sikhs have the highest proportion of 'other' households with 20 per cent and 21 per cent respectively. The national figure for other households is 7 per cent. However Muslims have the highest proportion of two or more dependent children in such households with 9 per cent compared with only 1 per cent nationally, 6 per cent of Hindus and 8 per cent of Sikhs. The 'Other households' category includes all student, all pensioner and 'other' which includes those households with more than one family unit such as the extended or joint family household and unrelated persons.[3]

Of this third subcategory, Hindus, followed by Sikhs, Buddhists and then Muslims have the highest proportion. As described above the most common type of complex household is that of a couple living with an adult child or children. The literature cited above suggests that Muslims produce children over a longer time span and therefore are likely to still have dependent children even if some of their children are no longer dependent[4] . The Census data does not provide figures for how many dependant and non-dependent children there are in a single household, and only provides data for non-dependant children, providing all children in the household are non-dependent. In other words, if there is a mixture of dependent and non-dependent children in a household the figure for non-dependents will not be left out. This is important because it could in theory be masking complex households.

It appears from the analysis detailed here that Sikhs and Muslims and to a lesser extent Hindus have higher proportions of complex households than both the total sample for the Health Survey and all people as measured by the Census. Sikhs and Muslims have similar proportions of households with large numbers of adults, although Muslims were the only household reporting seven adults households. Sikhs also demonstrate slightly higher proportions of three or more family unit households.

Census findings on 'Other' households again demonstrate that Sikhs and Muslims have similar proportions reporting these types of households. However when broken down further the position of Muslims within such household types become ambiguous due to the potential masking of adult children living with parents who may also have siblings still classed as dependent.

The data is unable to provide clear-cut answers regarding extended families although the finding that over 60 per cent of Sikh, Muslim and Hindu households in the Health Survey reported three or more adults and around 20 per cent of Muslim and Sikh households in the Census were classed as 'other' does suggest that these groups are more likely than others to be represented among non-nuclear type households. The data does clearly show however that Muslims are not the most likely to report or be living in complex households as this appears to be equally the case for Sikhs as it is for Muslims. It is important to remember that such data cannot provide any indications regarding quasi joint families as discussed previously.

When looking at intra-Muslim differences and household size the Health Survey data shows that Indian Muslims have the highest percentage of 1 person household of the three ethnic groups with 4 per cent compared 3 per cent of Pakistanis and 2 per cent of Bangladeshis. Indians have the highest proportion of 'smaller' households, which is 2–4 person households at 59 per cent, compared with 35 per cent of Pakistanis and 33 per cent of Bangladeshis. For 5 or more person households Indians reported 37 per cent compared with 62 per cent of Pakistani and 66 per cent Bangladeshi households. The mean household size for Pakistani and Bangladeshis is 5 whereas for Indians it is 4. However Bangladeshis have higher percentages at the higher end of the scale compared with the other two groups.

In sum, Pakistanis and Bangladeshis reported similar proportions of children to the Muslim average, whereas Indian Muslims reported smaller numbers in comparison.

For household size, Pakistanis and Bangladeshis reported similar proportions of small (2–4) and 5 or more person households. The majority of Indian Muslim households were classed as small. However Bangladeshis were twice as likely as Pakistanis to have 9 or more people households.

Conclusion

The aim of this chapter was to explore Muslim family formation, both by evaluating previous studies and through the secondary data analysis of the 2001 National Census for England and Wales, the 1999 Health Survey for England and the 2001 the Home Office Citizenship Survey for England and Wales.

In doing so two broad research questions were discussed:

- What appears to be the main trends for Muslim groups with regards to household composition and family formation? and
- Do these differ from both other groups and the national trends?

In the first section it was argued that marriage is normative for Muslims and the only accepted or legitimate means for reproduction according to Islam. The analysis of the data supported the studies discussed on the topic. As a result Muslims have higher rates of marriage, however the figure was not the highest, coming third, after Sikhs and Hindus. These three groups however do differ considerably in this regard to the national average. The data did undoubtedly show that Muslims have higher rates of marriage among younger age cohorts than all other groups. Muslims also clearly have the highest proportions of dependent children and the percentage of household containing children was the highest for Muslims, compared with all groups.

The analysis also found that as with Hindu and Sikhs, Muslims had lower rates of cohabitation compared with all other groups and here religion was explicitly a factor in not choosing this type of partnership for these three faith groups.

A finding which did not appear in the literature was the higher than average proportion of lone parent families among Muslims. The analysis of the Census data showed this to be case. This area clearly requires further exploration. There has been an established association between high levels of unemployment and lone parent families more generally (Blackaby et al. 1999) and as will be demonstrated in the following chapter, Muslims have the highest rates of economic inactivity. This is also something which requires exploration in order to understand whether there is a correlation between unemployment and lone parent families for Muslims. There is a lacuna in the literature and little discussion of Muslim separation and divorce.

As already shown by the FNSEM, Muslims are most likely to conceive within a formal marriage which means that a significant proportion of lone parents (those who are not classed as such due to geographical distance or in a polygamous marriage for example) are separated, either legally or otherwise, and that there has been a break up in marital relations.

The second section looked at altruism within the family and co-residence. Here it was argued that due to the norms regarding maintenance and expectations of responsibility towards family members, Muslims were more inclined to live in joint family households. The assertion that Muslims are more inclined towards this family type was reinforced by the arguments presented by those such as Mistry (2000) that Muslims are less acculturated than other South Asian groups.

The discussion throughout this chapter on altruism, stronger cohesion and emphasis on obligations and *izzat* is particularly relevant to the theory of social capital discussed during this chapter. The analysis found that the Muslim elderly were least likely to be living either on their own in pensioner households or as residents in care homes, suggesting they are most likely residing with family members. The data also found that Muslims reported the largest number of individuals, more importantly adults, residing in a household compared with all other groups. This perhaps is to be expected when considering Muslim fertility rates.

When looking at extended families however Muslims appear just as likely as Sikhs to reside in joint family households. The figures for such households, considering the emphasis placed on family responsibility for caring and maintenance of all members as suggested by the literature, are lower than one would at first imagine. However it is important to bear in mind that the data did not measure quasi joint families or attitudes towards joint families, which are significant when discussing social capitals in terms of family cohesion and obligation.

Whether Muslims are less acculturated when compared with Hindus and Sikhs is difficult to measure. In terms of education and economic activity, Muslims appear to be less so than the other two groups, who as discussed in Chapter Three, fare considerably better in comparison. Here the interpretations of certain conventions by the three faith groups has clearly played a part at least initially on settlement to Britain. Ballard writes,

A further source of differentiation was the strictness with which the conventions of *purdah* – female seclusion – were interpreted as between Hindus, Sikhs and Muslims ... The greater strictness with which the conventions were interpreted the more nervous their members tended to be of the prospect that their commitment to female modesty might be undermined in a British context, and the more resistant they were to the prospect of women taking waged employment outside the home once they reached the UK (2004: 7).

Clearly Muslims, Hindus and Sikhs retained their preferences for formal marriage, however if Hindus and Sikhs demonstrated later ages of marriage and less children per couple compared to Muslims prior to migration, it is not necessarily the case that on settling in Britain Hindus and Sikhs have become more acculturated when it comes to family formation.

When looking at intra-Muslim differences, in terms of ethnicity, cultural preferences such as the practice of consanguinity were more apparent for some groups, namely Pakistanis than others such as Bangladeshis. The data from the Health Survey did find differences between the three Muslims groups. There appeared to be a step like gradient with Pakistanis taking the middle position. For example, Indian Muslims reported fewer numbers of children compared with Bangladeshis.

The discussion of the literature and the analysis of data provided in this chapter demonstrate that Muslims do appear to have preferences and trends in family formation which differ from the national profile, with the exception for lone parent families, for which the Muslim figure is 3 per cent higher than the national figure. Muslims clearly place greater emphasis and importance on entering into formal marriages when compared with the national trends (and at younger ages compared with Hindus and Sikhs). Muslims families also visibly value the production of children and have the highest fertility rates. The implications of having large numbers of children and reporting the highest proportion of large households is explored in the next chapter.

5

Housing, Service Provision and Disadvantage

The predominately Muslim groups have been repeatedly described as presenting the highest levels of disadvantage. This has been discussed in a number of studies on various topics, both explicitly and implicitly. Such studies will be evaluated throughout this chapter.

In identifying whether Muslims report greater levels of disadvantage, three main areas will be explored in this chapter:

- Housing tenure, type and suitability in terms of amenities
- Unemployment and income
- Service provision and need for outside assistance

Housing in relation to ethnic minority communities is a well researched area. It is relevant for Muslim communities for two main reasons; firstly because of the subject of overcrowded housing and secondly, as housing type and neighbourhoods are indicators of poverty and disadvantage (Berthoud 1998).

In addition some ethnic minority groups have been shown to report higher levels of economic inactivity and as will be discussed, Muslim groups have been found to be amongst those reporting the

highest percentage of long term unemployment. In addition to unemployment, low levels of income, coupled with higher numbers of
dependents (as demonstrated in the previous chapter) often point to
Muslims being amongst the most severely disadvantaged both economically and socially.

A discussion of disadvantage and need would be lacking an essential area of focus without exploring service provision for ethnic minority communities, particularly families. Service provision can cover
all statutory bodies, however to explore each area of provision and
each type of service, be it hospital care, care of 'looked after' children
or respite facilities for parents of disabled children, would require far
greater discussion than this chapter is able to provide.

The main aims of this chapter therefore are to provide housing
profiles, particularly for Muslims groups and to discuss whether or
not Muslims show greater levels of need for services and to what extent these needs are being met.

Housing and Amenities

The 2001 Home Office Citizenship Survey for England and found that,

> For the most part, respondents with a religious affiliation lived
> in places with low to moderate level area deprivation; the ex-
> ception to this was that of respondents affiliated to the Muslim
> faith community. A significantly larger proportion of Muslim
> respondents lived in areas with the highest levels of area de-
> privation. (Attwood et al. 2003: *viii*)

The survey demonstrated that Muslims had higher levels of disadvantage in areas of residence. Several studies have attempted to understand why some groups have poorer housing and differ in housing tenure. A historical understanding of community settlement and
socio-economic profiles are key in understanding these patterns.
However, it has also been suggested that preferences for types of residential areas and tenure are equally important when discussing minority communities and housing.

When most ethnic minority communities arrived in Britain after the Second World War it was to take up work. They were forced
into a segregated labour market, taking on poorly paid manual and
unskilled jobs that were difficult to fill using the indigenous workforce. Just as they were at the bottom end of the labour market, they
also found themselves at the poorest end of the private sector housing

market because it was cheap and indiscriminate, as indigenous communities had rejected it. Chain migration led to clusters of communities on both regional and intra-urban levels. As the reality of long term residence in the UK became apparent and the 'myth of return' no longer prevailed, legislation pre-empted families joining their relatives in the UK (Anwar 1979). This meant that communities began to evaluate their housing situations and the various communities dealt with their needs differently.

Peach's (1998) study on neighbourhoods and clustering of ethnic groups argued that certain communities opted to purchase accommodation, whilst others opted for private and social renting. The option of buying was tied into economic activity. Here it is argued that Indian communities were in a more advantaged economic position when compared to other minority groups, however there appears to be evidence that purchasing is a cultural preference also. Although Pakistanis were not as financially successful, Ballard (1990) argues that there was a trend for pooling together resources among this community and this often resulted in over crowding. However the areas in which housing was purchased was largely undesirable. The main reasons for this was that communities had already settled into these areas and to remain clustered allowed a certain degree of cultural autonomy and safety in numbers.

The Local Authority housing sector which ironically had not been an option for these communities who were amongst those most in need, was opened up to applicants from ethnic minorities in the late 1960s. This bought some de-concentration of communities particularly amongst Caribbeans previously living in the private rented sector. Ethnic minority applicants, however, were often given the poorest choice in run down estates which indigenous communities refused to accept (Phillip 1998).

Housing Careers and Static Communities

This had long-term repercussions on the pattern of minority community settlement. In addition, many minority households were to find themselves trapped in marginal urban areas in regions of industrial decline. Research conducted by Owen and Johnson (1996) and Phillips (1998) has demonstrated that there has been little significant change in the types of areas of residence for many groups and therefore no considerable decline in segregation has occurred. Indeed where groups have been mobile, such as Pakistanis in search of employment, it had not resulted in de-concentration of communities but

rather the trend was to join other Pakistani communities in conur-
bations. Of all ethnic minorities communities Bangladeshis have remained the most segregated not only from both the White ethnic majority but other ethnic minority groups. The Fourth National Survey
of Ethnic Minorities (FNSEM) found that many ethnic minority individuals preferred to live in close proximity to people from other ethnic
minorities and particularly people from their own ethnic group. This
suggests that for many, concentration in itself is not the problem but
that essentially it is the disadvantaged areas that they are concentrated
in that is the concern (Modood et al. 1997).

The process of suburbanisation is one often associated with the
length of settlement of an ethnic minority population, as successive
generations are often better equipped when entering the work place
than their parents. For ethnic minorities on the whole those second
and subsequent generations who are in work do appear to be doing
equally well or better than their parent's generation. However unemployment is higher for British born ethnic minorities than for their
parent's generation and this contributes to the lack of economic improvement of these communities. The 1991 National Census found
that unemployment for British born Black Caribbeans was 31 per cent
and Pakistanis was 42 per cent compared with the immigrant generation Black Caribbean at 18 per cent and Pakistanis at 28 per cent. This
clearly has far reaching implications for housing options. However,
some communities have appeared to be experiencing greater rates of
suburbanisation and de-concentration, namely Indians and African
Asians, yet the proportions are still relatively low when compared to
the ethnic majority. Research by Wallace and Denham (1996) found
that all minority groups were underrepresented in the most affluent
Local Authorities.

It is here where debates of choice and constraint in housing type
and location are particularly vocal as some research suggests ethnic
or cultural preferences are in force rather than simple constraints of
economic disadvantage and racial discrimination. Peach writes, 'discrimination is not the preserve of a single group. Housing patterns
may be understood much more as the product of autonomous ethnic
culture and choice, moderated by chain migration and differing rates
of diffusion' (1998: 1658).

Here it is argued that due to different levels of possession of
human capital in the form of skills and qualifications for different communities, some groups, namely Indians and Asian Africans
had speedier economic advancements compared with Pakistanis and

Bangladeshis (Ballard 1990; Peach 1998). High rates of unemployment amongst some ethnic groups however plays a key role in their continued cycle of disadvantage and poor housing. This throws doubt on the level of choice available to such communities when opting to live in other areas or property types.

Tenure

As mentioned above Indians and Pakistanis were more likely to opt for owner occupation compared to other ethnic groups at around 80 per cent of households having this tenure in 1991. For Black Caribbean and Bangladeshi households living in social rented housing the percentage was double the national figure in 1991. The FNSEM suggested that the relatively low proportion of owner occupiers among Caribbean, Chinese and Bangladeshis was related to their concentration in inner London, and for Chinese and Caribbeans in particular, their smaller household sizes (Modood et al. 1997).

The findings from the FNSEM showed that the two Muslim groups had different tenure profiles: Pakistanis had higher rates of owner occupiers, whereas Bangladeshis had a higher percentage of households living in social rented accommodation. The 2001 Citizenship Survey found that for Muslims, approximately half reported owner occupation, and this was the lowest percentage for all groups. In addition, Muslims reported the highest percentage living in social rented accommodation, at just under a quarter of respondents.

Lakey (1997) argues that although occupation is often seen as the most attractive option and the promotion of ownership has been an important feature of housing policy, home owners from Pakistani backgrounds were found to have poorer living conditions than those in social rented accommodation. The 1991 National Census demonstrated that Indian owner occupiers had the best living conditions of all the ethnic minorities groups, 44 per cent of Indian home owners lived in detached or semi-detached properties. The number of Pakistanis, Bangladeshis and Black Caribbean owners with this type of property were significantly less. Although like Indians, Pakistanis had a high proportion of home ownership, as many as 30 per cent of these lived in terraced houses.

Housing Quality

There is an array of research including statistics derived from the 1991 Census suggesting Pakistanis and Bangladeshis have the worst overcrowding of the main ethnic minority groups. The English House

Condition Survey (DoE 1993) found that 20 per cent of both Pakistanis and Bangladeshis were assessed as having the 'worst' housing
in England. The FNSEM found that although conditions were poorer
for all minorities than for the White indigenous majority, the majority group, when compared with those living in similar circumstances,
were more likely to express dissatisfaction with their local area and
dissatisfaction with their accommodation after Caribbeans.

The FNSEM also shows that Pakistanis and Bangladeshis have the
highest levels of overcrowding when compared with all other groups.
Lakey (1997) describes this,

> The size of household was more important than is tenure in
> determining the likelihood of overcrowding, suggesting that
> this problem was associated with the general inability to ac-
> cess accommodation spacious enough for the needs of large
> households. (1997: 223)

Harrison (1998) argues that service providers, although working
in a multi-cultural setting often accept some lifestyles over others and
that 'differences may serve as a denigrating label' (p. 795). It is argued that this is a key issue which service providers should address;
those households that are seen as difficult because they do not fit the
conventional model, in this case due to their size, are stigmatised
and viewed as problematic instead of being sufficiently catered for.
Ansari (2002) also comments on this, 'One form of discrimination
is prejudicial and stereotypical assessment of need by personnel, resulting in policies that create differential access to housing' (p. 9). A
report by the IHRC (Ahmed et al. 2001) after the Oldham riots described how Pakistani and Bangladeshis spent longer on waiting lists,
were more likely to be offered lower quality housing and were segregated into specific estates around the centre of the town (2001).

Areas for Exploration
In order to discuss some of the key issues outlined in this section in
relation to Muslims, the following points will now be explored us-
ing the 2001 National Census for England and Wales, the 2001 Home
Office Citizenship Survey for England and Wales and the 1999 Health
Survey for England data:

Are Muslims Highly Concentrated in Urban Areas?
According to the 1999 Health Survey of England, Muslims have the
highest proportion of people living in urban areas when compared to

all faith groups. 59 per cent of Muslims compared with 30 per cent of Christians were classed as having residence in urban settings. 40 per cent of Muslims live in suburban areas compared with 69 per cent of Hindus and 71 per cent of Sikhs. Both Muslims and Sikhs had proportions close to 0 per cent living in rural areas compared with 1 per cent of Hindus and 6 per cent of Christians.

Amongst Muslims, Bangladeshis are most likely to live in urban areas both compared with the other two Muslim groups and in absolute terms, with 85 per cent of Bangladeshis Muslims in the survey compared to 48 per cent of Indians Muslims and 39 per cent of Pakistanis. Pakistanis had the highest proportion of households in suburban areas with 61 per cent compared with 52 per cent of Indians and 14.5 per cent of Bangladeshis. Less than 1 per cent of all groups lived in rural areas, however Indians were most likely to do so than the other groups.

The 2001 Citizenship Survey also looks at degrees of urbanisation and includes an 'inner city' category. As demonstrated below by 6.1 Muslims are found to have the highest proportions of households residing within inner cities with 62 per cent. This is closely followed by Jews with 61 per cent. All other groups reported less than 50 per cent within this category.

Therefore Muslims are more likely to live in urban areas when compared with all other groups. There is intra-Muslim differentiation however with Bangladeshi Muslims having the highest proportion of households in urban areas, when compared with Pakistani and Indian Muslims. Although there are Muslims in more prosperous areas it should not be assumed that they are better off than Muslims living in disadvantaged or poor areas. In the 1970s the Education Priority Areas demonstrated that children suffering from the greatest levels of deprivation did not live in the most disadvantaged areas and the majority of children who did were not deprived (Berthoud 2000).

In Scotland the vast majority of Muslims (79 per cent) reside in large urban areas and this compared with 39 per cent of the total population of Scotland. When compared with all other groups, Muslims were least likely to reside in remote rural and accessible rural areas.

Do Muslims Show Preferences Towards Certain Types of Tenure and Is There Significant Intra-Faith Group Differentiation for Ethnic Groups and Geographical Location?

The data from the 2001 National Census on housing tenure and religion found that Muslims make up nearly 2 per cent of all households in England and Wales. 51 per cent of Muslims households are owner

Figure 5.1: Percentage of respondents residing in inner city areas by religion.

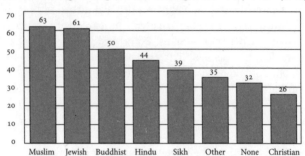

Taken from the Home Office Citizenship Survey for England and Wales (2001).

occupiers and compared to the national figure of 69 per cent as shown by Figure 5.2 Muslims who own their own homes are more likely to do so with a mortgage or loan, with two thirds of owner occupiers doing so compared to half of all owner occupiers nationally. A closer look at this figure reveals that that in actual terms, due to the lower percentage of Muslims owner occupiers, 33 per cent of all Muslim households have loans or mortgages, slightly less than the figure for all households at 39 per cent. In addition Muslims are just as likely to have shared ownership of their homes as all people.

The Census findings showed that 28 per cent of Muslim households live in social rented housing and within this category Muslims are most likely to rent from councils rather than housing associations[1]. This figure is not only higher than the national figure for households living in this sector at 19 per cent but the highest for all groups.

Muslims households are twice as likely as 'all households' to live in accommodation renting in the private rental sector. An explanation for this could be recent arrival of newer communities. Lakey (1997) argues that private tenancy is often the preferred or only option available to new arrivals, while they seek properties to buy or establish eligibility for social rental. It is also, however, likely to result from inability to purchase a property and the lack of suitable social housing. There have been criticisms of the social rented sector for their smaller sized properties and unsuitability for larger families for many sections of the community not just recent arrivals (Phillips 1998).

Muslims also reported a greater number of households living rent free, 4 per cent compared to 2 per cent of all households in England

Figure 5.2: Percentage of people within each broad tenure category by religion.

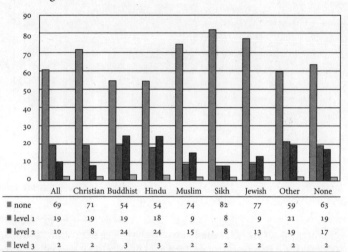

	All	Christian	Buddhist	Hindu	Muslim	Sikh	Jewish	Other	None
none	69	71	54	54	74	82	77	59	63
level 1	19	19	19	18	9	8	9	21	19
level 2	10	8	24	24	15	8	13	19	17
level 3	2	2	3	3	2	2	2	2	2

Source: taken from the Census for England and Wales (2001: Census table M324).

and Wales. Muslim households are most likely to be living rent free than any other religious group.

Analysis of the 1999 Health Survey found that of the three Muslim groups Bangladeshis are the least likely to own a property outright and 9.5 per cent of these respondents reported this compared with 26 per cent of Pakistanis and 31 per cent of Indian Muslims. Pakistanis were the most likely to be buying with a mortgage or a loan of the three groups, 46 per cent compared with 35.5 per cent of Indians Muslims and 21 per cent of Bangladeshis. Indians have similar proportions renting their homes as they do owning outright and owning with a mortgage. Bangladeshis however are highly concentrated in the 'renting' category, with 67 per cent of this group renting their homes, compared with a quarter of Pakistanis and almost a third of Indian Muslims.

The data illustrate that proportionately more Muslims live in social rented accommodation than any other faith group and are twice as likely to rent their homes within the private sector as all people nationally. Amongst Muslims, Pakistanis are the least likely of the three Muslim groups to rent their homes and most likely to be owner

Figure 5.3: Percentage of Muslims within each tenure category.

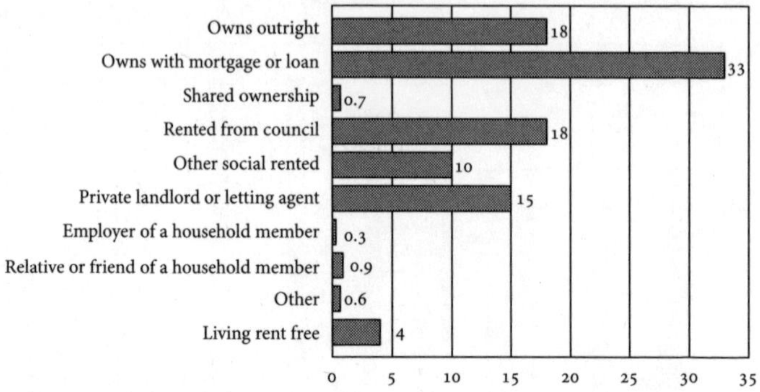

Source: taken from the Census for England and Wales (2001: Census table M324).

occupiers. In terms of tenure Pakistanis have a closer profile to Indian Muslims than Bangladeshis and the step like gradient described in the previous section changes order.

District Level Analysis

District level analysis shows that unlike owner occupiers, for whom the data is slightly negatively skewed (as most districts fall between the 40 to 60 percent range) data for social renting is positively skewed (most districts are concentrated towards the lower percentage end). This shows that renting is associated more with certain local authorities than with Muslims.[2]

Those with higher proportions in the owner occupier category are more equally distributed throughout England and Wales, whereas Muslims who are social renting appear to be concentrated largely in London, and the data shows that Tower Hamlets, Islington, Camden, Hackney, are the highest 5 districts for Muslims social renting ranging from 40–60 per cent. This is also the case for those living rent free. The areas with the highest concentration of Muslims living rent free are Red car and Cleveland and Gateshead

Are Muslims most likely to live in overcrowded dwellings than all other groups and is there evidence to suggest that Muslims have poorer qualities of housing and amenities when compared with other groups?

In addition to levels of urbanisation the Citizenship Survey also provides data on the desirability of areas in which people live using

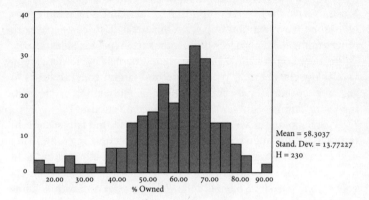

Figure 5.4: shows the distribution of local authorities containing Muslim
households reporting owner occupancy.

Source: taken from the Census for England and Wales (2001: Census table s156).
Local Authorities containing less than 100 Muslim households have been removed from the analysis.

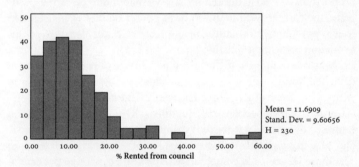

Figure 5.5: shows the distribution of local authorities containing Muslim
households reporting renting from council.

Source: taken from the Census for England and Wales (2001: Census table s156).
Local Authorities containing less than 100 Muslim households have been removed from the analysis.

ACORN (A Classification Of Residential Neighbourhoods) categories. Muslims have the highest proportion of households in 'multi ethnic high unemployment and overcrowding' areas both compared with other groups and compared with all other area types for Muslims. The figure, over 16 per cent is also the highest percentage for any group within any classification type. The second largest concentrations in any area type are 14 per cent for Hindus in 'multi ethnic home owning young families' and Jews in 'mature well off suburbs'.

When looking at Muslims specifically, the second largest concentration is within 'multi ethnic large families overcrowding' with 10 per cent followed by 'multi occupied terraces in multi ethnic areas' with 8 per cent. The fourth highest figure is 6 per cent in 'multi ethnic severe unemployed lone parents' followed by 5.5 per cent within 'home owning multi ethnic young families' and 5 per cent within 'multi ethnic areas, White collar workers'. What is most noticeable from this data is that Muslims have the highest concentrations within some of the most disadvantaged and overcrowded neighbourhood types as categorised by ACORN.

In the section above it was argued that tenure type alone is insufficient in indicating the degree of housing success or deprivation. Here it was argued that the type of area or neighbourhood as well as accommodation type should also be considered. Even though high proportions of Pakistanis and Indians were found to be owner occupiers, the former were found to have poorer quality of housing. As well as providing information on tenure, the Census also provides information on accommodation type.[3]

Muslims demonstrate the lowest percentage of people residing in detached houses or bungalows. This figure is 10 per cent compared with 25 per cent of all people nationally, and have the second lowest proportion of people, after Buddhists, living in a semi-detached house or bungalow, 22 per cent compared with 37 per cent nationally. Muslims have the highest proportion of people living in terraced accommodation when compared with all groups, with 36 per cent of Muslims having this accommodation type compared with 26 per cent of all people. The lowest proportion of people living in terraced accommodation is 10 per cent for Jews. Muslims are third most likely to live in a purpose built flat, after Jews and Buddhists, fifth most likely in a flat which is part of a converted or shared house and fourth most likely to live in a flat which is part of a commercial building.

When broken down by occupation class (table M317) Muslims still have the highest proportion of people living in terraced accommodation compared to all other groups in the same occupation class, however the proportions are lower for Muslims in the higher classes than for Muslims in the lower classes. 25 per cent of Muslims in higher managerial and professional occupations live in terraced accommodation compared with 41 per cent of Muslims within semi-routine occupations for example. The purchasing of cheap urban housing by some groups as described in the section above is clearly represented in the data on Muslims. There still appears to be a preference for this type of accommodation when compared with other groups regardless of class.

Shared Dwellings

Data from the 2001 Census (table S159) found that Muslims have the second largest percentage of households, after Buddhists, living in shared dwellings. The percentage of Muslims in shared dwellings is over three times that for all households nationally. A shared dwelling is defined by the Census as 'part of a converted or shared house' where not all the rooms, including toilet and bathroom are behind a door that only one household can use. There also must be at least one other household space at that address at which it can be combined to form a shared dwelling (Census output prospectus, 2001: 4).

Figure 5.8 on dependent children provides information on whether children live in households where they have sole use of a bath and/or shower and toilet. No more than 1 per cent of all groups do not have the sole use of these amenities; however findings show that Muslims are most likely not to have the sole use of such amenities of all the religious groups, although closely followed by Buddhists. In this regard Muslim children are over four times more likely to share than children in all households nationally. Given the higher proportion of Muslim households living in shared dwellings this is perhaps to be expected.

Central Heating

Muslim households are the least likely to have central heating in their homes, that is 12 per cent of Muslims compared with 8 per cent of all households and 4 per cent Jewish and Hindu households who have the lowest figure for all groups.

When looking at Muslims at local authority level, the data on central heating is positively skewed. Those locations with percentages of households without central heating ranging from 30 per cent to 40 per cent – Bradford, Leeds and Pendle are outliers or at a substantial distance away from the range for the majority of locations. Here tenure

Figure 5.6: Percentage of people living in accommodation within each occupancy rating by religion.

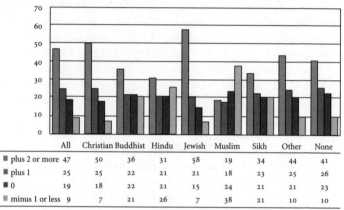

	All	Christian	Buddhist	Hindu	Jewish	Muslim	Sikh	Other	None
■ plus 2 or more	47	50	36	31	58	19	34	44	41
▨ plus 1	25	25	22	21	21	18	23	25	26
■ 0	19	18	22	21	15	24	21	21	23
▨ minus 1 or less	9	7	21	26	7	38	21	10	10

Source: taken from the Census for England and Wales (2001: Census table S159).

type could play a key part. In the previous section literature discussed suggested that those home owners with terraced houses were often living in a poorer quality of accommodation than those renting from the social rented sector. The fact that social rented property is maintained by an outside body could explain why areas such as London, with higher concentrations of Muslims living in social rented accommodation do not have the highest percentages reporting homes without central heating.

Overcrowding

Over crowding and poor housing was also discussed in the section above.[4] Muslims have the highest percentage of households with the highest rating of overcrowding when compared to all religious groups, and more than four times the national figure.

Although overcrowding, when looking at district level is normally distributed for Muslims, the areas with the highest concentrations of overcrowding are found in London. The local authorities with the highest percentages of children living in occupancy rating of -1 or less are Tower Hamlets, Camden, Westminster, Islington and Southwark ranging from 74 per cent to 63 per cent. Here it appears that areas with the highest proportions of Muslims living in social rented accommodation also have the highest percentages of people living in overcrowded accommodation. This is another example as with central heating, where tenure type appears to be associated with certain

Figure 5.7: Map showing proportions of Muslims living in overcrowded accommodation (occupation rating - 1) by Local Authority in England and Wales

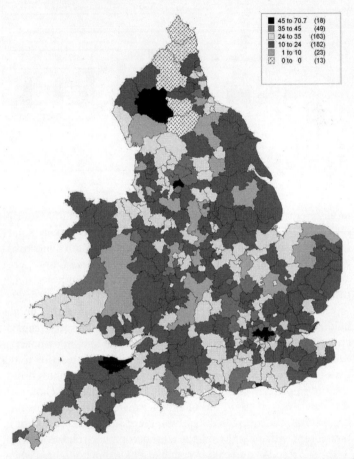

Local authorities represented by 'zero' are outliers due to smaller numbers of Muslim residents within these areas.

types of disadvantage or poverty indicators.

Lowest Accommodation Level

A variable often used as an indicator of the quality and suitability of accommodation is the lowest floor level of a flat or apartment. The table on dependent children shows that Muslims are least likely, after Buddhists to live on the ground or first floor and most likely

Figure 5.8: Percentages of dependent children by accommodation floor level by religion for England and Wales

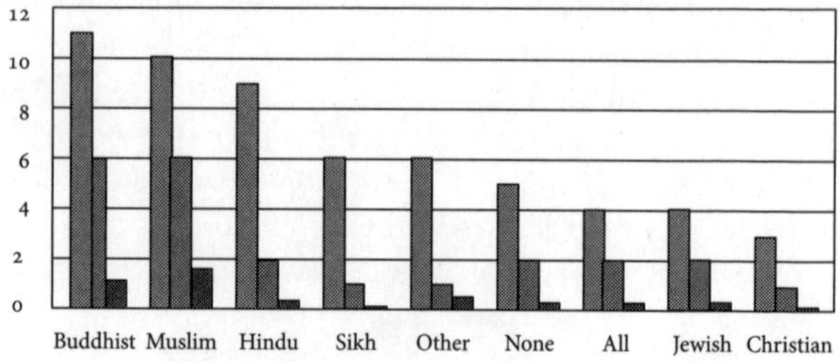

	Buddhist	Muslim	Hindu	Sikh	Other	None	All	Jewish	Christian
■ 1st floor	11	10	9	6	5	5	4	4	3
■ 2nd to 4th floor	6	6	2	1	2	2	2	2	1
■ 5th floor or higher	1.2	1.6	0.4	0.1	0.5	0.3	0.3	0.3	0.2

Source: taken from ONS (2001: Census table T52).

of all groups to live on the second to fourth floor and fifth floor or higher. The figures for these latter two levels are substantially higher for Muslim children than all children. Muslims children living in accommodation on the second to fourth floor are three times higher and those living on the fifth or higher floors are over four times higher than the figure for all children.

The Scottish Census output produced a table measuring household deprivation. 40 per cent of all Muslim households were considered deprived compared with 17 per cent of the total households in Scotland. The figure remained high for Muslim in comparison to the national average even when occupational class was taken into consideration. 24 per cent of Muslim households where the household representative person (HRP) was of a higher managerial or professional occupation was considered deprived, compared with 8 per cent of households with the HRP from the same occupational class nationally. At the other end of the scale, over half of all Muslim household where the HRP was long time unemployed were classed as deprived (55 per cent) compared with 30 per cent for the similar occupational class nationally.

Summary

The literature on housing discussed in the first section suggests that ethnic minorities generally have poorer housing conditions and live in worse areas than households from the White majority with similar demographic profiles. Proportionately Indians fared better in the type of housing and also in the type of location they resided. Although on the surface Pakistanis appeared to fare better than Caribbeans and Bangladeshis in that they have a larger proportion of households with owner occupation, this housing is just as likely to be lacking essential amenities as that of Bangladeshis, suggesting housing tenure makes little positive difference to the quality of housing although of course it can make a difference to possession of total assets. This coupled with the greater likelihood of these communities than all others live in overcrowded premises suggests that a greater proportion of Muslims live in the most disadvantaged housing.

In many aspects the results from the data on Muslims do correspond with finding on the two Muslim ethnic groups studied above. This is particularly the case for poor housing and amenities in which Muslims have the highest proportion of households with overcrowding, the lowest proportion of households with central heating and the highest percentage of children living in accommodation on high floor levels. Where Muslims did not have the highest poverty indicator, they were often second highest after Buddhist and those with 'any other religion'. Muslims are also shown to reside in areas which would suggest poor amenities.

Greater Levels of Need and Lower Service Take Up

At the level of community rather than individual, Berthoud (1998) argues that evidence shows the resources available to Britain's ethnic minorities vary widely from one group to another. In this section a brief outline of issues relating to income will be provided to demonstrate levels of need. A brief exploration of employment will also be provided.

The 2001 National Census data however will be particularly useful in unpicking some of the issues relating to those who are in employment, such as the types of industries Muslims are most concentrated in and whether these are traditionally areas with lower salaries.

The main purpose here is to demonstrate that Muslims, due to their lower levels of income and higher numbers of dependents, are a community that should be prime candidates for services and formal support.

Poverty

In the previous chapter on family structure, when exploring acculturation, figures from the 2001 National Census for England, Wales and Scotland on economic activity were discussed. Muslims

demonstrated the highest levels of economic inactivity when compared with all other groups. When discussing Muslims, literature concerned with employment or rather unemployment focus on Muslim
women and on the two Muslim ethnic groups cited already such as
Dale and Heath (1994) and O'Brien and Husain (2000). Here a brief
discussion on these groups' levels of unemployment will be provided.

In Berthoud's study of household income of ethnic minorities,
when taking out affects of age and family structure for the analysis,
comparing like with like, Africans, like Pakistanis and Bangladeshis
were two and a half times more likely to have no earners in the family
than White people.

Blackaby et al. (1999) describe in their study of the differential
unemployment rates of ethnic minority groups, how consistently for
the decade prior to their study the unemployment figures for Britain's
non-White population have been double that of the indigenous population. Just as with the case of educational attainment and housing
profiles however, when broken down by specific ethnic categories,
the various non-White groups show different employment profiles.
As described in their work,

> Ethnic minorities have experienced higher levels of unem-
> ployment than Whites yet a striking feature is that diversity of
> experience across minority groups. Pakistanis/Bangladeshis
> generally have experienced the highest levels of unemploy-
> ment; roughly double that of the Indian group. (p. 2)

In Enneli et al.'s (2005) study of Turkish speaking communities
(TSCS), it was found that 36 per cent of males and 28 per cent of females experienced unemployment for over 20 month periods. 55 per
cent of the Kurdish people interviewed for the study experienced 3 or
more spells of unemployment for this period. The overwhelming majority of Turkish speaking people interviewed, who were employed,
were in unskilled occupations and only 7 per cent were managers
or professionals. The study found that there is clearly an ethnic en-
clave with most young people reporting their most recent job to be in
a small shop or superstore, with the employer most often a relative.
Poor employment prospects have been reported by studied of other
Muslim minority groups also, including high levels of unemployment
among Somalis (Harris 2004; Khan and Jones 2002) and highly qualified and skilled Arabs, Bosnians, Turks and Somalis who worked as
professionals prior to their arrival in Britain (Mehmet Ali 2001; Dick
2002; Al-Jalili 2004).

Ethnic Penalty

Several theoretical issues are raised when discussing the possession of wealth or the persistence of disadvantage through differential labour market participation for minorities. Human capital amongst these is a key area and much has been made of education as a means of tackling racial disadvantage in order to accelerate social mobility (Berthoud 2000) however expectations, alienation, stereotyping and the greater discrimination of some groups are also areas discussed. Crucially it has been found that disadvantage remains after controlling for a range of individual and area factors. At the forefront of minority labour market progress and participation is the discussion of 'ethnic penalties'. Cheng and Heath describe ethnic penalties as referring to, 'All sources of disadvantage that might lead an ethnic group to fare less well in the labour market than to similarly qualified Whites' and that 'discrimination is likely to be the major component' (1993: 1).

The FNSEM (1994) found that 20 per cent of non-White respondents believed they had been refused a job because of their ethnicity and nearly half of those reporting this claimed to have had such an experience in the five years prior to the survey.

There have been several studies exploring this using empirical data (Owen 1997; Fieldhouse and Gould 1998; Brown 2000). The theoretical basis for such analysis is that an individual's job prospects will be affected by their ability or human capital, which is measured by their qualifications. The most commonly used indirect approach towards determining the impact of discrimination, while controlling for individual characteristics is multivariate regression analysis.

Two studies using data from the Labour Force Survey found that although all ethnic minority groups suffered an ethnic penalty these weren't at the same rate. It has in the past been suggested that Caribbean men especially faced an ethnic penalty, however as Berthoud found African, Pakistani and Bangladeshis were in a very similar position. And he wrote 'Part but only a small part of disadvantage in the labour market could be explained on the basis of the relatively low educational qualifications achieved earlier in life: degree for degree, A-level for A-level young Pakistani and Bangladeshi men were worse off than their White equivalents' (2000: 412). Carmichael and Woods (2000) also found that all minority groups under study were more likely to be unemployed than equally qualified Whites, however Pakistani and Bangladeshi males suffered the highest penalty and Indian males the smallest. In addition analysis of similarly qualified candidates for courses in higher education it was discovered that Caribbean and Pakistani students had lower chances of entry to the red brick and more prestigious universities (Modood et al. 1997).

Carmichael and Woods (2000) argue that penalties vary considerably between minority groups. For their analysis they used maximum likelihood methods to demonstrate that ethnic penalties experienced by minorities are not fully explained by differences in human capital and personal characteristics. They concluded that at least some of the disadvantage experienced by ethnic minorities can be credited to discriminatory selection practice by employers. Becker (1971) wrote extensively on the economic study of discrimination, in which he argued that employers discriminate, sometimes even subconsciously, justifying this on beliefs about an individual simply not being 'right' for a job because he or she didn't share common lifestyles or personal aspirations with the employer and therefore the employer feeling as though the position would be in safer hands with someone who they believed had a similar mind set. Here it is argued that this is more to do with culture than qualifications. Carmichael and Woods write, 'They (recruitment decisions) are likely to be justified in terms of subjective interpretations about who is more qualified than whom and supported by statements such as "she wasn't right for the job" or "he wouldn't fit in." ' (2000: 72).

Becker also argues that when hired the discriminated group are paid a wage lower than their actual productivity. Discrimination in selection processes is therefore consistent with lower occupational status as well as higher unemployment and lower average earnings for ethnic minorities. This certainly fits in with descriptions of Muslim graduates who managed to gain employment within successful companies but who felt that they did not fit in with the 'office culture', were unable to participate in many aspects of 'team building' particularly where they are limited in socialising with colleagues or felt uncomfortable with the pub lunches and after work business dinner venues.

Finding such as those discussed above raise the prospect that culturally determined group characteristics other than colour may be influencing the relative penalties and therefore disadvantage of minority groups. For South Asians in particular researchers adopting a more anthropological approach have emphasised the importance of language, caste and religion in determining group identity and discrimination (Robinson 1986; Ballard 1994).

Blackaby et al. (1997b) suggest that the higher rates of unemployment for some groups may be more socially damaging than simple wage inequality. There are arguments regarding groups who are aware that they face greater levels of marginalisation and differential incorporation resulting in a loss of desire for social mobility within a society which is viewed as alien. Young men who see themselves as being denied jobs on grounds of their ethnicity may adopt alternative lifestyles in which resentment of the social structure can lead to conflict with the establishment (Smith 1991). This can have early effects in the case of labelling and self-fulfilling prophecies within schools has most commonly been discussed with regards to Caribbean boys (Mac an Ghaill 1988). Cross (1994) has pursued this line of enquiry however he argues that unlike Caribbean's, Pakistanis and Bangladeshis have not become politically alienated as a result of economic marginalisation. In this view the latter two groups are still committed to socio-economic progress and this will eventually take place via investment in human capital acquisition as with other South Asian groups. However Modood et al. (1997) argue that this, 'grossly understates the current scale of the disadvantage of Pakistanis and Bangladeshis, and takes no account either of cultural differences between South Asians, or political alienation sometimes expressed in terms of a political Muslim identity' (p. 247).

Blackaby et al. found that the presence of educational qualifications for Pakistanis and Bangladeshis did not reduce the probability of unemployment to as great and extent as it did for other groups, such as African Caribbeans, for whom the presence of qualifications had the most positive impact. This would suggest that when comparing like with like, some groups, in this case the two Muslim subgroups, do still appear to face greater barriers into employment than other non-White groups. As Blackaby et al. point out,

> The considerable differences between the predominately Muslim Pakistani/Bangladeshi and the predominately non-Muslim Indian communities were the particular examples designed to illustrate the fact that it is not simply a matter of a fixed amount of White prejudice directed against all. (p. 27)

Discrimination is clearly a factor for the lack of success some groups find within the labour market. However it is not yet obvious whether discrimination is the only or even main factor in differential unemployment rates and commentators have argued that other factors should also be explored when trying to understand the differential positions for Muslim groups.

Economic Geography

A common argument for higher rates of unemployment among Muslims is that of the unequal impact the decline certain industries had on producing long term unemployment among some communities. As Iganski and Payne (1999) argue,

> The outcome [of economic restructuring] has taken different forms, according to people's employment status, industry, geographical location, age, occupational class and gender. That this had a differential impact on ethnic groups would seem naturally to follow. (pp. 195–196)

Key variables in this differential impact for the Muslim groups were industry and geographical location. Many Muslims communities are concentrated in areas which faced the greatest decline of traditional industries, meaning that they were among the most severely affected in terms of loss of jobs. This coupled with the fact that the majority of these communities had no formal training or skills (human capital) meant that they were unable to find opportunities in other sectors. This led to long term unemployment.

There have also been debates surrounding the extent to which such communities actually strive towards their betterment in terms of increasing human capital, through the pursuit of education and training. The fact that many British Pakistanis and Bangladeshis, regardless of their levels of poverty in a British setting are far more financially advanced than some of the communities they left behind could be taken as evidence that relatively speaking these communities are content with their lot or tolerate their position believing that they will not succeed through traditional means and see themselves on the fringes of society.

Thomas (1998) when looking to explore explanations for higher rates of unemployment amongst some communities attempted to measure how cultural or neighbourhood sociological models of behaviour impacted on differential unemployment rates. In this view, in response to discrimination and low employment opportunities, some communities have become comparatively more tolerant of joblessness. Thomas writes

> Many live in communities where unemployment is prevalent among their peers which engenders forms of what psychologists call 'resigned adapting' with restricted aspirations and a decreased desire for work. This is reinforced by the high probability that employment may not result in any financial gain compared to the benefit or other non-market income ... as joblessness becomes less extraordinary, the incentive to

acquire human capital and skills to help offset discrimination becomes less important.' (p. 139)

In this view some communities accept their position and show little will, motivation or belief in their abilities to change their employment status.

Thomas used attitudinal data to assess whether there is a correlation between attitudes towards living conditions and employment and actual employment status. The data showed that higher unemployment rates among minority groups such as Pakistanis and Bangladeshis could not be explained by attitude or behaviour and lack of aspirations within these communities. Thomas describes this,

> Using a hazard model we test one central implication of this culture-based view; namely, that excess minority unemployment spells can be explained, at least partially by such attitudes. However our findings run counter to this prediction. Not only are ethnic spell differentials more robust to the inclusion of attitudes but they actually widen. (p. 148)

Blackaby et al. (1999) explain the higher levels of Muslim unemployment as a combination of higher levels of discrimination in society towards these group and responses to discrimination in the form of 'isolation'. In this view Muslims remain more 'enclaved' and that isolation has more to do with choice than necessity, although the presence of racism and hostility would intensify any such inclination. A result of such isolation is that these groups can not participate fully within society. This view is in keeping with the negative impact of bonding social capital as discussed by Browning at al. (2000), a concept further explored later in this chapter. It was argued that there is a threat that such communities by remaining 'insular' and isolated can reproduce social disadvantage instead of promoting mobility.

Although it would be possible to find numerous examples of this I would argue that this view is over simplistic. Rather than a result of straight forward choice, as argued in the above section on housing when discussing choice versus restraint, Muslim communities clearly began their lives as communities in Britain with less human capital and therefore less opportunities were available to them as a result. This has clearly impacted on the position of second and subsequent generations within the labour market, however as discussed in the chapter on education, Muslims do demonstrate a drive to increase their qualifications and as a result, employability. If discrimination is a greater factor for Muslims it is within the process of admission to better institutions, recruitment for vacancies and 'burn out' experienced by Muslims once slotted into main stream industries, rather than a prompt for Muslims to remain more introverted, isolated and less willing to participate through traditional means of increasing human capital.

Family Income

The variations in household structure lead to differences in household income and expenditure. In particular the majority of lone parent families in Britain are claiming basic social security benefits and have low incomes. This is likely to affect the welfare of Caribbean families. The large household sizes in Muslim communities could increase the potential number of workers bringing in an income; on the other hand, it means an increase in the number of people depending on that income (Berthoud 1998). It has already been argued that Muslims have the highest levels of economic inactivity and with higher numbers of dependents it follows that Muslim families will be proportionally more dependent on state benefit as their primary source of income.

In Berthoud's study he found that non-working families with children are over three times more likely to have an income below the poverty line than working families with children (75 per cent compared with 22 per cent). In his analysis the more weight that was attached to additional household members the more households fell below the poverty line. If extra people, including children, living in the same household are assumed each to require almost as much income as a single person living alone, three quarters of Pakistanis and Bangladeshis were found to be in poverty.

State benefits are an important source of income for some groups in particular. Child Benefit is paid to all parents regardless of their employment status or income. The distribution of Child Benefit between minority groups mirrors the presence of children. Berthoud's analysis showed that two fifths of White families compared to two thirds of Pakistani and Bangladeshi families were in receipt of Child Benefit. However, very few ethnic minority couples with children received means tested benefits. Pakistani and Bangladeshis were particularly noticeable in this respect, with only 29 per cent of two parent families in this group claiming Family Credit.

Housing Benefit and Council Tax rebates were also of some importance for Pakistanis and Bangladeshis with children and also for

African two parent families. However, it was found that such families were still extremely disadvantaged and that the welfare effect is
simply not strong enough. Ginn and Arber's (2001) research found
that due to a combination of low private pension coverage, high rates
of unemployment, and the types of occupations some ethnic groups
have higher levels of employment within, Pakistani and Bangladeshis
women particularly, will be disproportionately dependent on means-
tested benefits in later life.

More than a quarter of Pakistani and Bangladeshi working families had a net income lower than their family needs. Even the combination of earnings and in-work benefits had not protected this group
from poverty. For unemployed families the figure was more than
half. Most strikingly, Berthoud's analysis found that working Pakistani and Bangladeshi families had a greater chance of poverty than
non-working White families.

Despite lower household incomes and higher numbers of dependents, Blakemore (2000) argues the reality is that groups are thrown
back on their own recourses when faced with the needs of their own
dependents. The lack of amenities makes it more difficult to care for
the old and frail and other dependents.

In a study by Radcliffe (1997) the key facilities that helped families
provide care, such as ownership of a vehicle, accommodation that is
not overcrowded and central heating have been found to be amenities
Bangladeshi and Pakistani families lack the most. This coupled with
higher child dependency rates make it difficult for some families to
cope with the extra demands of caring for elderly relatives, especially
if the older relatives are suffering from a long term illness or their
consequences, such as disability resulting from a stroke.

Lacking amenities have also been highlighted as 'practical barriers' for some families in accessing services (Becher and Husain 2003).
Pankaj (2000) identified in how issues of location of services and dis-
tances families may have to travel to reach services are more problematic for those without access to vehicles and especially so for those
with large numbers of dependent children and other family members
to care for. In addition Butt and Box's (1998) survey of 84 family centres found that the majority of centres were not accessible to families
in need from 'Black' communities.

What the Data Demonstrates

It has already been noted in the previous chapter that Muslims, both
men and women report higher proportions of economic inactivity

than all other groups. Clearly with the higher proportions of children it would follow that a larger percentage of women and men would be taking care of the home and family and this is the case. However when looking at those who are unemployed[5] in younger age cohorts, Muslims show differentiation by age and sex. Census table s153 covers those in England and Wales aged 16–74. It further differentiates by age (16–24 and 25–74) and sex. When looking at Muslims, both those in the first age cohort and the older age cohort report the highest proportions of people who are economically inactive and unemployed.

Economic Inactivity and Unemployment

When looking at economic inactivity Muslim males in the younger cohort report the third highest proportion (51 per cent compared with 32 per cent nationally) and Muslim females share the highest position with Buddhist females with 64 per cent.

Muslim males in the 25–74 bracket report the highest proportions for economic inactivity. Muslim women in this age cohort also report the highest proportion of economically inactivity and this figure is significantly larger than all groups with 71 per cent compared with a national average of 41 per cent and the lowest figure for those reporting no religion with 30 per cent.

The proportions of Muslim when differentiated by sex within the younger cohort presents a marginally more promising picture in that Muslim males do not have the highest proportion of economic inactivity.

Unemployment

When looking at Muslim males and females separately in the younger age cohorts they share the highest figure for unemployment with those reporting 'any other religion', 9 per cent for males and 5 per cent for females.

Muslim males in the 25–74 bracket report the highest proportions for unemployed (3 times greater than the national average) Muslim women in this age cohort, along with Buddhists, Sikh, Hindu and those with 'any other religion' have the highest proportion of unemployed (twice that of the national average).

Therefore in terms of both economic inactivity and unemployment Muslims report higher proportions compared with the national average. The issue of unemployment is important in that those within this category are 'actively seeking employment'. It would follow that less Muslim women would be actively seeking employment given their child care responsibilities. However Muslim men who are seeking employment are not only the least likely to have been successful in obtaining employment but 3 times less likely to be so than the national average.

Types of Employment and Earning Potential

As well as having lower percentages of economic activity and higher proportions of unemployment, the 2001 Census data (s153) has also found that Muslims are concentrated in certain industries and in some of the lowest paid occupations.

In terms of industry type Muslims are most highly concentrated in retail trade, restaurants, health and social work, 'Other business activities' and education. When broken down further however it is possible to see areas in which Muslims have higher concentrations than the national average. These include some more 'prosperous' categories such as restaurant and catering managers, software professionals, medical practitioners, chartered and certified accountants and civil service administrators and assistants. However the largest percentage differences begin to appear in areas such as cooks, sales assistants/retail cashiers/check out operators, process plant and machine operatives, assemblers and routine operatives, sewing machinists, taxi; cab drivers, labourers in foundries, waiting staff and security guards and related occupations.

In terms of occupational class Muslims are most highly concentrated in the lowest social classes. Clearly as there was a polarisation shown Chapter Three, it would be expected that there are concentrations of Muslims within some of the professional occupations and this has been demonstrated by the breakdown of industry type. However as also expected there are higher concentrations of Muslims in the manual and service industries also. These data provides an interesting insight into the types of industries Muslims have entered either by choice or accessibility.

Summary

The higher rates of economic inactivity found amongst Muslims will clearly impact on family income, this coupled with the larger average family sizes means that Muslims are at a greater risk of poverty.

The higher levels of economic inactivity found among Muslim women is also clearly a contributor to the economic position of Muslims in comparison to other groups.

Higher rates of unemployment amongst some communities have

already been discussed and a core element of the debate on differential levels of unemployment is discrimination within the labour market. As a result of an EU directive[6], there is now legislation within the UK which outlaws discrimination in employment and training of grounds of religion. This covers recruitment, appointment, any treatment during employment and dismissal. However as with other legislation the real test will be in areas of indirect discrimination, which in effect requires employers to consider reasonable accommodation of the observation of faith within the workplace. The aim here is to counter practices which do not overtly discriminate against Muslims, but have a negative impact on members of this community.

Family Services

A study of the literature on minority community disadvantage would be lacking an essential area of focus if it were not to discuss services provision for ethnic minority families and children. Service provision can cover all statutory bodies, however to explore each area of provision and each type of service (be it hospital care, care of state 'looked after' children or respite facilities for parents of disabled children) would require far greater discussion than the scope this chapter is able to provide. Due to the importance of the issue of service provision for ethnic minority families, an overview of some of the key discussions focusing on areas with particular reference to Muslims will be covered within this section.

One key area of debate within the area of families and services is the low take up of services by ethnic minorities. As will be discussed later in this section, some communities, including Muslims, have higher levels of poverty indicators, suggesting greater need and support from outside formal services (Beer 2004).

In O'Neale's (2000) study of service provision for ethnic minority families and children, an inspection of eight Local Authorities with substantial numbers of non-White communities was conducted. One of the primary objectives of the study was to understand why Pakistani, Bangladeshi and the Caribbean families, despite facing greater pressures, (such as higher numbers of dependents or higher proportions of lone parent families and lower incomes and amenities), had a lower take up rates for family support services than the White community.

O'Neale's study has been supported by other research which has identified ethnic minorities as being underrepresented in terms of usage of community support services such as day care facilities

(Blakemore 2000). In addition, research by Bywaters et al. (2003) on ethnic minority parents of children with impairments also found that there was low service take up by these parents in comparison to parents of White disabled children. An important finding in this study, however, was that some ethnic minority families did request respite support in a variety of kinds other than overnight care away from home, such as day time care in the school holidays or care support at home, but these services had not been made available. In short, the authors found little evidence that it was the families' lack of willingness to share the care of their children that resulted in low uptake. The services offered were either not fully articulated to the parents or were found to be inappropriate.

Cultural inappropriateness is a key feature in literature when discussing low take up. In addition to this however, are debates surrounding discriminatory service provision more generally. Bywaters et al. study found evidence of discriminatory and stereotypical attitudes among personnel working in services for families and children. Bywaters et al. argued that acknowledging the existence of such attitudes is particularly important as some service providers have simply dismissed the issue of low service use by some groups as being more related to group preferences than any other factor. With this in mind a great deal of care is required when discussing group preferences, as often there appears to be a strong element of directing blame towards the victim and thus deflecting attention away from institutional discrimination. Preferences and need will be discussed in greater detail under communities in need and the group preferences headings.

From a service provision perspective therefore, three main areas are explored when examining low take up: discriminatory conduct, cultural inappropriateness, and lack of communication or successful targeting of information. From a community perspective, the issue of preferences and availability of informal support are highlighted.

In O'Neale's report some of the families under study reported that they felt some workers had stereotypical views about ethnic minorities, however it was also reported that there were workers who behaved in a sensitive manner and who were willing to do their best for clients. One area which was highlighted in the report was that in some of the authorities there was a reluctance to sufficiently utilise family support systems by ethnic minority groups.

This has also been supported by Ochieng (2002) in her study on family centred care. Here it is argued that staff dealing with ethnic minority families do not fully appreciate or understand the family dynamics in play. For example, one worker refused to place children with their grandparents because they felt the accommodation was inadequate. The children were placed with foster carers whose accommodation had the same number of bedrooms and were felt to be inadequate by the parents of the children. The placement was found to be unsympathetic to the religious needs of the children. It was felt here that social workers should have given greater consideration to the first option of placement with grandparents. The onus of good quality service provision often fell on individual workers. This means that better monitoring of staff decisions and increasing the level and quality of training on culturally specific responses to such issues is imperative. Ansari also supports this view, he writes,

> Cultural barriers in Health and Social Services can also disadvantage ethnic minority groups, including Muslims. Instances of discrimination raise concerns that neither Health nor Social Services departments adequately meet the needs of Muslims in Britain. (2002: 18)

O'Neale's report demonstrates that all but one of the Local Authorities lacked any kind of monitoring of staff decisions in terms of service provision for ethnic minorities,

> We found that whilst authorities had anti-racist and equal opportunities policies and strategies there was little evidence that they had been implemented. There was only one council that had taken race issues seriously. Many authorities talked about 'mainstreaming' the issues, but in practice this often meant that no one took responsibility for them and they were ignored.

Furthermore on the monitoring of information on service users there appeared to be lack of clarity about what should be collected, by whom and more importantly why it should be collected at all, 'This basic lack of understanding of the rationale for ethnic monitoring by some has led to their services for ethnic minority families being poorly planned, poorly delivered and poorly considered at a strategic level' (O'Neale 2000:43).

The study acknowledged that whilst ethnicity in various forms is recorded by most councils across the country, language and religion to a lesser extent is documented. This is of course particularly important for Muslims, for example when considering placement issues for children who are looked after.

Understanding religious needs of families and children is essential in providing culturally appropriate services. Becher et al. (2003) write, 'Previous research has repeatedly highlighted the importance of 'cultural sensitivity' in providing services for minority ethnic groups. However, within this broader theme, the importance of religious sensitivity has received less attention' (p. 8).

Failure to provide placements which recognised the religious needs of children was highlighted in O'Neale's study. Some young people were concerned that staff in residential units who were atheists did not fully support and encourage them to fulfil their religious duties.

O'Neale's study also reveals mixed levels of satisfaction with the range and type of service provided with regards to religious adherence. There were concerns about how religious needs of children were being met. A frequently quoted example was the unavailability of halal meat. There were some children's homes that would provide halal meat for everyone, however, this was most likely to be the case for those with higher numbers of Muslims in the locality.

Vydelingum (2000) also argued that areas of dissatisfaction found in his study of hospital services and after care provision, 'have similarly been reported previously (and) consistently demonstrated levels of dissatisfaction with utilisation of hospital services by South Asian patients in relation to the provision of meals to meet religious needs' (p. 104).

It is clear from Muslims' interpretation on Islam being a way of life, that religious considerations are imperative when providing appropriate services for these communities. As O'Neale writes,

> The 1989 Children Act (section 22(5) (c)) is clear that on issues of service delivery councils should 'give due consideration to the child's religious persuasion, racial origins and cultural and linguistic backgrounds'. This Act has not been repealed nor has the guidance changed. There was therefore an expectation that close attention would be given to such issues. (p. 15)

In addition to monitoring, consultation with ethnic minority families was identified by the report as being a key means for providing appropriate service provision. Although it was felt that there was a good representation of ethnic minority staff in the authorities, the report highlighted that most authorities had poor consultation histories with ethnic minority communities themselves.

The presence of staff from minority communities has been highlighted as a potential issue for caution when addressing the subject of representation by Johns (2004) in his study of ethnic diversity policy perceptions within the National Health Service. Here it is argued that there is a significant danger that by hiring staff to deal with ethnic diversity, White professionals can wipe their hands of minority issues. It is not sufficient to assume that staff from a particular community will either have the inclination, want or ability to assist with minority issues.

Johns points out several flaws with such assumptions. Firstly it was found through his interviews with NHS employees that there were suspicions regarding some staff misusing their influence to attain their goals under the guise of a community representative. Secondly there is research to suggest that successful individuals from minority communities in other fields do not always feel an affinity or want to take on the responsibility of assisting the betterment of the community from which they originate (Young 2000). Thirdly Johns argues that there can be a clash of identities, the professional or class identity versus the ethnic identity. Here it is argued that some professionals choose to ally themselves with the culture of their profession rather than of their ethnic background.

This can allow for complacency and the attachment of blame by service providers when it comes to dealing with diversity and community consultations, as Johns writes, 'The message appears to be, "If you want a better service it is your responsibility". However when a better service fails to emerge due to marginalisation or individual choices, it will allow policy makers to underline deviance of minority ethnic cultures. Even 'they; cannot solve the problems they present' (p. 85).

Targeted information provision was also an area that appeared to be problematic. O'Neale argued that families seeking support often experienced difficulty in accessing services because they did not understand the role of Social Services, particularly if English was not their first language. Bywaters et al. study supported this argument, they write, 'Lack of information about or experience of appropriate services was likely to be the main reason why parents had what might be described as low expectations' (p. 508).

In their study of Pakistani and Bangladeshi families, Bywaters et al. (2003) also found that many parents had very little idea about what caused their child's disability and impairments. The study argued that there was clear evidence of the impact of language barriers to understanding with the absence of interpreters in many medical consultations. In addition he argued that parents were also missing essential support and information by voluntary organisations. There was no evidence of any of the families in this study having been touched by the wider disability rights movement or that they were linked with any organisation of and for families with disabled children. This seems to be further evidence of the predominately White membership and the orientation of the movement.

Social Capital

Social capital has been identified as having many forms yet there are some tenets common to all definitions. For Putman, social capital is about 'features of social organisations, such as networks, norms, and trust that facilitates action and cooperation for mutual benefit.' (1993: 35) For Baker, social capital is 'a resource that actors derive from specific social structures and then use to pursue their interests' (1990: 619). Therefore social capital is particularly relevant when exploring the characteristics of communities and preferences for taking care of themselves autonomously rather than accessing state services due of the emphasis placed by this theory on strong networks and social ties.

Within sociology the actor is seen as socialised and actions as administered by social norms, rules and obligations. The primary asset of viewing the actor in this way is in the ability to explain action in social context and to illustrate the way action is moulded, restricted and transmitted by social context. Definitions of social capital which may be of particular relevance to minority communities are those focussing on family support and the strength within families to promote the internalisation of certain norms. For Coleman families who are intact most likely have the greatest social capital and it is the children from such homes that are the most successful in reaping the benefits of parental investment and support.

It has been pointed out that social relations which lead to positive outcomes for one group of people or in a certain situation do not for another group. Putnam discussed the flip side to bonding social capital and dense communities, in that they often resulted in keeping people outside the community at arms length. There is also a threat that such communities can reproduce social disadvantage instead of promoting mobility. Portes and Zhou (1993) commented on

how residence in inner city communities supported alternative cultural style which can stunt manoeuvrability within wider society. In
addition the tight social control and the transmission of some norms
can stunt certain members opportunities for mobility and betterment,
particularly where control is enforced more rigidly on some rather
than others. Empirical data has found that Pakistani and Bangladeshi
women marry at younger ages than women from other ethnic groups.
There is a strong correlation with age of marriage and educational attainment for these women (Dale et al. 2000) and therefore community encouragement for women from such communities to enter marriages earlier can have a negative effect on their acquisition of human
capital. There is the risk that just as social structures promote the internalisation of norms and provide sanctions to ensure control, some
of these norms and control may well be counterproductive.

Community Preferences?

When discussing low levels of service take up, it was highlighted above
that some service providers view the issue as being more related to
group preferences than any other factor. With particular reference to
Muslims, issues such as preferences for the utilisation of available informal care in the shape of extended family members, is often cited.

Blakemore (2000) argues that stereotypes of extended family life
and minority communities feed the assumption among service plan-
ners and providers that South Asian people are more willing to look
after their own, than the White majority. This is an assumption that
not only relies on the fact that those in need of support have extended
families members at hand, but also that such families members are
willing if able to provide support. In addition, some studies have argued that the presence of extended family members only adds to the
difficulties of those needing additional support, for example young
mothers who care for elder family members as well as young children
(Pels 2000; Ginn and Arber 2001).

Despite the fact that presence of extended families should not be
relied on by service providers to offer the support they are meant to,
some studies have shown that extended family support can be extremely beneficial within some communities as has been argued by
Coleman (1998) when discussing social capital. Hackett et al. (1991)
attributed the greater well being of South Asian children to structural
features of the traditional Asian family. They suggest that the protec-
tive nature of South Asian families generally and extended families in
particular promotes psychological well being in children.

This is in line with the large body of literature that suggests

that extended family living is beneficial for children. This traditional
extended family type holds benefits for other dependents also, such
as grandparents. Mistry (2000) argues that in those studies in which
South Asian adults do display higher levels of disorder than their indigenous counterparts, this tends not to be reflected in the well being
of their children who are often better adjusted than their classmates.

Although the above studies demonstrate that extended families
can be beneficial for their members in a variety of ways; what is also
emphasised is that this most certainly is not always the case and therefore should not be assumed to be a valid reason for low take up of
services. Furthermore whether or not such informal care appears to
be successful in the maintenance of dependents, the expectations on
women in particular (either by family members or service providers)
to provide such care could be unfair if not detrimental. This is keeping
with definitions of negative social capital discussed above.

Unfair Burden?

When exploring the issue of informal care in minority communities Ginn and Arber (2001) argue that due to the higher rates of unemployment among economically active Pakistanis and Bangladeshi
women (being even higher than among their male counterparts)
some service providers conclude that despite problems of poverty, the
presence of these women at home implies a plentiful supply of potential carers. The paper points out several objections to this argument.
Firstly it cannot be assumed that traditional expectations of uncon-
ditional support for older people will or should be maintained indef-
initely.

In a survey carried out by Blakemore (2000) of public sector organisations working with ethnic minority elderly people, he found
that 91 per cent of organisations included statements which pointed
to losses of family support within the previous 5 years to the survey
being conducted. There were other signs identified in his study, point-
ing to the changing nature of care for the elderly, such as an increase
in extra familial ways of meeting needs among minority older people.
For example, sheltered housing developments for older couples or for
older people to live alone have met with instant and strong demand. If
traditional norms of joint family residence and the three-generation
household were showing little sign of change, one would expect only
lukewarm demand for housing specifically for older people.

In the above view changes (with regards to family structure
and household composition) may be relatively subtle and gradual,
involving modifications to extended family support for older people,

such as through the non-residential extended family rather than an outright loss of support. However it is important to be aware of signs of change and to consider their significance in relation to assumptions about family members willingness and ability to provide care.

In addition, the 'plentiful supply of care' assumption also implies that older women will be cared for as well as older men. But given the ambivalent or uncertain position that some women occupy in their husbands families (widows with no sons to protect their interests) age in itself is not always the guarantee of devoted care. Such older women are particularly disadvantaged in terms of being able to seek help outside the family if they are ill or distressed (Ginn and Arber 2001).

Another objection pointed out by Ginn and Arber is that this assumption is essentially sexist in that women are expected to shoulder the burden of caring. One study that explores the benefits of extended family living is Mistry's (2000) work on Hindu and Muslim women coping with depression. This paper suggests that extended family living is not beneficial to some family members, namely mothers. Mothers in extended families had significantly higher levels of depression and anxiety than those in nuclear families. In this view, in extended families where social support was likely to be most available, mothers were at greatest risk, while their children profited and this advantage seemed to be linked to the grand maternal presence. Blakemore's study of Muslim parents with disabled children found that only two families were receiving significant support from their extended families, although most were in contact with other adult family members, it was clear that the burden of care again fell largely on the mothers.

In addition, even where women are working, Pels's (2000) study of Muslims living in the Netherlands, demonstrated that employment outside the family hardly effects the division of household tasks. One third of younger generation Muslim women expected help around the house from their husbands and all women saw their husband's primary role as the breadwinner. The important finding here being that men did not help as much as their wives suggested or hoped (see Chapter Four) and this was the case not only with domestic tasks but also with caring for dependants.

Areas for Exploration

In this section it has been argued that Muslim groups such as Pakistanis and Bangladeshis have greater needs due to higher numbers of dependents and higher rates of poverty coupled with poorer living conditions. Yet despite this there are arguments that although their circumstances would suggest greater levels of need for formal support, in reality service take up, as with other minority groups is less than that for White families.

There is a risk that services can be culturally inappropriate, that is, not appropriately catering for needs of some communities or recognising community specific issues, such as the importance of religious practice and therefore providing services that are inadequate in meeting such community needs and at worst discriminatory and/or offensive.

The issue of adequate information delivery and communication with families from such communities was also raised and O'Neale's report described the ambivalence surrounding consultation and monitoring by service providers. Issues to do with poor understanding of information needs can seriously affect communities where not only language barriers are apparent (where English is not the first language) but also where they are less obvious. Bernstein's (1971, 1981) research on restricted codes of speech and the bureaucracy of language is of particular relevance to ethnic minority communities and how those with 'restricted codes' are subsequently treated when seeking advice and information about provision.

Another argument for low service take up is the preference to remain independent from outside authorities and bodies and to deal with problems 'in house'. This has been suggested by some service providers to be the case for South Asians as they are more insular and community oriented. Furthermore it has been argued that South Asian preferences for extended families results in access to assistance from other adult family members, namely women, who are more likely to remain at home rather than partake in formal outside employment.

As already discussed above, Muslim groups, namely Pakistani and Bangladeshis, are associated with higher levels of female economic inactivity, larger families and complex households. Therefore this argument would be seen as especially relevant when explaining the low service take up by Muslims. However, research cited in this section found that extended family support was not always available and in addition due to higher levels of poverty among these communities, amenities were often lacking. Therefore reliance on extended families to provide support or indeed to use a community preference argument for the lower take up of services by Muslims is a problematic one.

Therefore when looking at the above in conjunction with the previous section, there appears to be a strong assertion that coupled with poor quality housing and overcrowding these communities should be prime candidates for service provision.

Is There Evidence That Suggests Muslims Have Lower Take-Up Rates of Services Than a) the Majority Population and b) Other Minority Groups?

There is strong evidence from the Census table s161 that shows Muslims do not utilise medical and care establishments to the same extent as other groups, as they have the lowest proportion in these establishments. However this only covers specific establishments and not day care or drop in centres.

Of the communal establishments listed in s161 there are significant difference in the proportion of people from each faith groups in medical and care communal establishments. 48 per cent of all people who are in communal establishments are in medical and care establishments, this compares with 54 per cent of Christians, who have the highest proportion, to 6 per cent of Buddhist who have the lowest. Muslims also have a significantly lower figure 9 per cent, which is the second lowest. The highest proportions of Muslims who are in such establishments are in NHS hospitals at 4 per cent.

Muslims have the lowest proportion of people in local authority communal establishments (less than 1 per cent compared with 5 per cent of all people). Despite this however the figure for Muslim children in local authority children's homes is the same as the figure nationally for all children.

In both private and local authority nursing homes Muslims have the second lowest proportion of people, 1 per cent compared with 16 per cent of all people in the former. This is also the case with residential care homes, where less than 1 per cent of all Muslims in communal establishments are in local authority residential cares homes and under 2 per cent are in private residential care homes. This compares with 4 per cent of all people in local authority and 21 per cent in private residential care homes.

In other establishments Muslims have the highest proportion of people in hotel, boarding houses and guest houses at 6 per cent and this is double the national percentage. Muslims also have the highest proportion of people in 'Hostels' this includes youth hostels, hostels for the homeless and people 'sleeping rough' and the proportion of Muslims in such establishments is over 4 times greater than the national percentage at 12 per cent.

Proportionately there are more Muslim males than females in communal establishments, 69 per cent and 31 per cent respectively. Muslims have the greatest gender gap across all faith groups in this respect. In medical and care establishments Muslim males and females have very similar proportions of residence. However when percentages of residence in types of communal establishments for Muslim females are compared with females of other faith groups Muslims have the highest percentage of females in NHS establishments with 4 per cent. Amongst males, Hindus have the highest percentage in NHS establishments with nearly 10 per cent. As with the percentage for Muslims as a whole, Muslim males and females have the highest proportions of people in hotel, boarding houses and guest houses and in 'Hostels' including youth hostels, hostels for the homeless and people 'sleeping rough'. For Muslims 6 per cent of all Muslim males and females in communal establishments are in the first category. However there is a higher proportion of Muslim females 14 per cent in the second category than males, 12 per cent.

In many respects Muslims men and women have a similar profile to each other in the proportions living in different types of communal establishments, and the figures are consistently similar which is not the case nationally for males or females. However Muslims do have the largest gender gap over all, in that the majority of Muslims in communal establishments are men.

Seeking Advice

When discussing community preference specifically for the use of services providing support and advice on childcare and related matters data from the 2001 Citizenship Survey found that Muslims, like other groups, stated their preferred sources of advice and information on child rearing came from professionals. Approximately 50 per cent of all groups stated that their GP was one of three preferred sources of advice, and figures for advice from health visitors, nurses and other health professionals was similar for all groups. However two groups had higher figures for preferences for information from religious leaders and organisations, with 25 per cent for Jews and 15 per cent for Muslims. Hindus and Sikhs followed with 8.5 per cent and 7 per cent respectively.

Muslims were amongst the lowest to report the media as a preferred source with only 3 per cent stating this to be the case for magazines and newspapers and 1 per cent for websites and TV and radio.

Sikhs and Christians had the highest percentage reporting schools and colleges as a preferred source jointly with 37 per cent and Muslim had the second largest percentage with 22 per cent again preferring advice and information from professionals. Voluntary organisations were a low preference for all groups and those with no religion had the highest percentage reporting this type of source as a preference with only 4 per cent.

Here it appears that Muslims do value the information and advice from health professionals and those who are believed to be trained to understand child rearing issues such teachers and those working within educational establishments. Religious leaders are also a key source or information and advice however this is also the case for Jews and doesn't appear to undermine the importance placed on other professionals by Muslims and Jews.

Do Muslims Provide More Unpaid Care and Have Stronger Support Networks?

The Census provides information on unpaid care in both the theme table on dependent children, T52 and a commissioned table, M314. The Census defines unpaid carers as,

> A person is a provider of unpaid care if they give any help or support to family members, friends, neighbours or others because of long-term physical or mental health or disability, or problems related to old age. Note that there is no specific reference to whether this care is provided within the household or outside the household. Therefore, no explicit link can be created to infer that an individual providing care is providing it to a person within the household who has poor general health, or a limiting long-term illness, disability or health problem. (Census Definitions 2001: 12)

According to Figure 5.9, proportionately less Muslim provide unpaid care, with 9 per cent, than all other faith groups. However they do provide more care than those reporting no religion, with 7 per cent. The national figure for all people providing care is 10 per cent. Those with 'any other religion' have the highest proportion of people providing unpaid care with 16 per cent.

However of those who provide unpaid care Muslims have the highest percentage of people caring for 50 or more hours per week than any other groups, with 25.5 per cent of Muslim carers compared

Figure 5.9: Percentage of carers providing 50 hours or more of unpaid care per week by religion.

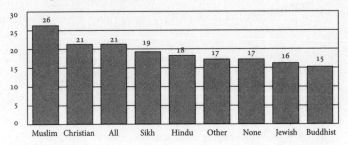

Source: taken from the Census for England and Wales (2001: table M314).

with 21 per cent of all carers nationally.

When broken down by age however 16–24 year old Muslims have the highest proportion of carers in this age band when compared with all groups, 10 per cent compared with 5 per cent nationally. Muslim carers in this age cohort also have the highest proportion of providing care for 50 or more hours per week when compared with all other groups.

For those aged 25–34 Muslims and Sikhs have the highest proportions of carers in this cohort, with 12 per cent of both groups providing care compared with 7 per cent of all people in this age band. Muslims again have the highest proportion of people providing 50 or more hours of care per week. From the ages 35 upwards Muslims decrease in their proportions of carers when compared with all other groups, except those with no religion.

Therefore the figures for unpaid care are not as straight forward as they first appear. Clearly age is a significant factor when looking at who is more likely to be a carer for some groups including Muslims.

Perceived Social Support

Questions regarding attitudes towards social support were included in the health survey. When presented with the statement 'People I know can be relied upon', 69 per cent of Muslims felt that this statement was certainly true for them compared with 62 per cent of Hindus and 66 per cent of Sikhs. Despite close family ties and value placed on altruism these were the lowest three figures answering 'certainly true' across all the groups. 84.5 per cent of Christians answered with the same response, followed by those with other religions (75 per cent) and those with no religion (71 per cent).

Gender differences in responses were taken into account for the analysis of responses to the statement 'People I know will see that I am taken care of'. Here 71 per cent of Muslim men and 68.5 per cent of Hindu and 73 per cent of Sikh men answered certainly true. This compares with 84 per cent Christian males. 75 per cent of Muslim women, 69 per cent of Hindu women and 67 per cent of Sikh women responded with certainly true to this statement. 89 per cent of the total female adult sample responded certainly true and the lowest figure for women responded this way was for Buddhists with 59 per cent.

What is worth noting is that Muslims are not most likely to respond certainly true to these above statements measuring social support, and this is both the case for men and women. Although these results are highly subjective and dependent upon cultural interpretations of what 'care' and 'reliance' consists of they by no means indicate that Muslims feel to a greater degree than any other group of the availability of sufficient social support to ensure they are taken care of and who can be relied upon. This therefore suggests that they would be as dependent on outside formal networks for support as other faith groups.

There are two key areas of discussion however, that cannot be explored further here by using the data. Firstly, to what extent services are culturally appropriate and secondly to what extent do Muslims have greater religious needs than other groups, thus requiring careful planning and consideration, as well of awareness promotion among staff. When examining service take up and needs of Muslims throughout England and Wales, differences in levels of take up could indicate to Local Authorities where examples of good practice or targeted information campaigns have resulted in greater service use by Muslims, however they could also simply reflect greater levels of need among Muslims in certain localities.

Conclusion

This chapter set out to discuss the levels of disadvantage faced by Muslims and whether as a group Muslims were more deprived than other faith groups. In doing so an exploration of key housing concerns for minority groups, and more specifically Muslims was provided and through the analysis of data an understanding of Muslim housing profiles was attempted.

The analysis shows that Muslims are most highly concentrated in urban areas compared with all other groups. A larger percentage of

Muslims owned their accommodation with a lone or mortgage than any other tenure type, and this is similar to the percentage for all people nationally. When compared with all groups however, Muslims are most likely to live in social rented accommodation. When looking at intra-Muslim differences, Bangladeshis were most likely to report this tenure type.

Significantly Muslims were shown to have the highest proportion of households living in overcrowded accommodation, poorer quality and less desirable housing and fewer amenities (even amongst those reporting owner occupancy).

In the previous chapter it was established that Muslims report the highest rates of economic inactivity and through the discussion of previous studies an attempt to understand the higher levels of unemployment among Muslims was presented. This was primarily to highlight the fact that Muslims have lower incomes and higher numbers of dependents, thus demonstrating that as a group they are proportionately at higher risk of living in poverty.

In addition to demonstrating that Muslims are the most highly concentrated in some of the worst living conditions, the data provided some evidence to suggest that Muslims also have low service take up, as demonstrated by Census table s161. It was argued that some groups, including Muslim groups, have stronger support networks and often rely on care provided by family members (this has also been suggested by the previous discussions of social capital). It was also argued that their may be a preference to keep care 'in house'. However the data did not provide evidence to suggest this is the case for Muslims, in fact Muslims were found to be second least likely to provide unpaid care (although of those providing care, Muslims are most likely to provide fifty hours or more).

Muslims as a group clearly demonstrate greater levels of need and this has been presented explicitly through the finding from the analysis. Muslims reported the highest proportions living in some of the least desirable living conditions, the highest levels of economic inactivity and were found to be amongst those requiring greater targeting of services, for example when considering the large proportion of Muslims residing in social rented accommodation the need for service providers to take note of the average Muslim household size and demographic profile is particularly imperative. Previous empirical findings from studies such as Weller et al.'s (2001) *Religious discrimination in England and Wales* of how half to two thirds of Muslim organisations interviewed identified staff, policies and practices of landlords, local authorities, housing associations and estate agents as sources of unfair treatment, are supported by the findings from this chapter as key areas for concern and review.

6

Conclusion

This book set out to provide a greater understanding of the social position of Muslims living in Britain. The research was timely in that Muslim communities as 'Muslims' rather than Bangladeshis, Pakistanis or Somalis had come under the spotlight due to key global and local events. Muslims spoke about being viewed as a fifth column within the 'West', greater levels of Islamophobia were recorded and public opinion on Muslims was split. Yet prior to 2001 there had already been evidence to suggest that Muslims were facing both higher levels of discrimination and suffering from greater levels of disadvantage compared with other groups.

In terms of discrimination, the discourse had already changed to accommodate the fact that prejudice on the grounds of religion existed for Muslims and this was evident from reports such as those by the Runnymede Trust (1997).Yet within the social sciences, when discussing disadvantage, the discourse was still very much in terms of race and ethnicity rather than religion or faith communities. Although the evidence pointed towards the severe disadvantage and 'difference' of two groups, both of whom adhered to the Islamic faith, it was still problematic to discuss this disadvantage in terms of religion for two reasons, which are discussed here:

Firstly, the social sciences had largely relegated the subject of religion, and when discussing minority communities, religion was seen as one of many facets of ethnicity. Ways of exploring religion and disadvantage therefore had not yet been properly thought through. A potential question that may have been addressed was whether Islam, as a belief system, caused certain phenomena to occur within this faith community. Certainly with regards to Muslim women, a topic which was discussed using rhetoric on religion as well as ethnicity, inferences about the relationship between religious doctrine and the social position of women were commonly referred to. In other words the question of deciphering 'in what ways the spiritual converts into the social?' had already been raised. During a conference organised by the Association of Muslim Social Scientists in 2004 on the jurisprudence for Muslims living as minorities, there appeared to be concern regarding the position of sociologists attempting to link the social with the theological, and although experts on the social, in the vast majority of cases sociologists were not scholars of Islamic jurisprudence. The general feeling of the delegates was that sociologists should be confined to describing and not prescribing. This was something the author has been particularly aware of throughout this research and established early on that this project is first and foremost a descriptive effort. Although to steer clear of the influences theological regulations play on the social outcomes of a community is also unavoidable and this clearly is an area in which greater deliberation would be of benefit. Even though in the UK Pakistanis and Bangladeshis make up two thirds of British Muslims, Islam is pan-ethnic and there are Muslims in Britain originating from a vast range of countries. In addition there are many differing faith traditions within Islam whose practises and profiles are different to the majority of South Asian Muslims.

Secondly, prior to the Census, when discussing faith communities and disadvantage, due to the limitations of the available data, it simply was not possible speak of Muslim disadvantage with any real authority. Of course it was established that the two groups facing the greatest levels of disadvantage on the largest numbers of measures were largely adherents to the Islamic faith, but it was not possible to translate this into Muslims facing the greatest levels of disadvantage.

Areas Investigated

Areas for investigation were of course limited to the space available and the topics researched were identified through previous studies which were both of interest to the author whilst also appearing to be prominent areas of concern. The three areas for research were:

Do Muslims Suffer from Greater Educational Disadvantage Than Other Faith Groups?

Most strikingly the analysis in Chapter Three found that Muslims were most likely to be without qualifications. This was not simply a matter which was related to generation or which could be explained by migration, as Muslims of school leaving age were still the most likely to leave at sixteen without qualifications. Has this been a result of the education system failing Muslims? Are there greater needs to be met for this section of society? Discussions of well-documented phe- nomena within schools and how these could apply to Muslims were raised, such as labelling, self-fulfilling prophecies and bullying.

There was of course the discussion of theory throughout the book, exploring concepts such as of human capital, the possession of which is likely to be reproduced in subsequent generations. Clearly Muslims on average are low in human capital and this certainly has an effect on the acquisition of human capital for their children. Yet despite this, analysis shows that Muslims do not shy away from academic pursuits. Education is an area which appeared to be of importance to this com- munity, however it should be noted that participation rates were not the same as those for Hindus and Sikhs and in terms of social tra- jectories this will no doubt have played a key role. Although there is evidence to suggest that Hindus possessed greater levels of human capital on migration; Sikhs and Muslims did appear to start off from a similar footing. The higher participation rates of women for Hindus and Sikhs will have undoubtedly had positive implications for these communities and this is something which will need to be mirrored by Muslim women.

There is therefore a conundrum. Muslim participation rates in post-compulsory education are higher than the national average, yet Muslim school leavers demonstrate the highest proportions with no qualifications. Post-compulsory participation demonstrates willing- ness for betterment through the acquisition of human capital, to the extent that in many cases this will mean having to retake the exams for the same qualification both at school and then again in further education.

Do Muslim Families Households Differ from Other Faith Groups?

In many regards the analysis in Chapter Four on household struc- ture demonstrates how Muslims have a very similar profile to that of Hindus and Sikhs and it was in this area that the three faith groups showed the most similarity. Certainly with regards to household size, Muslims had the largest households, yet Sikhs also had large households and both groups appeared to be equally as likely to have complex households. All three groups were more likely to report married couple households and significantly less likely to report cohabiting couple households. What are described as traditional lifestyle choices in terms of family formation therefore were apparent for all three groups. Yet there were some unexpected findings in the analysis, the most prominent being the proportion of lone parent households amongst Muslims. Previous studies on the two ethnic groups had not indicated that this would be the case and it is likely that newer Muslim communities have contributed to the higher proportion of single parents for this faith community.

Are Muslims Poorer & More Deprived Than Other Faith Groups?

There are various indicators of disadvantage that are available in the census and when looking at this area, geographical location is one of these that could have been explored more since this is one of the census's main strengths. Health is also a useful variable to examine when discussing disadvantage and service provision. Both of these were touched on during the chapter on disadvantage (Chapter Five) and provide interesting opportunities for further work using the data.

In terms of location, Muslims were found to be the most concentrated in urban areas and are often living in accommodation which is overcrowded and with poor amenities. Although the census does not measure income, there are clear poverty indicators namely high economic inactivity, high numbers of dependents, large families and, as already mentioned above, poor housing in some of the least desirable areas according to the ACORN classifications. When looking at employment the contrast between Muslims and all other groups is very striking: approximately one third of Muslims are long term unemployed or have never been in employment.

Did the Data Tell Us Anything New?

At the outset of this work it was stated that a question to be answered, once the analysis had commenced, was whether the data confirmed what was suspected, and here it is argued that it has done. Yet in many regards it has demonstrated levels of disadvantage over and above what some of the studies cited had indicated. The heterogeneity of Muslims is masked by the Census data employed and the separation of various communities would provide some insight into the extent of uniformity of disadvantage faced by Muslims.

This work was not only concerned with disadvantage (although this appears now to have become one of two themes running through this study due to the outcomes of the analysis) but also with exploring and describing Muslim social structures and in this case the family or families, both as a unit and a household. The analysis of this subject did indicate areas of interest which had not been covered in previous studies and these have already been mentioned above. The analysis has provided some additional findings for the discussion of social capital and Muslim communities. As a 'traditional' community with dense social networks and strong family structures, it would be assumed that Muslims have high levels of positive social capital and although lacking in human capital the possession of social capital will eventually pull Muslims up in terms of socio-economic status. Apart from the research findings by those such as Modood (2004), supported by the data on participation rates from the Census, there is no demonstrable evidence that Muslims as a group or community are climbing up the social ladder. This could be due to the heterogeneous nature as discussed at various points in this thesis, more recent settlers may hold the percentage average back whereas longer established Muslims may well be on their way to socio-economic advancement like Sikhs and Hindus, and certainly there was polarisation found within the data on qualifications amongst Muslims. However, if period of settlement is the key variable contributing to social advancement, then the picture presented of those longer established communities, such as Pakistanis, is not a particularly inspiring one. If they as a Muslim community are at the higher end of the scale due to the period of settlement and they are still largely fairing poorly when compared with Sikhs and Hindus, then we can assume there will be a long process before any real progress will be demonstrated by Muslims as a whole. An exploration of the data on Pakistanis from the 1991 and 2001 National Census would provide an indication of the rate of advancement for some measures.

Social capital was presented as having both positive and potentially negative outcomes. In terms of community cohesion it was described as being a double-edged sword. There is the danger of communities reproducing disadvantage, and where there was a particularly strong moral code (which of course religion provides), the application of greater social control on certain members of a community. With regards to communities reproducing disadvantage there was a discussion of choice verses constraints on remaining within disadvantaged neighbourhoods. Although the ghettos referred to by Portes (1998) when discussing this subject are argued to not exist in Britain as they do in the United States (Peach 1998, 2002). Muslims were undoubtedly shown to reside in some of the worst types of neighbourhoods and housing. Whether this is a matter of choice remains unclear and with arguments surrounding ecological fallacy it cannot be assumed that people do not wish to remain in poorer neighbourhoods even if they did have the means to relocate. An important motivation for people to remain is the community element. However as Modood et al. (1997) argue, it is not the 'segregation' which is problematic, these communities appear to want to remain as communities, what is problematic is the fact that whole communities cannot uproot and relocate to more desirable neighbourhoods, even if individual households can afford to do so.

Women

A brief overview of the key debates surrounding Muslim women has been provided by this book. A more in depth discussion of Muslim women would have required far greater room than this book was able to provide, as the topic is one which has acquired one of the largest spaces within academia when discussing Muslims in the West. The subject of the position of Muslim women is a particularly prickly one and in many regards standpoint theory is very much applicable in understanding the often contrasting debates on Muslim women: the outsiders looking in can paint a very different picture to the insider when it comes to matters most commonly raised.

Yet women have been a running theme throughout this book and this has perhaps been presented in a far more implicit way than disadvantage. Participation rates in post-compulsory education, although higher than the total population, were lower than those for Hindu and Sikh women. The figures for those aged 16–24 showed the difference of one percentage between Sikh and Hindu women's participation (65 per cent and 58 per cent respectively) compared with their male counterparts (66 per cent and 59 per cent). For Muslim men and women there is a gender difference of 10 per cent (57 per cent and 47 per cent respectively).

Muslim women, like men had the highest levels of economic inactivity, however in terms of the male-female ratio compared with all other groups, Muslim women were more likely to be economically inactive in both absolute terms and when compared with their male counterparts. When broken down by age, however, although still demonstrating asymmetry, it is not to as great a degree. There is a 3 per cent difference for economic activity for Hindu and Sikh women aged 16–24 (47 per cent and 51 per cent respectively) compared to their male counterparts (50 per cent and 54 per cent). For Muslims within this age bracket there is a 13 per cent difference, 36 per cent of women compared with 49 per cent of men who are economically active. The important point here is that for the younger generation there are still greater gender gaps within this community compared with all others. A key factor contributing to this is clearly the fertility rates for Muslims and therefore the importance placed on marriage, motherhood and family found within this community. Therefore it is clear that the absence of women from the formal labour market impacts greatly on the Muslim populations' economic activity as a whole.

The findings raise important questions, such as whether the outcomes from the analysis on Muslim women are a direct result of unequal social control, be that in terms of specified gender roles or sexual control limiting their participation within wider social institutions (namely the education establishments and the labour market). Or whether it is not a matter of negative social capital and control at all but rather a lifestyle choice, which has resulted in Muslim women demonstrating a more divergent profile when compared with Hindus and Sikhs. Does the data provide evidence that Muslim communities, and women as part of those communities, choose to place greater emphasis on the family rather than the individual? In many ways this appears to be a 'choice verses constraints' debate also. Of course specified gender roles and greater participation within wider society and institutions are not mutually exclusive and yet Muslim women have been presented, certainly when compared to Hindu and Sikhs (who it should be noted have similar family profiles in many regards), as demonstrating greater levels of asymmetry within the most common means for socio-economic advancement – education and economic activity.

Discrimination

Along with disadvantage, religious discrimination has been identified as being a key issue for Muslims in Britain. The aftermath of 11 September 2001 and more recently and relevantly for the British context, the events in London on 7 July 2005, have heightened the sense of 'moral panics' surrounding the British Muslim community. Such backlash is to be expected at every such juncture due to the rhetoric on terrorism becoming synonymous with Islam and Muslims. The mayor of London, Ken Livingstone (2005) was quick to point out that the attack on the London transport network was indiscriminate of religion and emphasised that Muslims will have been affected by the acts, as will have members of other religious groups. The Archbishop of Canterbury (2005) also talked about the unity of faith groups in condemning the attacks, again specifically mentioning Muslims amongst these. The increase in religious hatred post 11 September 2001 is clearly still in the minds of these men and no doubt the Muslim community in Britain. British Muslims continue to make headline news for terror attempts, becoming so numerous since 2001 that it would require more space than this chapter is able to provide to explore them all individually. No doubt collectively, such incidences contribute to the ongoing negative rhetoric and discourse used to describe Muslims in the public and private domains.

Some of the studies cited pointed towards greater discrimination of some groups and in particular ethnic penalties. There was research presented that suggested Muslim groups (Pakistanis and Bangladeshis) when equally qualified, were not as successful in the labour market. There have been references above to figures found by the analysis of the differential participation of Muslim women within wider society and institutions. What has not been discussed or presented is the extent discrimination plays in this participation. The impact religious discrimination has on the greater levels of disadvantage faced by Muslims is not measurable using the data employed here. Yet this is likely to be one of the most significant contributors to the continued disadvantage of this community.

Although legislation has been introduced to outlaw religious discrimination in the work place, there are currently debates taking place regarding the extension of the Race Relations Act (2000) to include the discrimination of Muslims and other faith based groups not currently covered by the Act; the events of 7 July 2005 have fuelled the debate even further.

Concluding Thoughts

Muslims appear to suffer from a vicious cycle of poor educational qualifications, low percentages of economically active, poor job prospects leading to unfavourable tenure patterns, when compared with the other minority faith communities and the national profile. Although economically challenged, Muslims in the UK have strong social networks and dense family organisation, as well as being a greatly religious and practising population.

Policy makers, social scientists, political philosophers and all those in the business of equality agree that class, gender and ethnicity are important variables for recognition, distribution and representation[1], however this is not the case with religion. Conceptual grounds for the relegation of religion as a factor in the study of society have been revisited throughout this book and these are mainly tied to concepts about secularisation in the West. Yet this study has explicitly shown how religious affiliation is an important measure for deprivation and disadvantage for Muslims. This research then is part of an unfolding and evolving study of minoritiesindexminorities!religious in which religious identity has come to feature and thus requires attention and analysis. The recognition of faith group affiliation has resulted in the study of minorities in Britain becoming more multifaceted, rather than viewing religious identity, class stratification or ethnic background as areas for separate study. In other words, religious affiliation should be viewed as one of a number of important variables that feature and be treated as one of the various streams within the study of minorities in Britain.

In terms of policy development, all the areas discussed above are relevant for service delivery and engaging with Muslim communities. Chapter Five showed greater levels of deprivation for this faith group and as the government have in place deprivation areas schemes such as Single Regeneration Budget and Neighbourhood Renewal programmes, religion as an additional facet of disadvantage should also be monitored. The targeted allocation of resources may well not be enough when it comes to tackling the severe disadvantage of Muslims. There is a danger that this community is bypassed by such schemes and even where ethnicity is monitored, Muslims who are not Pakistani and Bangladeshi could fall through the net completely.

With regards to future planning and services, the fact that Muslims are not only a young faith community but also that they have more dependent children per household on average than any other community needs to be recognised and catered for. Such a young community profile has far reaching implications, which cross into many areas of consideration, be they government youth training initiatives or areas such as paediatrics and health care. In order to understand and counter deprivation among Muslims, it is imperative that there is monitoring of religion within such areas, which will inevitably be of particular significance to this community.

The schooling system as an institution is of real relevance for communities with such a young demographic profile. This coupled with the alarmingly poor results for the educational attainment of Muslims requires a serious revision of the way religious minorities are accommodated for within the system.

Due to key global and local events, politically, Muslims as a minority group are at the centre of some policy debates, particularly those on discrimination. This study is especially significant at the moment because it provides a greater understanding of issues that require policy attention. Gaps in the research are not a reflection on the existence and importance of the issues themselves but rather an indication of inconclusive data. This study has been equally valuable in identifying both areas for greater policy consideration and also sociological themes requiring greater exploration and investigation.

Notes

Chapter 1

1. Mohammed Abdul Kahar of Forest Gate, London was shot in the shoulder during a police anti-terror raid on 2 July 2006.
2. The Danish newspaper Jyllands-Posten printed cartoons depicting the Prophet Muhammad as a terrorist in January 2006.
3. Deputy Prime Minister of Britain and MP for Blackburn stated that he would prefer Muslim women constitutes who veil their faces (in accordance with some interpretations of Islamic law regarding dress code) to remove their veils in his presence.
4. MCB eventually took over the role of UKACIA which as a result now ceases to exist.
5. In all previous Censuses in Great Britain, when a question on religion was included it was compulsory to answer it.

Chapter 2

1. These figures for asylum applications exclude dependent children.

Chapter 4

1. A married couple family consists of a husband and wife with or without their child(ren). In most tables, the term 'married couple household' is used to describe a household that comprises a married couple family and no other person.
2. The subject of caring has appeared in this chapter several times either when looking at altruism or parental responsibilities towards adult children and adult children towards elderly parents. Informal caring will be explored in greater detail in Chapter Five.
3. Other households are classified by the number of dependent children or whether all student or all pensioner. See ONS (2001b) for further information on terminology.
4. A dependent child is a person aged 0–15 in a household (whether or not in a family)

or aged 16–18 in full-time education and living in a family with his or her parent(s). This is a change from the 1991 definition which was a person aged 0–15 in a household or a person aged 16–18, never married, in full-time education and economically inactive. See 2001 See ONS (2001*b*) for further information on terminology.

Chapter 5

1. Table M324.
2. When conducting local level analysis, Unitary and District Authorities containing less than 100 cases have been filtered out prior to analysis due to the production of meaningless outliers.
3. Tables T52 and M317.
4. The Census measures overcrowding through occupancy ratings and households are rated on the actual number of rooms to the number of rooms required by households. This was based on members of household's relationships and ages.
5. Those who are classified as unemployed come under 'economically active', because they are actively seeking employment.
6. On November 27, 2000, the EU passed the Employment Framework Directive (No. 2000/78/EC).

Chapter 6

1. Fraser (2000) discusses these in her essay 'Rethinking recognition', New Left Review, 3.

References

Abbas, T. (2003). 'The impact of religio-cultural norms and values on the education of young South Asian women', *British Journal of Sociology of Education*, 24(4): 411–428.

———— (2006). *Seeds of Discontent*, Institute of Race Relations, <http://www.irr.org.uk/2006/july/ak000022.html>.

Abd al'Ali, H. (1997). *The family structure in Islam*, USA: American Trust publications.

Acheson, D. (1998). *Independent inquiry into health report – part two*, <http://www.archive.official-documents.co.uk/document/doh/ih/part2h.htm>.

Afkhami, M. (1995) (ed.). *Faith and Freedom: Women's Human Rights in the Muslim World*, Syracuse, NY: Syracuse University Press.

Ahmad, F. (2006). 'British Muslim Perceptions and Opinions on News Coverage of September 11', *Journal of Ethnic and Migration Studies*, vol. 32, no. 6, August 2006, pp. 261–982(22).

Ahmad, W. (1999). 'Ethnic Statistics: better than nothing or worse than nothing?' in Dorling, D. and Simpson S. (eds.), *Statistics in society: the arithmetic of politics*, London: Arnold.

———— (2000). *Ethnicity, disability and chronic illness*, Buckingham: Open University Press.

Ahmed, L. (1992). *Women and Gender in Islam, Historical Roots of a Modem*

Debate, New Haven: Yale University Press.

Ahmed, N. M., F. Bodi, and R. Kasim (2001). *The Oldham Riots: Discrimination, Deprivations and Community Tension*, Islamic Human Rights Commission.

Akhtar, S. (1989). *Be Careful with Mohammad! The Salman Rushdie Affair*, London: Beller.

Al-Ali N., R. Black, and K. Koser (2001). 'The limits to 'transnationalism': Bosnian and Eritrean refugees in Europe as emerging transnational communities', *Ethnic and Racial Studies*, vol. 24, no. 4, pp. 278–600.

———— (2002). 'Gender relations, trans-national ties and rituals among Bosnian refugees', *Global Networks*, 2:3, 249–262.

Al-Jalili, Ismail (2004). *Arab population in the UK: an ethnic profile*, <http://www.naba.org.uk/content/theassociation/Reports/arabPopUK_04.htm>.

Al-Masyabi, Mohammad (2000). *The Yemeni Community in the UK*, <http://www.caabu.org/press/focus/masyabi.html>.

Ali, Z. (2003). 'Attitudes towards disability amongst Pakistani and Bangladeshi parents of disabled children in the UK: considerations for service providers and the disability movement', *Health and social care in the community*, 11:6, 502–509.

Allen, A. (1998). 'What are ethnic minorities looking for?' in Modood, T. and T. Acland *Race and Higher education*, London: Policy Studies Institute.

Anderson, M. (1971). 'Family, household and the industrial revolution', in Anderson, M. (ed.), *Sociology of the Family*, Harmandsworth: Penguin.

Ansari, H. (2002). *Muslims in Britain*, published by Minority Rights Group International.

———— (2004). *The infidel within: Muslims in Britain since 1800*, Hurst and Co.

Anthias, Floya and Yuval-Davis, Nira (1992). *Racialized Boundaries. Race, Nation, Gender, Colour and Cass and the Anti-Racist Struggle*, London: Routledge.

Anwar, M. (1979). *The myth of return: Pakistanis in Britain*, London.

———— (1993). *Muslims in Britain: 1991 Census and Other Statistical Sources*, The Centre for the Study of Islam and Christian–Muslim Relations, Selly Oaks Colleges, Birmingham.

AP (2004). 'Thousands of Muslims in Britain practicing polygamy, Islamic leaders say', <www.statistics.gov.uk/census2001/pdfs/glossary.pdf>.

Arber, S. (2001). 'Pension prospects of minority ethnic groups: inequalities by gender and ethnicity', *British journal of sociology*, 52:3, pp. 519–539.

Archbishop of Canterbury (2005) Press release to British media, 7 July 2005,

<http://www.catholic-ew.org.uk/cn/05/050711b.htm>.

Archer, L. (2001). 'Muslim Brothers, Black lads, traditional Asians: British Muslims young men's construction of race, religion and masculinity', *Feminism and Psychology*, 11:1.

Aspinall, P. (2000). 'Should a Question on Religion be Asked in The 2001 British Census? A Public Policy Case in Favour', *Social Policy and Administration*, vol. 34, no. 5, pp. 284–600.

Attwood, C., G. Singh, and D. Prime (2003). *2001 Citizenship Survey: People, Families and Communities*, Home Office.

Azam, N. (1997). 'How Many Muslims Are There?', *Q news*, June 1997.

Baker, W. (1990). 'Market networks and cooperate behaviour', *American Journal of sociology*, 96/3, pp. 289–625.

Baker, D. (2002). 'Inequalities in morbidity and consulting behaviour for socially vulnerable groups', *British journal of general practice*, pp. 224–130.

Ballard, R. (1982). 'South Asian Families: Structure and Process', in Rapaport, R. and M. Fogarty (eds.), *Families in Britain*, London: Routledge.

———— (1990). 'Migration and kinship: the differential effect of marriage rules on the processes of Punjabi migration to Britain', in Peach, C. and S. Vertovec (eds.), *South Asians overseas: Contexts and communities*, Cambridge University Press.

———— (1994a). *Desh Pardesh: South Asian presence in Britain*, London: Hurst.

———— (1994b). *Ethnic Dimensions of the 1991 Census: A Preliminary Report*, Census Microdata Unit.

———— (1994c). 'Negotiating Race and Ethnicity: Exploring The Implications of The 1991 Census', *Patterns of Prejudice*, vol. 30, no. 3, pp. 3–33.

———— (1996a). 'The Pakistanis: Stability and Introspection', in Peach, C. (ed.), *The Ethnic Minority Populations of Great Britain: Ethnicity in the 1991 Census*, vol. 2, London: Central Statistical Office, pp. 121–149

———— (1996b). 'Islam and the Construction of Europe', in Shadid, W. A. R. and P. S. van Koningsveld (eds.), *Muslims in the Margin: Political Responses to the Presence of Islam in Western Europe*, Kampen: Kok Pharos Publishers.

———— (1998). *Upward mobility: the socio-economic and educational achievements of Britain's visible minorities*, CASAS, University of Manchester, <http://www.art.man.ac.uk/CASAS/pdfpapers/mobility.pdf>.

———— (2004). *Riste and Ristedar: The significance of marriage in the dynamics of transnational kinship networks*, CASAS, University of Manchester, <http://www.art.man.ac.uk/CASAS/pdfpapers/ristedari.pdf>.

Barkat-E-Khuda, M. (1985). 'The nuclearization of the joint family household in a rural area of Bangladesh'. *Journal of Comparative family studies*, 16 (3).

Basit, T. (1997). 'I want more freedom but not too much': British Muslim girls and the dynamism of family values, *Gender and education*, 9:4, pp. 425–439.

Bate, R. (1999). 'Housing Projections: A sheep in wolf's clothing', in Dorling, D. *Statistics in Society*, Oxford University Press.

Becher, H. and F. Husain (2003). *Supporting minority families: South Asian Hindus and Muslims in Britain*, National family and parenting institute.

Beck, U. and E. Beck-Gernsheim (1995). *The Normal Chaos of Love*, Cambridge: Polity Press.

———— ———— (2002). *Individualization*, London: Sage.

Becker, G. (1964). *Human Capital*, Princeton: Princeton University Press.

———— (1993).*Human Capital*, 3rd ed, University of Chicago Press, Part 1.

Becker, H. (1971). 'Problems in the publication of field studies', in Vidich, A., J. Bensman and W. Stein (eds.), *Reflections on community studies*, New York: Harper and Row, 267–84.

———— (1988). 'Family Economics and macro behaviour', *The American economic review*, vol. 78, no. 1, pp. 2–13.

Beer, J. (2004). *Race Equality through leadership in social care*, Health and social care directive.

Bernstein, B. (1971). 'Social class, language and socialisation', in Bernstein, B. (ed.), *Class, codes and control*, vol. 1: *Theoretical studies towards a sociology of language*, London: Routledge and Kegan Paul.

———— (1981). 'Codes, modalities and the process of cultural reproduction – a model', *Language in Society*, 10, pp. 327–63.

Berrington, A. (1994). 'Marriage and family formation among the white and ethnic minority populations in Britain', *Ethnic and Racial Studies*, vol. 17 (3), pp. 517–46.

Berthoud R. and S. Beishon (1997). 'People, families and households', in Modood, T. *Ethnic minorities in Britain: Diversity and disadvantage*, Policy Studies Institute.

———— (1998). *The incomes of ethnic minorities*, Institute for social and economic research.

———— and K. Robson (2003). *Early motherhood and disadvantage: a comparison between ethnic groups*, Institute for social and economic research.

———— and J. Gershuny (2000). *Seven years in the lives of British families*, Institute for social and economic research, the policy press.

Bishtawi, Adel. (1999). 'The Arab community in Britain: The absent presence', Paper presented at the 3rd Arab Communities Conference, October 16–17, 1999.

Black, Edwin (2001). *IBM and the Holocaust*, Little Brown publishers.

Blackaby, D., D. Leslie, P. Murphy, and N. O'Leary (1999). 'Unemployment among Britain's ethnic minorities', *The Manchester School*, vol. 67 (1).

Blakemore, K. (2000). 'Health and social care needs in minority communities: An over problemised issues?', *Health and social care in the community*, 8:1, pp22–30.

Bodi, F. (2000). 'A Question of Numbers?', *The Guardian*, 27 May 2000.

Bose R. (2000). 'Families in transition', in Lua, A. (ed.), *South Asian children and adolescents in Britain*, London: Whurr.

Boulton, M. (1995). 'Patterns of bullying victim problems in mixed race groups of children', *Social development*, 4, p. 277–293.

Bourdieu, P. (1997)., 'The forms of capital', in Halsey, A. H., H. Lauder, P. Brown and A. S. Wells (eds.), *Education: Culture, Economy, Society*, Oxford, Oxford University Press, p. 46–68.

Boyle, P. and D. Dorling (2004). 'Guest editorial: the 2001 UK census: remarkable resource or bygone legacy of the 'pencil and paper era'?', *Area*, vol. 36, no. 2, pp. 201–110.

Bowels, S., H. Gintis and M. Osbourne (2001)., 'The determinants of earnings: a behavioral approach', *Journal of economic literature*, 39:4.

Bowen, J. (2004). *Islam, Law, and Equality in Indonesia: An Anthropology of Public Reasoning*, Missouri: Washington University.

Bowes, A. M., N.S. Dar and D. F. Sim (2002). 'Differentiation in Housing Careers: The case of Pakistanis in the UK', *Housing Studies*, vol. 17, no. 3, pp. 281–400.

Brah, A. (1993). 'Race and culture in the gendering labour markets: South Asian young Muslim women and the labour market', *New Community*, 19:3, pp. 241–458.

Brown, C. (1984). *Black and White Britain: The third PSI Survey*, London: Heinemann.

——— and P. Gay (1985). *Racial discrimination: 17 years after the act*, London: Policy Studies Institute.

Brown, M. (2000). 'Religion and economic activity in the South Asian Population', *Ethnic and racial Studies*, 23 (6)., pp. 1035–1061.

Browning, C. R., R. Dietz and S. L. Feinberg (2000). 'Negative' Social Capital and Urban Crime: A Negotiated Coexistence Perspective, URAI Working Paper No. 00–07.

Bullock, K. (2000). 'Challenging Media representations of the veil: Contemporary Muslims women's re-veiling movement', *American Journal of Islamic social sciences*, 17:3, pp. 1–20.

Burke, J. (2006). 'Muslim anger: the real story', *The Observer*, 20 August.

Burt, R. S. (1992). *Structural Holes: the social structure of competition*. Cambridge, MA: Harvard University Press.

Butt, J. and L. Box (1998). *Family Centred: a study of the use of family centres by black families*, London: Race Equality Unit.

Bywaters, P., Z. Ali, Q. Fazil, L. A. Wallace and G. Singh (2003). 'Attitudes towards disability among Pakistani and Bangladeshi parents of disabled children in the UK: considerations for service providers and the disability movement', *Health and social care in the community*, 11 (3). pp. 502–509.

The Cabinet Office (2002). 'Ethnic Minorities and the Labour market: Interim analytical report', <http://www.strategy.gov.uk/downloads/files/interim.pdf>.

Carens, H. (2000). *Culture, Citizenship and Community*, Oxford: Oxford University Press.

Carmichael, F. and R. Woods (2000). 'Ethnic penalties in unemployment and occupational attainment: evidence for Britain', *International review of applied economics*, vol. 14, no. 1, pp. 21–98.

Carvel, J. (2003). 'Census in doubt after figures prove unreliable', *The Guardian*, 23 October.

Chambaz, C. (2001). 'Lone parent families in Europe: A variety of economic and social circumstances', *Social Policy and Administration*, 35 (6). pp. 258–671.

Cheng, Y. and A. Heath (1993). 'Ethnic origins and class destinations', *Oxford Review of Education*, 19:2, pp. 251–166.

Clarke, A. (2001). 'Research and the policy making process', in Gilbert, G. N. (ed.), *Researching Social Life*, London: Sage, pp. 28–44.

Clifford, J. (1994). 'Diasporas', *Cultural Anthropology*, 9, No. 3, pp. 202–338.

Coleman, J. S. (1988). 'Social capital in the creation of human capital', *American Journal of Sociology*, 94, pp. 95–120.

Coleman, D. (1999). 'Census Plans to 'Pry' into Religion', *The Times*, 12 January.

Craig, S. (1999). *Experience of racial bullying in two secondary schools*, unpublished, Department of Psychology, University of Central Lancashire.

Cumper, D. (1990). 'Muslim schools: implications of the education reform act of 1988', *New community*, 16:3, pp. 279–389.

Dale, A. and Marsh, C. (1993). *The 1991 Census User Guide*, London: HMSO.

——— and Heath, S. (1994). 'Household and family formation in Great Britain: the ethnic dimension', *Population Trends*, pp. 77, 5–13.

——— , E. Fieldhouse and C. Holdsworth (2000)., *Analyzing Census Microdata*, 1st ed., London: Edward Arnold.

————, N. Shaheen, V. Kalra and E. Fieldhouse (2002). 'Routes into education and employment for young Pakistani and Bangladeshi women in the UK', *Ethnic and racial studies*, 25:6, pp. 242–968.

Demie, F. (2001). 'Ethnic and gender differences in educational achievement and implications for school improvement strategies', *Educational research*, 43:1, pp. 247–159.

Diamond, I. (1999). 'The census' in Dorling, D. and L. Simpson (eds.), *Statistics in society: the arithmetic of politics*, London: Arnold, 9–18.

Dick, Malcolm (2002). *Celebrating Sanctuary: Birmingham and the Refugee Experience 1750–2002*, <http://www.Birmingham.gov.uk>.

Dispatches (2006). Channel 4, 7 August.

Dodd, V. and A. Travis (2005). 'Move to limit backlash against Muslims', *The Guardian*, 9 July.

Domesday Book Online (2004). <http://www.domesdaybook.co.uk/>.

Dorling, D. and P. Boyle (2004). 'The UK Census: Remarkable resource or bygone of the 'pencil and paper era'?', *Area*, (co-editors of special issue).

Drew, D. and Grey, J. (1990). 'The fifth year examination achievements of black young people in England and Wales' *Educational research*, 32:2, pp. 117–207.

Edwards, R., J. Ribbens McCarthy and V. Gillies (2003). *Making Families: Moral Tales of Parenting and Step-Parenting*, Routledge-Cavendish.

Edwards, R. (2004, forthcoming) (ed.). *Social Capital in the Field: Researchers' Tales*, Families & Social Capital ESRC Research Group Working Paper, London South Bank University.

El-Solh, C. (1992). 'Arab communities in Britain: cleavages and commonalities', *Islam and Christian-Muslim relations*, 3, 2.

Enneli, Pinar (2002). 'Social exclusion and young Turkish speaking people's future prospects: economic deprivation and culturalisation of ethnicity' in Fenton, S. and H. Bradley (eds.), *Ethnicity and Economy – Race and Class Revisited*, Basingstoke: Palgrave Macmillan.

————, T. Modood and H. Bradley (2005). *'Young Turks and Kurds: A set of 'invisible' disadvantaged groups'*, Joseph Rowntree Foundation.

Ermes, Ali Omar (2002). *Invisibility of the Arab Community in Britain*, <http://www.aliomarermes.co.uk/resources/view_article.cfm?article_id=10>.

Esmail, A. and P. Dewart (1998). 'The failure of Asian students in clinical examination: the Manchester Experience' in Modood, T. and T. Acland *Race and Higher education*, London: Policy Studies Institute.

Esposito.J (1999). *The Islamic threat: myth or reality?*, New York: Oxford University Press.

Eslea, M. and K. Mukhtar (2000). 'Bullying and racism among Asian schoolchildren in Britain' *Educational Research*, 42: 2, pp. 207–17.

Fekete, L. (2005). 'Deporting Muslim Clerics: Lessons from Europe', *The European Race Bulletin*.

Fernea, E. W. (1998). *In Search of Islamic Feminism: One Woman's Global Journey*, Doubleday.

Field, J. (2003). *Social Capital*, London: Routledge.

Fieldhouse, E. and M. Gould (1998). 'Ethnic minority unemployment and local labour market conditions in Great Britain', *Environment and Planning*, vol. 30, pp. 233–53.

Finch, J. and J. Mason (1991). 'Obligations of kinship in contemporary Britain: Is there normative agreement?', *British Journal of Sociology*, 42:3, pp. 345–67.

Foster, P. (1990). *Policy and Practice in multi-cultural and anti-racist education: case study of a multi-cultural school*, London: Routledge.

——— (1993). 'Some problems in establishing equality of treatment in multi-ethnic schools', *British Journal of Sociology*, 44: 3.

Francis, L. (1998a). letter sent to RAG member, 20 October.

——— (1998b). Aide memoir of the first meeting, 25 June.

——— (2000c). Communication, 15 August.

Fraser, N. (2000). 'Rethinking Recognition', *New Left Review*, 233, 107–20.

Gale, R. (2005). 'Representing the City: Mosques and the Planning Process in Birmingham, UK', *Journal of Ethnic and Migration Studies*, vol. 31, no. 6, pp. 1161–79.

Gardener, D. (2005). 'The west's role in Islams' war of ideas', *The Financial Times*, 8 July.

Garvie, D. (2001). *Far From Home: The Housing of Asylum Seekers in Private Rented Accommodation*, Shelter.

Gellner, E. (1992). *Postmodernism, Reason and Religion*, London: Routledge.

Ghuman, P. A. S. (1997). 'Assimilation or integration? A study of Asian adolescents', *Educational research*, 39:1, pp. 11–29.

Giddens, A. (1991). *Modernity and Self-Identify: Self and Society in the Late Modern Age*, Cambridge, England: Polity Press.

——— (1992). *The transformation of Intimacy: Sexuality, Love and Eroticism in Modern Societies*, Oxford Policy Press.

Gilbert, N. (2001). *Researching Social Life*, London: Sage.

Gillborn, D. (1990). *Race ethnicity and educational: teaching and learning and multi-ethnic schools*, London: Unwin Hyman.

——— and C. Gipps (1996). *Recent research on the achievement of ethnic mi-*

nority pupils: OFSTED reviews of research, London: HMSO.

———— (1998). 'Race and ethnicity in compulsory schooling' in Modood, T and T. Acland *Race and Higher Education*, London: Policy Studies Institute.

Gilliat S. (1997). 'Muslim youth organisation in Britain: a descriptive analysis', *The American Journal of Islamic Social Sciences*, 14:1, pp. 29–111.

Gillies, V. (2003). *Family and Intimate Relationships: A Review of the Sociological Research*, Published by South Bank University.

Ginn, J. and S. Arber (2001). 'Pension prospects of minority ethnic groups: Inequalities by gender and ethnicity', *British Journal of Sociology*, 52(3), pp. 519–29.

Goffman, E. (1959). *The Presentation of Self in Everyday Life*, New York: Anchor Books.

Goldthorpe, J. H., C. Llewellyn and C. Payne (1980). *Social Mobility and Class Structure in Modern Britain*, Oxford: Clarendon Press.

———— (1996)., 'Class analysis and the reorientation of class theory: the case of persisting differentials in educational attainment', *British Journal of Sociology*, 47, 481–505.

Goode, W. (1963). *World Revolution and Family Patterns*, Gencoe, New York: Free Press

Gull, D. (2001). unpublished doctoral dissertation, Faculty of Health, University of Salford.

Guthrie, J. (2005). Fear and Frustrations for Muslims, *The Financial Times*, 9 July.

Hackett, L., R. Hackett and D. Taylor (1991). 'Psychological disturbance and its association in the children of the Gujarati community', *Journal of child psychology and psychiatry*, 32, pp. 251–6.

Hai, N. (1999). *Britain's South Asian Muslims a Statistical Profile*, Department of Sociology Manchester Metropolitan University.

Hakim, C. (1994). *Secondary analysis in social research: A guide to data sources and methods with examples*, London: Allen & Unwin.

Halliday, F (1992). *Arabs in Exile: Yemeni Migrants in Urban Britain*, London.

Halstead M. (1991). 'Radical feminism Islam and single sex school debate', *Gender and education*, 3:3, pp. 263–78.

Halstead, M. J. (2001). 'Baudrillard, Simulation and the Debate about Collective Worship in Schools', in Francis, L. J., J. Astley and M. Robbins (eds.), *The Fourth R for the Third Millenium: education in religion and values for the global future*, Dublin: Lindisfarne Books.

Harb, Z. and Bessaiso, E. (2006). British Arab Muslim Audiences and Television after September 1, *Journal of Ethnic and Migration Studies*, vol. 32, no. 6, August 2006, pp. 2063–76(14).

Harris, Hermione (2004). 'The Somali community in the UK: What we know and how we know it', The Information Centre about Asylum and Refugees in the UK (ICAR).

Harrison, M. (1998). 'Theorising exclusion and difference: specificity, structure and Minority ethnic housing issues', *Housing studies*, vol. 13, pp. 293–306.

Hassouneh-Phillips, D. S. (2001). 'Marriage is half of faith and the rest is fear Allah; marriage and spousal abuse among American Muslims', *Violence against women*, 7:8, pp. 926–46.

Haw, K. (1998). *Educating Muslim Girls: Shifting Discourses*, Buckingham: Open University Press.

Hawtin, M., G. Hughes and J. Percy-Smith (1999). *Community profiling: auditing social needs*, Buckinghamshire: Open University Press.

Heath, T., R. Jeffries and J. Purcell (2004). *Asylum statistics: United Kingdom 2003*, 11/04, 24 August, London: Home Office.

Heelas, P., S. Lash and P. Morris (1996). *Detraditionalization*, Oxford: Blackwell.

Hellyer, H. A. (2005). *The European union and its Muslim populations*, Ph.D thesis, University of Warwick.

Hennink, M., I. Diamond, and P. Cooper (1999). 'Young Asian Women and Relationships: Traditional or Transitional?', *Ethnic and Racial Studies*, vol. 22, Issue 5: 867–91.

Hillery, G. A. (1955). 'Definitions of Community: Areas of Agreement', *Rural Sociology*, 20, p. 111–23.

Holloway, J. and Valins, O. (2002). 'Editorial: Placing Religion and Spirituality in Geography', *Social and Cultural Geography*, 3 (1)., pp. 5–9.

Hopkins and Kahani-Hopkins (2006). 'Minority group members' theories of inter-group contact: A case study of British Muslims' conceptualisation of Islamophobia and social change', *British Journal of Social Psychology*, 45, 245–64.

House, J. (1997). 'Muslim Communities in France', in Nonneman, G. (ed.), *Muslim Communities in the New Europe*, Reading: Ithaca Press, pp. 219–41.

Huntington, S. P. (1993). 'Clash of Civilations: The Next Pattern of Conflict', *Foreign Affairs*, vol. 72, no. 3, pp. 22–8.

Hussain, S. (2005). *A Statistical Mapping of Muslims in Britain*, unpublished doctoral thesis, University of Bristol.

———— (2004). An Annotated Bibliography of Recent literature on 'Invisible' Muslim Communities and New Muslim Migrant Communities in Britain, published by the Centre on migration policy and so-

ciety, as part of the 'Muslims and Community Cohesion in Britain'
project, <http://www.compas.ox.ac.uk/publications/papers/Muslim\
%20Communities\%20Annotate\%20Bibliography\%20090306.pdf>.

—— (2003). *An Introduction to Muslims in the 2001 National Census*,
<http://www.bristol.ac.uk/sociology/ethnicitycitizenship/intromuslims\
_census.pdf>.

Husain, F. and M. O'Brien (2000). 'Muslim communities in Europe: recon-
struction and transformation', *Current Sociology*, 48:4, pp. 1–13.

Hutnik, N. (1985). 'Aspects of Identity in a Multi-Ethnic Society', *New Community*, vol. 12, 2, pp. 298–309.

Hymowitz, K. (2003). *The Women Feminists Forgot, The Wall Street Journal online*, <http://online.wsj.com/article/0,,SB104700907962016300,00.
html?emailf=yes>.

Iganski, P. and G. Payne (1999). 'Socio-economic restructuring and employment: the case of minority ethnic groups', *British journal of sociology*, vol.
50 (2). pp. 195–215.

Imaginate (n.d) 'Attitudes of Living in Britain – A Survey of Muslim Opinion',
<http://www.imaginate.uk.com/MCC01_SURVEY/Site\%20Download.
pdf\#search=\%22NOP\%20muslim\%20survey\%22>.

Jacobson, J. (1997). 'Religion and Ethnicity: Dual and Alternative Source of
Identity Among Young British Pakistanis', *Ethnic and Racial Studies*, vol.
20, no. 2, pp. 238–56.

Johnson, H. and M. Castelli (2002). 'How to understand the culture of Muslim
schools in England: some methodological reflections', *International journal
of education and religion*, 3:1, pp. 23–45.

Jamieson, L. (1998). *Intimacy: Personal Relationships in Modern Societies*,
Cambridge Policy Press.

Johns, N. R. (2004). 'Ethnic Diversity Policy: Perceptions within the NHS',
Social Policy and Administration, 38, 1, pp. 73-88.

Jowell, R. and C. Airey (1984). *British Social attitudes: the 1984 report*, Social
and Community Planning Research.

Kelly, Lynette (2003). 'Bosnian refugees in Britain: Questioning community'
in *Sociology*, vol. 37, no. 1, pp. 35–49.

Kelso, P. and J. Vasgar (2002) 'Muslims reject image of separate society', *The
Guardian*, 17 June.

Kendall, L. (1998). *Report on the analysis of 1997 examination results: NFER?
AMA project on examination results in context*, London association of
metropolitan Authorities.

Kettani, A. (1986). *Muslim Minorities in the World Today*, London: Mansell
Printing Ltd., for Institute of Muslim Minority Affairs.

Khan, S. and A. Jones (2002). *Somalis in Camden: Challenges faced by an emerging community*, The Refugee Forum.

Khan, V. S. (1979). *Minority families in Britain*, Social Science Research Council.

Khan, Z. (2000). 'Muslim Presence in Europe: the British Dimension – Identity, Integration and Community Activism', *Current Sociology*, vol. 48, No. 4, pp. 29–43.

Knott, K. (1982). *Muslims, Sikhs and Hindus in the UK: Problems With Estimating Religious Statistics*, Religious Research Paper, Department of Sociology, Leeds University.

———— and S. Khokher (1993). 'Religious and Ethnic Identity Among Young Muslim Women in Bradford', *New Community*, 19, no. 4, pp. 601–2.

Kong, L. (2001). 'Mapping 'new' geographies of religion: politics and poetics in modernity', *Progress in Human Geography*, 25 (2)., 211–33.

———— (1990). 'Geography and religion: trends and prospects', *Progress in Human Geography*, 14 355–71.

Koser, K. (1998) 'Social networks and the asylum cycle: the case of Iranian asylum seekers in the Netherlands', *International Migration Review*, 31 (2).: 411–47.

Kosmin, B. (1999). 'Divine and Divide', *The Guardian*, 4 August.

Kucukcan, T. (1996). *The politics of ethnicity, identity and religion among Turks in London*, Ph.D thesis, University of Warwick.

Lakey, J. (1997). 'Neighbourhoods and Housing' in Modood, T. *Ethnic Minorities in Britain: Diversity and Disadvantage*, Policy Studies Institute.

Laslett, P. (1972). *Household and Family in Past Time*, Cambridge: Cambridge University Press.

Lehrer, Evelyn (2004). 'Religion as a Determinant of Economic and Demographic Behavior in the United States', *Population and Development Review*, 30(4): 707–26.

Lesthaeghe, R. (1995). 'The Second Demographic Transition – An Interpretation', in Mason, K. O. and A. M. Jensen (eds.), *Gender and Family Change in Industrial Countries*, pp. 27–62, Oxford: Clarendon Press.

Lewis, B. (2002). *What went wrong?*, Oxford University Press.

Lewis, P. (1994). *Islamic Britain: Religion, Politics and Identity Among Young British Muslims*, London: IB Tauris.

Lewis, M. (2005). 'Hostility to asylum seekers has risen most among the middle class', *The Guardian*, <http://society.guardian.co.uk/asylumseekers/comment/0,8005,1517104,00.html>.

Little, A. (2003). 'Motivating learning and development of human capital', *Compare*, vol. 33, no. 4, pp. 237–444.

Livingstone, K. (2005) Press release, 7 July, <http://66.102.9.104/ search?q=cache:tEx8zYooIekJ:www.london.gov.uk/view_press_release. jsp\%3Freleaseid\%3D5565+press+statement+livingstone+7th+july+ bombing\&hl=en>.

Loewenthal, K. M., M. Cinnirella, G. Evdoka, and P. Murphy (2001). 'Faith conquers all? Belief about the role of religious factors in coping with depression among different cultural-religious groups in the UK', *British journal of medical psychology*, 74, 293–303.

London Civic Forum (2002) 'The Arab Community in Britain', Voices for London Policy Commission, March.

Loury, G. (1981). 'International transfers and the distribution of earnings', *Econometrica*, 49, pp. 243–67.

Maalouf, A. (1998). Les Identities meurtriers (Mortal Identities), *Grasset et Fasquelle*, Paris.

Mac an Ghaill, M. (1988). *Young, gifted and black*, Buckingham: Open University Press.

Macey, M. (1999). 'Class, gender and religious influences on changing patterns of Pakistani Muslim male violence in Bradford', *Ethnic and Racial Studies*, 22(5) 845–66.

Mabey, C. (1981). 'Black British literacy', *Education Research*, vol. 23, no. 2, pp. 83-95.

Macdonald, K. (2001). 'Using Documents' in Gilbert, N. (ed.), *Researching Social Life*, London: Sage, pp. 194–210.

Majid, N. (2005). *Working together to prevent extremism*, <www.homeoffice. gov.uk>.

Marks, A. (2000). 'Life long learning and the breadwinners ideology', *Educational Studies*, 26, 3, pp. 203-320.

Marsh, C. (1988). *Exploring Data: An Introduction to Data Analysis for Social Scientists*, Polity Press.

Masic, S. (2003). 'Resettlement of Bosnian refugees in the UK' in Listening to the Evidence: the future of UK resettlement. Verity Gelsthorpe and Lauren Herlitz (eds.), Communication Development Unit, pp. 19–25.

McLoughlin, S. (2005) 'Mosques and the Public Space: Conflict and Cooperation in Bradford', *Journal of Ethnic and Migration Studies*, 31(6), pp. 1045–1066.

McMahon, W. W. (1991) 'Relative Returns to Human and Physical Capital in the U.S. and Efficient Investment Strategies', *Economics of Education Review*, December 1991, pp. 283–96.

McPhee, S. (2005). *Muslim Identity: The European Context*, Sussex Migration Working paper no. 34.

McRoy, Anthony (2000). 'The British Arab', <http://www.naba.org.uk/content/articles/diaspora/british_arabs.htm>.

Mehmet Ali, Aydin (2001). *Turkish speaking communities and Education – No delight*, Fatal publications.

Merry, M. (2004). 'Islam versus (liberal) pluralism? A response to Ahmad Yousif', *Journal of Muslim Minority Affairs*, vol. 24, no. 1, pp. 223–139.

——— (2000). 'The effect of extended family living on the mental health of three generations within two Asian communities', *British journal of clinical psychological society*, 39, pp. 129–41.

Mitchell, J. (1971). *Women's Estate*, Harmondsworth: Penguin.

Model, S. (2002). The cost of not being Christian: Hindus, Sikhs and Muslims in Britain and Canada', *International migration review*, pp. 2061–92.

Modood, T., S. Beishon and S. Virdee (1994). *Challanging Ethnic Identities*, London: Policy Studies Intitute.

——— and M. Shiner (1994). *Ethnic minorities and higher education: why are there different rates of Entry?*, London: Policy Studies Institute.

———, R. Berthoud, J. Lakey, J. Nazroo, P. Smith, S. Virdee, and S. Beishon (1997). *Ethnic Minorities in Britain: Disadvantage and Diversity*, London: Policy Studies Institute.

——— (1998). 'Ethnic minorities' drive for qualifications' in Modood, T. and T. Acland *Race and Higher education*, London: Policy Studies Institute.

——— (2001). 'Their liberalism and our multiculturalism', *British journal of politics and international relations*, vol. 3, no. 2, pp. 245–57.

——— (2003). 'Ethnic Differentials in Educational Performance', in Mason, D. (ed.), *Explaining ethnic differences: challenging disadvantage in Britain*, Policy Press.

——— (2004). 'Capitals Ethnic Identity and Educational Qualifications', *Cultural Trends*, 13 (2)., 50, pp. 87–105.

——— (2006). 'The Liberal Dilemma: Integration or Vilification?', Open Democracy, <http://www.opendemocracy.net/conflict-terrorism/liberal_dilemma_3249.jsp>.

Moffatt, P. G. and J. Thornburn (2001). 'Outcomes of permanent family placement for children of minority ethnic origin', *Child and family social work*, 6, pp. 13–21.

Moghadar, V. M. (1993). *Gender and National Identity: Women and Politics in Muslim Societies*. Karachi: Oxford University Press.

Mohammad, R. (1999). 'Marginalisation, Islamisation and the Production of the Other's Other', *Gender, Place and Culture*, vol. 6, no. 3, pp. 221–40.

Molokotos Liederman, L. (2000). 'Religious diversity in schools the Muslim headscarf controversy and beyond' *Social Compass*, 43: 3, pp. 253–366.

Mueller, Roland (2000). *Honor and Shame, Unlocking the Door*, Xlibris, PA.

Muslim Council of Britain (MCB) (2000). *Frequently Asked Questions on the 2001 census – the religion question*, <http://www.mcb.org.uk/faqs260500.htm>.

Nicholas, D. and M. Marden (1998). 'Parents and their needs: A case study of parents with children under the age of five', *Journal of librarianship and information science*, 30:1, 35–48.

Nielsen, J. (1995). *Muslims in Western Europe*, 2nd edition, Edinburgh: Edinburgh University Press.

Nurdin, A. A. (2006). 'Islam through the eyes of western media', MPACUK, <www.mpacuk.org/content/view/2104/34>.

Oakley, A. (1972). *Sex, Gender and Society*, London: Temple Smith Gower.

Ochieng, B. (2002). 'Minority ethnic families and family centred care', *Journal of child health care*, 7:2, pp. 223–32.

The Office for National Statistics, (1998). *Labour Force Survey*, 4th Quarter 1996, and 1st Quarter.

Office for National Statistics (ONS) (2001). 'Census Background', <http://www.statistics.gov.uk/census2001/cb_8.asp>, Accessed 12 March.

——— (2001). 'Glossary', <www.statistics.gov.uk/census2001/pdfs/glossary.pdf>.

——— (2001*b*) 'Census 2001: Definitions', <http://www.statistics.gov.uk/statbase/Product.asp?vlnk=12951>.

Ogbu, J. U. and H. D. Simson (1998). 'Voluntary and involuntary minorities', *Anthropology and Education quarterly*, 29:2, pp. 155–88.

O'Neale, V. (2000). *Excellence not excuses: inspection of services for ethnic minority children and families*, Department of Health.

Othieno, G. K. (1998). *African social and cultural structures*, London: African cultural promotion.

Ouis, P. S. (2004). 'Marriage strategies among young Muslims in Europe', Association of Muslim Social Scientists Conference, London, February 21–22.

Owen, D. and M. Johnson (1996). 'Ethnic Minorities in the Midlands' in Ratcliffe, P. *Ethnicity in the 1991 Census*, vol. 3, London: HMSO.

——— (1997). 'Labour force participation rates, self employment and unemployment', in Karn, H. (ed.), *Ethnicity in the 1991 Census, Volume Four: Employment, Education and Housing among the Ethnic Minority Populations of Britain*, London: HMSO, pp. 29–67.

Pacione, M. (2004). 'The relevance of religion for a relevant human geography', *Scottish Geographical Journal*, vol. 115, no. 2, pp. 131–217.

Pajwani, F. (2005). Agreed Syllabi and Un-agreed Values: Religious Education and missed opportunities for fostering Social Cohesion. *British Journal of Educational Studies*, 53 (3)., 375–95.

Pankaj, V. (2001). *Family Mediation services for minority ethnic families in Scotland*, The Scottish Executive Central Research Unit, The Stationery Office, Edinburgh.

Parekh, B. (2000). Rethinking Multiculturalism: Cultural Diversity and Political Theory, Palgrave.

Parker-Jenkins, M. (1992). 'Muslim Matters: An Examination of the Educational Needs of Muslim Children in Britain', *American. Journal of Islamic Social Scientists*, pp. 351–69.

Parson, S., J. H. Godson, S. A. William, and J. E. Cade (1999). 'Are there intergenerational differences in the diets of young children born to first- and second-generation Pakistani Muslims in Bradford, West Yorkshire?' *Journal of Human nutrition and dietetics*, 12, pp. 113–22.

Parsons, T. (1956). *Economy and society. A study in the integration of economic and social theory*, Glencoe, IL: Free Press.

Peach, C. (1990). 'The Muslim Population of Great Britain', *Ethnic and Racial Studies*, vol. 13, no. 3, pp. 214–419.

——— and G. Glebe (1995). 'Muslim Minorities in Western Europe', *Ethnic and Racial Studies*, vol. 18, no. 1, p. 26–45.

——— and S. Vertovec (1997). *Islam in Europe: The Politics of Religion and Community*, Baskingstoke: Macmillan.

——— (1998). 'South Asian and Caribbean Ethnic Minority Housing Choice in Britain', *Urban studies*, vol. 35, p. 1657–80.

——— (2002). 'Social geography: new religions and ethnoburbs – contrasts with cultural Geography', *Progress in Human Geography*, 26, 2, pp. 252–60.

Pels, T. (2000). 'Muslim families from Morocco in the Netherlands: gender dynamics and fathers roles in a context of change', *Current Sociology*, 48:4, 75–93.

Pettigrew, N. (2002). *Experiences of lone parents from minority ethnic communities*, Department of Work and Pensions.

Pillai, R. (2006). *Glorifying terror or silencing political views?*, Institute for Public Policy Research, <http://www.ippr.org.uk/articles/index.asp?id=2060>.

Phillips, D. (1998). 'Black minority Ethnic Concentration, segregation and Dispersal in Britain', *Urban Studies*, vol. 35.

Portes, A. and M. Zhou (1993). 'The New Second Generation: Segmented Assimilation and Its Variants', *The ANNALS of AAPSS*, 530: , pp. 74–96.

——— (1998) 'Social Capital: Its Origins and Applications in Modern Sociology', *Annual Review of Sociology*, 24(1): pp. 2–24.

Putnam, R. D. (1993). 'The prosperous community: social capital and public life', in the *American Prospect*, 4:13.

Putnam, R. (2000). *Bowling Alone*, New York: Simon and Schuster.

Prewitt, K. (1987). 'Public Statistics and Demographic Politics' in Alonso, W. and P. Starr (eds.) *The Politics of Numbers*, New York: Russell Sage Foundation, pp. 261–74.

Rajan, Nalini (2002). *Democracy and the Limits of Minority Rights*, New Delhi: Sage Publications.

Ramadan, T. (2004) *Western Muslims and The Future of Islam*, New York: Oxford University Press.

———— (2005). Living Together takes effort, *The Guardian*, 9 July.

Rampton, Anthony, (1981). *West Indian Children in our Schools: Interim, report of the Committee of Inquiry into the education of children from ethnic minority groups*, HMSO.

Rees P. and F. Butt (2004). 'Ethnic change and diversity in England, 1981–2001', *Area*, 36(2), 174–86.

Richardson, R. and A. Wood (1999). *Inclusive schools, inclusive society: Race and identity on the agenda*, Trentham Books.

———— (2004). *Islamophobia issues, challenges and action: A report by the Commission on British Muslims and Islamophobia*, Trent Books.

Rippin, Andrew (1993). *Muslims: Their religious beliefs and Practice*, London: Routledge.

Robinson, Vaughan (1986). *Transients, settlers and refugees: Asians in Britain*, Oxford: Clarendon Press.

The Runnymede Trust (1997). *Islamaphobia: A Challenge For Us All*, <http://www.runnymedetrust.org/publications/pdfs/islamophobia.pdf>.

Sacranie, I. (1996). letter written on behalf of UKACIA to John Dixie of the ONS, 14 October.

———— (1999). letter sent to Margaret Beckett, 18 May.

———— (2000). letter to ICRC, 14 January.

Saeed, A., N. Blain and D. Forbes (1999). 'New Ethnic and National Questions in Scotland: Post-British Identities Among Glasgow Pakistani Teenagers', *Ethnic and Racial Studies*, vol. 22, no. 5, pp. 221–844.

Saint-Blancat, A. (2002). 'Islam in Diaspora: between Reterritorialization and Extraterritorialization', *International Journal of Urban and Regional Research*, vol. 26, no. 1, pp. 138–51.

Savage M., A. Warde and F. Devine (January, 2004) 'Capitals, assets, and resources: some critical issues' *Cultural capital and social exclusion workshop*,

Oxford University.

Schultz, T. W. (1961). 'Investment in Human Capital', *The American Economic Review*, LI (1).

Scruton, R. (2005). 'I resent your success. I hate you and your kind. So I bomb you.', *The Times*, 9 June.

Sellick, P. (2004). *Muslim Housing Experince*, The Housing Corporation, Oxford Centre for Islamic Studies.

Shadjareh, M. (2001). *The Oldham Riots*, The Islamic Human Rights Commission, London.

Shah-Kazemi, S. N. (2001). *Untying the knot: Muslim women, Divorce and and the shariah*, The Nuttfield Foundation.

Shaw, A. (1988). *A Pakistani Community in Britain*, Oxford: Basil Blackwell.

——— (2000). *Kinship and continuity. Pakistani families in Britain*, Amsterdam: Harwood Academic Publishers.

——— (2002). 'Why Might Young British Muslims Join the Taliban?', *Anthropology Today*, vol. 18 no. 1, pp. 2–8.

Sheikh, A. and A. R. Gatrad (2000). *Caring for Muslim Patients*, England: Radcliffe Medical Press Ltd.

Sheridan, L and Gillett, R (2005). Major world events and discrimination, *Asian journal of social psychology*, 8, 191–97.

Sherif, B. (1999). 'Gender contradictions in families', *Anthropology Today*, 15(4).

Sherif, J. (2002). 'Historical roots of Islam in Britain', in *The Quest for Sanity*, Muslim Council of Britain. pp. 163–73.

Shuval, J. T. (2000). 'Diaspora Migration: Definitional Ambiguities and a Theoretical Paradigm', *International Migration*, vol. 38 (5), p. 41–57.

Simpson, L. (2003). *Are the census outputs fit for purpose?* Working paper Cathie Marsh Centre for Census and Survey Research, University of Manchester.

Skerry, P (2001a). 'Counting on the Census?' Stan. L. Rev. pp. 2077–1113.

——— (2001b). 'What's Wrong With Group Politics?', *NEXUS*, Spring.

Smart, K. (2004). *Navigation guide Refugee populations in the UK: Kosovars*, The Information Centre about Asylum and Refugees in the UK.

Smith, A. (1952). *The Wealth of Nations*, Regnery Publishing.

Smith, D. (1991). 'Discrimination against applicants for white collar jobs', in Braham, P., E. Rhodes and M. Pearn (eds.), *Discrimination and disadvantage in employment*, London: Harper and Row.

——— (2004). *Social work and evidence-based practice*, London: Jessica Kingsley.

Smith, P. and S. Wands (2003). *Home Office Citizenship Survey 2001 Technical Report*, Home Office.

Snow, J (2006). Muslim integration has come to a halt, *The Times*, 6 August 2006

Southworth, J. (1997). 'Should we collect Racial Statistics?' *Radical Statistics* 63.

———— (1998). 'My position on positionality', *Praxis*, 36, pp. 29–32.

———— (1999). 'The religious question: representing reality or compounding confusion?', in Dorling and Simpson (eds.), *Statistics in Society: the arithmetic of politics*, pp. 132–39.

———— (2001). 'Count me in?' *Radical Statistics* 78, pp. 32–39.

Stanton, M. (1982). *The Woman's Bible*, <http://www.undelete.org/library/library0041.html>.

Stephen, P. H. (2004). *Islam and Social Policy*, Nashville: Vaderbilt University Press.

Stewart, David and Michael Kamins (1993) *Secondary Research: Information, Sources, and Methods*, Thousand Oaks, CA: Sage Publications.

Stopes-Roe, M. and R. Cochrane (1990). *Citizens of this country: the Asian-British*, Multilingual Matters.

Swann, Lord (1985). *Education For All: The report of the Committee of Inquiry into the education of children from ethnic minority groups*, HMSO.

Tamimi, A. (1995). *Perceptions of Islam in the BBC and other Western Media*, Institute of Islamic Political Thought, <http://www.ii-pt.com/web/papers/media.htm>.

Taylor, C. 2002, *Varieties of Religion Today: William James Revisited*, Cambridge, MA: Harvard University Press.

Taylor, M. and S. Hegarty (1985). *The best of both worlds? A review of research into the education of pupils of south Asian origin*. Windsor: NFER-Nelson.

Teague, A. (2000). *New Methodologies for the 2001 Census*, online paper, Office for National Statistics <http://www.statistics.gov.uk/census2001/pdfs/NewMethodologies.pdf>.

Thernstrom, S. (1992) 'American Ethnic Statistics', in Horowitz, Donald L. and Gerard Noiriel (eds.), *Immigrants in Two Democracies: French and American Experience*, New York University Press, pp. 80–111.

Thomas, J. M. (1998). 'Who feels it knows it: work attitudes and excess non-white unemployment in the UK', *Ethnic and racial studies*, vol. 21 (1), pp. 238–50.

Time (2001). 'Islam in Europe', *Time*, 24 December.

Tomlinson, S. (2005). *Education in a Post-Welfare Society* (2nd Edition), Open

University Press.

Vanaik, Anvil (1997) *Communalism Contested: Religion, Modernity and Secularization*, London: Vistaar Publications.

Van de Kaa, P. J. (1987). Europe's Second Demographic Transition. *Population Bulletin*, 42(1), Washington DC Population reference bureau.

Van Dyke, R. (1998). 'Monitoring the progress of ethnic minorities students: A New Methodology', in Modood, T. and T. Acland *Race and Higher education*, London: Policy Studies Institute.

Verma, G. (1986). *Ethnicity and educational achievements*, London: Macmillan.

———— and D. S. Darby (1994). *Winners and losers. Ethnic minorities in sport and recreation*, Basingstoke: Falmer Press.

Vertovec, S. (1999). 'Three Meanings of Diaspora, Exemplified Among South Asian Religions', *Diaspora*, 7, 3, pp. 277–99.

———— (2002). 'Religion in migration, diasporas and transnationalism', *Research on Immigration and Integration in the Metropolis*, University of British Columbia Working Paper 02–07, (<www.riim.metropolis.net>).

Vydelingum, V. (2000). 'South Asian patients' lived experience of acute care in an English hospital: a phenomenological study', *Journal of advanced nursing*, 32:1, 100–7.

Wahhab, I. (1989). *Muslims in Britain: Profile of a Community*, London: The Runnymede Trust.

Walford, G. (2003) (ed.). 'Investigating Educational Policy through Ethnography', *Studies in Educational Ethnography*.

Wallace, M. and C. Dehnam (1996). *The ONS Classification of Local and Health authorities of Great Britain*, ONS, London: HMSO.

Weller, P. (1998). 'Counting Religion: Religion, Statistics and the 2001 Census', *World Faiths Encounter*, no. 21, pp. 29–37.

————, A. Feldman, and K. Purdam (2001). 'Religious Discrimination in England and Wales', Home Office Research Study 220, Research, Development and Statistics Directorate, The Home Office, London.

———— (2004). 'Identity, politics, and the future(s) of religion in the UK: the case of the religion questions in the 2001 decennial census' *Journal of Contemporary Religion*, vol. 19, no. 1, pp. 2–21(19).

Werbner, P. (2002). *Imagined Diasporas Among Manchester's Muslims: The Public Performance of Pakistani Transnational Identity Politics*, San Francisco: James Currey Publishers.

———— (2003). *Theorising Complex Diasporas, Hybridity and Purity in the South Asian Public Sphere in Britain*, Keele University, <http://www.crassh.cam.ac.uk/events/2003-4/WerbnerPaper.pdf\#search=\%

22werbner\%202003\%20south\%20asian\%22>.

Williams, F. (1989). *Social Policy: A critical Introduction*, Blackwells Publishers

Willmott, P. and M. Young (1957). *Family and Class in a London Suburb*, London: Routledge & Kegan Paul.

———— ———— (1975). *The Symmetrical Family*, Harmondsworth: Penguin.

Wright, C. (1992). *Race relations in the Primary school*, London: David Fulton Publishers.

Yavul-Davies, N. (1997). *Gender and Nation*, London: Sage.

Yilmaz, I. (2002). 'The challenge of post-modern legality and Muslim legal pluralism in England', *Journal of ethnic migration studies*, 28:2, pp. 243–354.

Young, G. (2000). 'Stars and bars', *The Guardian*, 9 October.

Yousif, Ahmad (2000). 'Islam, Minorities and Religious Freedom: A Challenge to Modern Theory of Pluralism', *Journal of Muslim Minority Affairs*, vol. 20, no. 1, p. 29.

Zellick, G. (1998). 'Religion an Issue in the Next Census?', *The Times*, 12 October.

———— (1999). 'Question of Morality', *The Times Higher Education Supplement*, 1372: 22.

Zokaei, S. and D. Phillips (2000). 'Altruism and intergenerational relations among Muslims in Britain', *Current sociology*, 48:4, pp. 25–48.

Index

Spanish, 107
standpoint theory, 180
stereotypes, 10, 56–8, 63, 70,
    72–3
    in schools, 89–92
Stopes-Roe, M., 118
Sudanese, 37
support networks, *see also*
    biraderi networks, 173
Swan Committee, The, 50
Swann Report, 69
Syrians, 37

Taylor, D., 65, 164
Taylor, M., 70
TEC performance, 13
terrorism, 3, 182
Thenstorm, xix
Thomas, J. M., 152–3
toleration, 4
Turkish Cypriots, 28, 34–6, 54,
    148
Turkish speaking communities
    (TCS)s, *see* Kurds, Turkish
    Cypriots, Turks
Turks, xiii, xxiv, 6, 12, 23, 28–9,
    34–6, 39, 54, 148

UK Action Committee on
    Islamic Affairs (UKACIA), 13,
    15
Ummah, the, 2, 10
unemployment, xv, 134, 148,
    150–4, 156–8, 173, 178
UNESCO, 116
UNHCR, 32
UNICEF, 116
Universities and Colleges
    Admissions Service (UCAS),
    51
urbanisation, 134, 137–8, 140

Van de Kaa, P. J., 96
Van Dyke, R., 52
veiling, *see hijab*

Vertovec, S., 10, 24, 40
Virdee, S., xiv, xviii, 3–5, 8, 51,
    56, 60, 99, 103, 105, 108,
    134–5, 150–1, 180
Vydelingum, V., 161

Wahhab, I., 38
Wales, xxii
Wallace, L. A., 159, 162
Wallace, M., 134
Weatherall, 16
welfare services, *see also*
    community housing
    services, *see also* family
    services, *see also* health
    services, *see also* social
    services, xxiii, xxiv, 154–5,
    158–69, 173, 183
    barriers to usage, 159–65,
        167, 173–4, 183
    care, informal, 164–7, 173
    care, unpaid, 170–1, 173
Weller, P., 2–3, 17, 19, 173
Werbner, P., viii, 5–7, 10–1
white extremists, 1
'White Others', xiii
Whites, xxi, 12
    demographics, 46–7
    discrimination, 72
    divorce, 102
    education, 50–2, 57–8, 63,
        65
    families, 98, 154–5
    households, 100–1
    housing, 136, 147
    marriage, 102
    poverty, 155
    unemployment, 148
    welfare services, 154, 158,
        167
Whites, women, 102–3, 107
Willmott, P., 94–5
women, 51–4, 64, 83–5, 91, 96,
    166, 172, 180